PELICAN BOOK

A739

HISTORICAL INTERPRETATION

Advisory Editor: J. H. Plumb

John J. Bagley was educated at Cowley School, St Helens, and the University of Liverpool. He graduated in 1930 and since then, apart from war-time service in the R.A.F., he has been teaching and studying history. He was first a schoolmaster at Rochdale and Upholland and then a staff tutor and senior staff tutor in the Extra-Mural Department of the University of Liverpool. He considers himself lucky that he had a grounding in the history of Medieval England from three such tutors as G. W. Coopland, May McKisack, and the late R. R. Betts.

John Bagley has published biographies of Margaret of Anjou and Henry VIII, histories of Lancashire and Up-holland Grammar School, and a social history, *Life in Medieval England*. Since the war he has developed a particular interest in the history of the north-western counties. He is one of the two honorary editors of the *Transactions of the Historic Society of Lancashire and Cheshire*, general editor of *A History of Cheshire*, and a Fellow of the Royal Historical Society.

HISTORICAL INTERPRETATION

Sources of English Medieval History
1066–1540

BY
J. J. BAGLEY

PENGUIN BOOKS

BALTIMORE MARYLAND

Penguin Books Ltd, Harmondsworth, Middlesex, England
Penguin Books Inc., 3300 Clipper Mill Road, Baltimore 11, Md, U.S.A.
Penguin Books Pty Ltd, Ringwood, Victoria, Australia

—

First published 1965

—

Copyright © J. J. Bagley, 1965

—

Made and printed in Great Britain
by Cox & Wyman Ltd, London, Reading, and Fakenham
Set in Monotype Bembo

To the many who have asked,

'How do we know?'

CONTENTS

FOREWORD

It would require a team of specialists and a far bigger book than this to achieve a comprehensive description of the sources available to those who study the history of England and Wales in the Middle Ages. All that I have been able to do here is to illustrate characteristic or outstanding sources for each century. Much has had to be omitted, and it has not been possible to mention a particular type of document more than once. I hope, therefore, that the reader will understand that, although he will find patent and close rolls, for example, discussed in the thirteenth-century chapter, they are indispensable sources for the fourteenth and fifteenth centuries as well, and that, in the archives, monastic chronicles or private letters are not confined to the twelfth or fifteenth centuries as they are here.

Those who wish to read more medieval documents should graduate from this outline to the appropriate volumes of *English Historical Documents* published by Eyre and Spottiswoode, and thence to the various sources listed in the bibliographies at the end of each chapter. Inevitably, only a small percentage of those who study history will ever possess the time, opportunity, and technical skill to read substantial parts of the manuscripts themselves, but primary sources, even in print and translation, make possible a closer affinity with the past than do histories and biographies, however scholarly or well written they may be.

Dr J. H. Plumb, of Christ's College, Cambridge, originally discussed with me the plan of this book, and, as on previous occasions, my friend and colleague, Dr A. R. Myers, has read the text of each chapter as it has been written, and made many constructive suggestions. I am most grateful to them both.

University of Liverpool
June 1964   J.J.B.

A historian needs manuscripts as a bricksetter needs bricks. Without them he can do no work at all. However ready a good bricksetter may be to use concrete, breeze-blocks, or stone in appropriate parts of his building, he relies on bricks for the main construction, and spends most of his working hours patiently and skilfully laying course upon course. In the same way a good historian, especially if he is a medievalist or an ancient historian, will use archaeological, place-name, numismatic, and topographical evidence whenever he finds it relevant and useful. He may not appreciate the technique of the archaeologist or aerial photographer, and he will probably fail to follow the linguistic arguments of the place-name scholars, but he will eagerly consider the conclusions of these experts to see if they supplement and verify his own knowledge. Yet, for him, nothing can take the place of the written word. Field-patterns, place-names, potsherds, and coins are impersonal compared with the most formal manuscript, and since the historian is essentially concerned with people, their lives, thoughts, actions, and beliefs, his truest and most valuable material must always be the words and the pictures which men and women have written and drawn on clay, stone, parchment, and paper.

To acquire manuscripts is only the beginning of the historian's work. All writing is subjective, and consequently liable to error and personal bias, so that the historian, who is himself subject to prejudice and capable of mistaken interpretations, has to attempt to assess the value of each piece of his raw material and fit it into his general picture of the age he is describing. It is essentially *his* picture, and the reader is free to accept or reject it according to his own preconceptions and knowledge of the period. Historians are ever disputing with each other about the interpretation of facts, and each new generation, shifting the emphasis made by its predecessor, feels it essential to re-write history. This will always be so, for young historians, adding occasional new discoveries to the well-known body of raw material, reassess the evidence, and often proclaim important certain facts which previous historians have tended to ignore or thrust into the background. Every history book, therefore, is the author's own interpretation of his own selection of facts. Even a history book such as this one, which merely describes and quotes documents, is as personal a work as an anthology of English poetry. Some documents, such as Domesday Survey, William of Malmesbury's chronicles, or the Paston Letters, would appear in all but the most eccentric collections of English medieval documents, but each historian has his own views about what is sound, revealing, trivial, or misleading. Fortunately there is a considerable measure of agreement, and where differences of opinion exist, they make the subject more, and not less, interesting to study.

Those who have read I. A. Richmond's *Roman Britain*, the first volume in the *Pelican History of England*, will realize that our knowledge of Roman Britain is based as much, if not more, upon the work of the archaeologist's spade and trowel as upon the written word of contemporaries. We possess the writings of Caesar and Tacitus, inscriptions upon scores of Roman tombstones, Ptolemy's map of the British Isles in the second century, and the evidence that can be distilled from the Antonine Itinerary, but without the comparatively recent and still continuing work of archaeologists in every county, our knowledge of the activities of the Romans in Britain would be much poorer than it is. Certainly it would not be increasing.

Manuscript evidence for Anglo-Saxon history is more plentiful, but still not sufficient for a complete story. In her book, *The Beginnings of English Society*, Dorothy Whitelock shows that the backbone of our knowledge of the period between the departure of the Romans and the coming of the Normans consists of such contemporary documents as the writings of the Venerable Bede, Asser's *Life of King Alfred*, and the various annals which are collectively known as the Anglo-Saxon Chronicle. But she also demonstrates how the study of place-names, the excavation of sites once occupied by English, Danish, and Norse settlers, and the study of their few material remains can help us to complete the skeleton of our knowledge. Unlike the historian of more modern times who often appears to have raw material to squander, the historian of pre-Conquest days has need to treasure every scrap of evidence. From each line of his scanty documents he must squeeze all the knowledge he possibly can, and he will ponder over a fragment of poetry, a single coin, the interpretation of a law, or the construction of a few feet of masonry to see if he can confirm an old speculation or find a reason for a new one. Nothing is so insignificant that he can afford to despise it.

1. DESCRIPTIONS OF THE CONQUEST

Once the narrative of English History reaches the second half of the eleventh century, more documents become available. It is possible, for example, to look through half-a-dozen pairs of contemporary or near-contemporary eyes at the events leading up to the Conquest. The Bayeux Tapestry is the best-known source. Its pictures and captions tell a prejudiced political and moral story, but the pictorial information it gives us about dress, arms, armour, and methods of fighting is invaluable. A full and sympathetic running commentary on the Tapestry could be constructed from the account of the Conquest written by Ordericus Vitalis in his *Ecclesiastical History of England and Normandy*. Orderic did not witness the Conquest. His father came over from Normandy as one of the followers of Roger de Montgomery, the Norman earl of Shrewsbury, but he himself was born in England in 1075. When he was only ten years old he entered the Benedictine monastery of Ouche near Lisieux as a novice, and apart from three journeys made to Cluny, Cambrai, and Worcester, he spent the rest of his life there. He began his *History* with an account of the life of Christ and the struggles of the early church, but its chief value as a primary source of information lies in his description of recent and contemporary events in Normandy and England. His birth and upbringing conditioned him to see things from the point of view of the Norman rulers. Harold was a usurper: 'before long', Orderic reported, 'the throne which had been wickedly seized was stained by horrible crimes'. Tostig was banished from England for protesting against the wrong Harold had done, and, after appealing successfully to William for help, he tried to invade England. But Harold's coastal defences kept him out at sea, and contrary winds forced him to sail for Norway, and seek aid from Harold Hardrada. This is the speech which Orderic puts into Tostig's mouth:

Great king, I come as a suppliant to your highness, offering myself and my faithful services to your majesty, in hope that by your aid, I may be restored to my hereditary rights. My brother Harold, who rightfully ought to submit to me as his elder brother, has treacherously opposed me, and even presumed, at the price of perjury, to usurp the English crown. Knowing therefore, your pre-eminence in power, and in armed men, and every excellence, I, as one ready to do you homage, earnestly entreat you to give me your powerful assistance. Humble the pride of my perfidious brother by a hostile invasion of England; and reserving one half of it for yourself, confer the other on me, who will ever after preserve my fealty to you unbroken as long as I live.

Orderic is not anti-English. In his account of the Conquest he shows his sympathy by praising the 'stout resistance' of the English soldiers at Senlac Hill – 'each man strained his strength to the utmost' – and by sympathizing with the victims whenever the Normans destroyed English property without good reason. Yet King William is his hero. He praises him for his personal bravery, his skilful leadership, and not least for his careful observance of his duties towards the Church.

Duke William having intelligence of Harold's approach, ordered his troops to take to their arms on the morning of Saturday [14 October]. He then heard mass, strengthening both body and soul by partaking of the consecrated host; he also reverently hung from his neck the holy relics on which Harold had sworn. Many of the clergy had followed the Norman army, among whom were two bishops, Odo, of Bayeux, and Geoffrey, of Coutances, with attendant clerks and monks, whose duty it was to aid the war with their prayers and counsels. The battle began at the third hour of the ides of October, and was fought desperately the whole day, with the loss of many thousand men on both sides. The Norman duke drew up his light troops, consisting of archers and men armed with crossbows, in the first line; the infantry in armour formed the second rank; and in the third were placed the cavalry, in the centre of which the duke stationed himself with the flower of his troops, so as to be able to issue his commands, and give support to every part of the army.

... Duke William surpassed them all [i.e. all his knights] in courage and conduct; for he nobly performed the duties of a general, staying the flight of his troops, re-animating their courage, their comrade in the greatest dangers, and more frequently calling on them to follow where he led, than commanding them to advance before him. He had three horses killed under him in the battle; thrice he re-mounted, and did not suffer his steeds to be long unavenged. Shields, helmets, and coats of mail were shivered by the furious and impatient thrusts of his sword; some he dashed to the earth with his shield, and was at all times as ready to cover and protect his friends as to deal death among his foes.

William of Poitiers, archdeacon of Lisieux and one of the Conqueror's chaplains, was a contemporary writer for whom William could do nothing that was not splendid and just. Like Orderic he detested Harold, 'that stupid Englishman', but in his biographical history, written in the early seventies and entitled *The deeds of William, duke of the Normans and king of the English*, he went further than Orderic in praising and flattering his hero. Most of William's advisers, he claimed, tried to dissuade him from crossing the Channel because they thought the invasion of England too difficult an enterprise. But William knew the valour of his men. Had Rome had the services of such warriors and counsellors as Robert of Mortain, Robert of Eu, Hugh of Lisieux, and Richard of Evreux, she would still be ruling the world; yet 'in every deliberation they all bowed to the prudent wisdom of the duke as if God had shown him what ought to be done and what avoided'. William of Poitiers attributed the duke's exceptional qualities to his piety. On the field of battle the hero felt no fear and instinctively shunned all dishonour. Many of his noblemen fell because the site did not favour their way of fighting, but William overcame all his difficulties and drove back the enemy. After the battle the pious duke gazed with pity on the dead, and even allowed those who wished to do so to give decent burial to the English who 'had richly deserved their fate'. But a day or two later we find him punishing the people of Romney 'at his pleasure', and burning down Dover and its castle. Neither plague among his troops, personal sickness, nor wicked opponents held back his steady, relentless advance on London. At length his knights pleaded with him to accept the crown. William demurred. He would prefer, he said, to continue settling and pacifying the country. He did not lust for power, and when he was crowned he would like his wife to be crowned by his side. But at length, in spite of these worthy sentiments, he yielded to the pressing desires of all his soldiers, which was most sensible, for, as William of Poitiers caused Haimo, the orator-soldier, to declaim, 'however much wise and prudent men might wish to increase their own wealth and status through their leader's advancement, they would never seek to give him a crown if they were not confident that he was fitted in every way to carry out his kingly duties most nobly'.

William of Jumièges, another contemporary, was not so fulsome an admirer of the Conqueror, but he has left us in no doubt whose side he was on. Indeed from among contemporary commentators only the writers of Anglo-Saxon Chronicle E and the unknown author of *The life of King Edward who lies buried at Westminster* had any praise for the English. The latter did not describe the Conquest, although he was certainly writing after 1066. Instead he protested that Edward the Confessor, despite his intelligence and devotion to duty and the

Church, had been most unjust to Earl Godwin. Norman friends and court favourites had blinded him to Godwin's loyalty and ability. For the most part the authors of the different versions of the Anglo-Saxon Chronicle were comparatively non-committal. Each had his own personal interests and bias, but compared with the two Williams, of Poitiers and Jumièges, they were free from passion. Manuscript E declared boldly that 'Harold succeeded to the throne of England as the king had granted it to him, and as men had chosen him', but the only comment any version of the Chronicle made on the verdict of Hastings was that 'the Frenchmen took possession of the battle-field – all as God granted them because of the people's sins'. Nevertheless, it is in the E version of the Chronicle that we find the frankest obituary of the Conqueror. The scribe praised his wisdom, his dignity, his respect for and his benevolence to the Church, and his ability to bring peace to England, but he also condemned his cruelty, his covetousness, his pride, and his stubbornness. 'Alas! that a man should be so proud, so exalt himself, and so consider himself above all men!'

2. ANGLO-SAXON CHRONICLES

There are no less than seven versions of the Anglo-Saxon Chronicle. Each surviving manuscript begins with a copy, or a copy of a copy, of the original chronicle written during Alfred's reign, but from early in the tenth century they all go their own way as different scribes in different religious houses kept them up to date or copied them afresh. For general convenience scholars now distinguish the manuscripts from one another by giving each a letter of identity. Manuscript A, which ends its story in 1070, was written first at Winchester and later at Canterbury. The texts of B and C, both in part written at Abingdon, are closely associated as far as 977. B then ceases, but C continues its narrative to the eve of the Conquest. D is a later version. Nothing of it seems to have been written down before Edward the Confessor's reign, yet its narrative ceases in 1079. E, written in Peterborough but partially based on a Canterbury manuscript, goes as far as 1155, the beginning of Henry II's reign. F was written in Canterbury as late as 1100, but its story stops short of the Conquest, and scholars think that G, a charred fragment and the last of the seven known manuscripts, is a copy either of part of A or of a common ancestor of both A and itself.

The texts of the six principal versions of the Chronicle differ considerably. One will describe an event in detail; others will dismiss it with a passing reference or not mention it at all. Sometimes, like the four gospels, the six versions are hard to reconcile; now and again they contradict each other. Because of these differences the Chronicle manuscripts occasion and reward detailed study. To illustrate how the versions often supplement one another, here, first from D and then from C, is the story of the events of 1066.

In this year King Harold came to Westminster from York at that Easter which followed the mid-winter in which the king [Edward the Confessor] died; and that year Easter was on 16 April. Then was seen throughout England such a portent in the sky as no man ever saw before. Some men said it was a comet, which some call the hairy star; and it was first seen on the eve on the Greater Litany [24 April] and so shone all the week. And soon afterwards Earl Tostig came across the sea to the Isle of Wight with as powerful a fleet as he could muster; and there they bought him off with money and food. And King Harold, his brother, gathered so great a company of sailors and soldiers as no king in this land had done before, because he learned that William the Bastard intended to invade and win this land; as it all happened afterwards. Meantime Earl Tostig sailed into the Humber with sixty ships; and Earl Edwin came with the fyrd and drove him out. And the butse-carls [bodyguard of sailors] forsook him, and he ventured to Scotland with twelve small ships. And there Harold, king of Norway, met him with three hundred ships, and Tostig submitted to him and became his liege-man. Then both sailed into the Humber until they came to York; Earl Edwin and his brother, Earl Morcar, fought against them there, but the Northmen gained the victory. Then news was taken to Harold king of the English that it had fared thus with them; and this battle was fought on the eve of St Matthew [20 September]. Then Harold our king surprised the Northmen, and attacked them beyond York at Stamford Bridge with a great force of Englishmen. During the day there was severe fighting on both sides. Harold Harfagr [a mistake for Hardrada] and Earl Tostig were slain, and the remaining Northmen fled; and the pursuing English pressed them hard until they reached their ships; some were drowned, and some were burnt. And so in different ways they perished so that few were left, and the English took possession of the battlefield. The king granted his protection to Olaf, son of the king of the Northmen, and to their bishop and to the earl of Orkney and to all the men left in the ships; and then they went ashore to our king and swore oaths that they would ever remain peaceful and friendly towards this land. And the king let them go home with twenty-four ships. These two battles were fought within five nights.

Then came Earl William from Normandy to Pevensey on the eve of Michaelmas [28 September], and as soon as they could, they built a castle at the port of Hastings. This was told to King Harold, and he gathered a great host and came to meet him at the hoary apple-tree; and William took him by surprise before his men were ready for battle. Nevertheless, the king fought strongly against him with those men who would follow him, and each side suffered great slaughter. King Harold, Earl Leofwin his brother, and Earl Gyrth his brother, and many good men were slain; and the Frenchmen took possession of the battlefield – all as God granted them because of the people's sins.

Manuscript C gives additional details. After describing Tostig taking money and food from the men of the Isle of Wight this version of the Anglo-Saxon Chronicle says:

And he sailed from there and did damage along the sea coast wherever he could until he came to Sandwich. King Harold, who was in London, received word that Tostig his brother had come to Sandwich. Then he gathered so great a force of soldiers and sailors as no king in the land had done before, because he had been told for a truth that Earl William from Normandy, King Edward's kinsman, purposed to come here and conquer this land, as it all happened afterwards. When Tostig heard that King Harold was on his way towards Sandwich, he sailed from Sandwich taking some of the butse-carls with him, some willingly and some unwillingly. He went north into [Humber?] and harried in Lindsey and killed many good men there. When Earl Edwin and Earl Morcar understood that, they came and drove him from the land. Then he made for Scotland; and the king of the Scots welcomed him and supplied him with provisions. And there he dwelt the whole summer. Then King Harold arrived at Sandwich, and waited for his fleet there because it took a long time before it could be gathered together. And when his fleet had been mustered, he sailed to the Isle of Wight and lay there during the whole summer and autumn; and in all places on the coast a force of soldiers [a land-fyrd] was maintained although in the end it achieved nothing. By the Nativity of St Mary [8 September], the men had eaten their supplies, and they could be kept there no longer. The men were then allowed to go home, and the king rode inland and the ships were taken to London, and many perished before they reached here. When the ships were back home, then Harold king of Norway unexpectedly sailed north into the Tyne with a very large fleet – no small one; it might be [space in MS.] or more. And Earl Tostig came to him with all those under his command – everything as they had agreed beforehand; and then both moved with the whole fleet inland along the Ouse towards York. In the south, when he had left his ship, King Harold learned that Harold king of Norway and Earl Tostig had landed near York. He then marched northward, day and night, as quickly as he could muster his fyrd. But before King Harold could reach there, Earl Edwin and Earl Morcar recruited from their earldom as great a force as they could; and fought against the army and slaughtered greatly; and many Englishmen were slain and drowned and driven to flight, and the Northmen took possession of the battlefield. And this battle was on the vigil of St Matthew the apostle [20 September]; and it was Wednesday.

And then after the battle Harold, king of Norway, and Earl Tostig entered York with as many men as seemed good to them. And the city gave them both hostages and provisions, and so they embarked again and arranged a full peace – that everyone should move south with him and conquer this land. While this was happening Harold king of the English brought the whole fyrd on the Sunday to Tadcaster, and there assembled his troops, and on Monday moved right through York. And Harold king of Norway and Earl Tostig and their forces had gone from the ships beyond York to

Stamford Bridge because it had been solemnly promised that there hostages should be brought from the whole shire to them. Then Harold king of the English fell on them unexpectedly beyond the bridge, and there they joined battle and were fighting very fiercely long in the day; and there Harold king of Norway and Earl Tostig were killed together with an unknown number of Northmen and Englishmen; and the Northmen fled before the English. Then one of the Northmen withstood the English, so that they might not cross the bridge nor gain the victory. An Englishman shot an arrow at him but it did no damage; and then another approached underneath the bridge and thrust him through the corselet. Harold king of the English then came across the bridge, his fyrd with him, and slaughtered many Northmen and Flemings. And Harold let the king's son, Hetmund, sail home to Norway with all his ships.

[This is the end of Manuscript C. The last few sentences, from 'and the Northmen fled before the English', were added at a later date.]

Manuscript E, with its good word for Harold here and there, tells the same story with much less detail. But after recording William's coronation, this chronicler added a postscript of special interest to Peterborough, which illustrates not only the confusion which followed Harold's defeat, but also the chroniclers' habit of incorporating local information in their general narrative.

Leofric, abbot of Peterborough, was with that army [probably Harold's] and fell sick there and returned home and died soon afterwards on All Saints' Eve; God rest his soul! In his day all was happiness and goodness in Peterborough, and he was beloved by everyone so that the king gave to St Peter and him the abbacy of Burton and that of Coventry which earl Leofric, his uncle, had founded, and that of Crowland, and that of Thorney. And he did so much good for the monastery of Peterborough with gold, silver, vestments, and land, more than anyone else before or since. Then the Golden Borough became a wretched borough. The monks then elected the provost, Brand, as abbot, because he was very good and very wise, and sent him to Edgar the Atheling because locally people assumed he would be king, and the atheling gladly assented. When King William heard of this he was most angry, and claimed the abbot had insulted him.

Then eminent men acted as intermediaries because the abbot was an eminent man himself. He then gave the king forty golden marks as a peace offering. And he lived a little while longer, but only three years. Afterwards all disturbances and evils visited the monastery. God take pity on it!

3. DOMESDAY SURVEY

Without doubt the most comprehensive and detailed English document of the eleventh century is Domesday Survey. As it has come down to us it consists of two main volumes (Domesday Book proper), three major manuscripts associated with the Survey, and a number of more local fragments. The first volume of Domesday Book contains 382 sheets of vellum each about $14\frac{1}{2}$ in. $\times$ $9\frac{3}{4}$ in., and it surveys every English shire with the exception of Essex, Suffolk, and Norfolk, which are the subject of volume 2, and of the four northern counties, Cumberland, Westmorland, Northumberland, and Durham. The second volume, often called 'Little Domesday', is fatter but smaller. It has 450 sheets, each about $10\frac{1}{2}$ in. $\times$ 7 in., and the entries are in single and not double column as in the first volume. The three chief associated manuscripts are the Exeter Book, *Exon Domesday*, which covers the south-western shires; the Ely Inquest, *Inquisitio Eliensis*; and the Cambridgeshire Inquest, *Inquisitio Comitatus Cantabrigiensis*. All five documents as well as the other fragments are based upon detailed returns made by the inquisitors or commissioners whom William I sent into the shires in 1086. In an oft-quoted passage Anglo-Saxon Chronicle E gives us a contemporary version of the purpose of the Survey.

Then at Christmas [1085] the king was at Gloucester with his witan, and there he held court for five days, and afterwards the archbishop and clergy held a synod for three days. Maurice was elected bishop of London there, and William elected to Norfolk and Robert to Cheshire. They were all king's clerks. After this the king had much thought and very intense discussion with his witan about this country, how it was occupied and with what kind of men. Then he sent his men all over England into every shire and caused them to find out how many hundred hides there were in the shire, or what land and cattle the king himself had in the country, or what dues he ought to have annually from the shire. Also he required to be written down how much land his archbishops had, and his bishops and his abbots and his earls and – though I tell my story at too great a length – what and how much in land or cattle had every man who was holding land in England, and how much money it was worth. So very closely did he cause it to be investigated, that there was not a single hide, nor a yard of land, nor even – it is shameful to tell though it seemed no shame to him to do – an ox nor a cow nor a pig that was overlooked and not included in the record. And all the records were brought to him afterwards.

Robert Losinga, bishop of Hereford at the time of the Survey, added a paragraph to the chronicle written by the Irish monk, Marianus Scotus. In it he claimed that William made a double survey, so that a second team of commissioners could check on the work of the first.

In the twentieth year of his reign by order of William, king of the English, a survey was made of all England, that is of the lands of the several shires of England, and of the possession of each and of all tenants-in-chief. This was done concerning ploughlands and habitations, and of men both bond and free, both those who lived in cottages, and those who had their homes and held land in the fields; and concerning ploughs, horses, and other animals; and concerning the services and payments due from all men in the whole country. Other commissioners followed the first; men were sent into areas they did not know and where they were unknown, in order that they could have an opportunity to check the first survey and, if necessary, denounce its authors as guilty to the king.

So far as we can tell there were at least seven teams of commissioners in each survey. They divided the English shires between them and set out on their inquiry. Their daunting task was to record who had held each manor from Edward the Confessor (Harold's name was pointedly omitted), who held it now, what changes had occurred in the size and value of each manor since 1066, how many freemen, villeins, cottars, and other people lived on the manor lands, how many plough-teams were used, how much land came under the plough, and how many mills and fisheries each landholder possessed. The commissioners used various methods of getting this information quickly. Probably they made informal inquiries about such things as the extent of woodland or the number of cottars, and reserved the open court proceedings for formally confirming such details as well as recording the holders' names and the values of estates. None at least of the second wave of com-missioners were local men. Methodically they progressed through the group of counties they were responsible for, but when they came to write their report they had to rearrange all their material. They had acquired it topographically, neigh-bouring manor after neighbouring manor, but the king required the information arranged according to the list of landholders, beginning with himself, followed in turn and precedence by the spiritual and temporal lords, and ending with the lesser men who chanced to hold a few acres of land directly from the crown. The commissioners were feudally-minded Normans. For them the manor was the obvious unit of land-holding, but they often found manors difficult to fit in with English land boundaries. Geld was traditionally assessed and collected by shires and hundreds, and manors were heedless of such divisions, for they could vary in size from a large collection of holdings scattered over two or more shires to a mere frag-ment of a village. Consequently in the writing of the report the commissioners faced some difficult editorial problems. They had to make the word *manor* [*manerium*] do all kinds of work.

Winchester was the ultimate destination of the commission-ers' reports. There the royal clerks condensed and regimented them. The clerks were primarily interested in land – who held it, its size, the use to which it was being put, and its value. They were not very interested in sub-tenants or in the details of farm stock. The first volume of Domesday Book is the outcome of their editorial work. It begins with Kent, Sussex, and Surrey, moves steadily south-westwards, and then advances irregularly north-eastwards to Yorkshire and Lincolnshire. Most of the county records follow the same general plan – a description of the main borough in the shire, a list of the landholders, and then the details of the royal manors followed by the holdings of the tenants-in-chief. The first page of this volume begins with a description of Dover written in the terse, abbreviated Latin characteristic of the whole Survey.

In King Edward's time, Dover returned 18 pounds [240 silver pennies weighed 1 lb.] of which the king had two parts and Earl Godwin the third. And to match this [moiety] the canons of St Martin had another moiety. Once a year for a fortnight's service, the burgesses provided the king with 20 ships, each manned by 21 men. They did this because the king allowed them to keep sac and soc [freedom from outside jurisdiction]. Whenever the king's messengers passed through the port, they paid 3d. in winter and 2d. in summer for the transporting of a horse. The burgesses supplied the navigator and one assistant, and if more help was required, the navigator hired it. From the feast of St Michael [29 September] to the feast of St Andrew [30 November] the king's peace was in force in the town. If anyone broke the peace, then the king's reeve took a common fine. Anyone living permanently in the town paid customary dues to the king and was free of toll throughout England. All these customs were established when King William came to England. On his first arrival in England, the town was burned, and therefore it has not been possible to reckon its value when the bishop of Bayeux received it. Now it is assessed at 40 pounds, but the reeve returns 54 pounds, of which he pays 24 pounds of pence (20 to the ora) to the king, and 30 pounds to the earl by tale.

In Dover there are 29 inhabited houses from which the king has lost customary dues; of these Robert de Romenel has 2, Ralph de Curbespine 3, William son of Tedold 1, William son of Oger 1, William son of Tedald and Robert the Black 6, William son of Geoffrey 3, amongst which was the burgesses' guildhall, Hugh de Montfort 1 house, Durand 1, Ranulf de Columbels 1, Wardard 6, and the son of Modbert 1. And all these men for all these houses appeal to the bishop of Bayeux as their warrantor and liberator or grantor. It is generally admitted that one half of the land belonging to Ranulf de

Columbels' house, which was owned by a certain outlaw, belongs to the king, and Ranulf keeps the whole of it himself. Humphrey the bandy-legged has 1 house half of which was forfeit to the king. Roger of Westerham has built a certain house on the banks of the king's water, and up to now he has not paid the king's customary dues. There was not a house there T.R.E. [*tempore regis Edwardi* – in the days of king Edward]. At the entrance of Dover harbour is a mill which damages nearly all the ships because it causes a great disturbance in the sea, and occasions very great loss to the king and his subjects, and it was not there T.R.E. Herbert's nephew says of this that the bishop of Bayeux allowed it to be built by his uncle Herbert son of Ivo.

The account goes on to describe details of the law prevailing in Kent, and then lists separately the lands held by the canons of St Martin's church in Dover. Then follow the lands held by the king and by twelve tenants-in-chief – the archbishop of Canterbury; the monastery of Christ Church, Canterbury; the bishop of Rochester; Odo, bishop of Bayeux and earl of Kent; Battle Abbey; St Augustine's Abbey, Canterbury; the abbey of Ghent; Hugh de Montfort; Count Eustace of Boulogne; Richard of Tonbridge; Haimo the sheriff; and Albert the chaplain.

The royal clerks retained from the commissioners' reports what was essential for their purpose, but it is very probable that the greater detail of those reports, or better still of the original returns made in the field during the Survey, would have solved many of the problems which Domesday Book has set historians. The second volume, Little Domesday, is a much fuller account than the first. It only covers the three East Anglian counties, and seems to be an unedited copy of the commissioners' report. Why it was not put into final form like the rest is a minor mystery. It might simply have been that William died before the clerks had finished their task, and that they then received orders to abandon it and turn to more pressing work.

The Exeter, Ely, and Cambridgeshire manuscripts, as well as the various fragments that have been found elsewhere, are based on the original drafts made in the field or on rearranged copies of them. The Exeter manuscript was written in 1086 or soon afterwards; the Cambridgeshire manuscript is a twelfth-century copy of an earlier document. The Ely manuscript seems to have been compiled from a selection of original returns expanded and recorded by a monk living in the abbey of Ely.

Because of the way the evidence has survived the hazards of nine hundred years, Domesday Survey does not give us a uniformly detailed picture of England at the end of the Conqueror's reign. East Anglia and part of south-west England are comparatively rich in detail. Most of the south and midlands is adequately covered, the north-west is hastily dispatched, and the extreme north ignored. Here are typical entries for manors haphazardly chosen from different counties.

KENT

The abbot of St Martin of Battle holds the manor of Wye, which T.R.E. as now was assessed at 7 sulungs [sulung was a Kentish measure of land about twice as large as the hide used in south-eastern counties]. There is land for 52 ploughs. On the demesne there are 9 ploughs, and 114 villeins with 22 bordars have 17 ploughs. There is a church and 7 serfs and 4 mills worth 23 shillings and 8 pence, and 113 acres of meadowland and woodland which yield 300 swine from pannage dues [pannage was the right to pasture swine in the woods]. T.R.E. it was worth 80 pounds and 106 shillings and 8 pence. When received 125 pounds and 10 shillings at 20 pence to the ora [a Danish coin]. Now it is worth 100 pounds by tale, and if the abbot had sac and soc it would be worth 20 pounds more . . .

NORFOLK

Stiffkey [Stivecai] is held by Toka in the hundred of Greenhoe. It consists of $1\frac{1}{2}$ ploughlands: then as now there are 11 bordars: then [i.e. T.R.E.] 6 serfs, and afterwards and now 3: both then and now $1\frac{1}{2}$ ploughs on the demesne. Then there was 1 plough belonging to the villeins, afterwards 1 plough belonging to the villeins, now half a plough; 5 beasts, 12 swine, 200 sheep, woodland for 8 swine, 2 acres of meadow, and half [share of] a mill.

And there belongs to this vill 1 berewick [outlying estate] Wells [Guella] which T.R.E. had 1 ploughland, but Godric found no stock: 4 bordars then had half a plough afterwards and now 1 ox, and 4 sokemen, (with) 8 acres of land, then as now half a plough. 13 sokemen belong to this manor with 40 acres of land T.R.E. and half a plough and the same now. Then it was worth 4 pounds, now it pays 6 pounds. And Stiffkey is 1 outlying estate which belongs to Aylsham [Helesham] (of) 4 bordars, 1 plough T.R.E. and when Godric received it, and now half a plough; half an acre of meadow. This all belongs to Aylsham and is valued with it.

DEVON

The church itself [the abbey of Tavistock] holds Milton. T.R.E. it paid geld for half a hide. There is land for 15 ploughs. In demesne are 5 ploughs and 12 serfs, and 14 villeins and 12 bordars have 10 ploughs; there are 20 acres of meadow, 400 acres of pasture, 10 acres of woodland. Formerly it was worth 4 pounds, now 8 pounds.

[*Exon Domesday* confirms all these facts, and adds that the demesne and the villeins' lands each measured a virgate [usually a quarter of a hide] and the abbey possessed in Milton 22 beasts, 12 pigs, 170 sheep, and 30 goats.]

NORTHAMPTONSHIRE

Peterborough abbey holds 6 hides in Oundle. There is land for 9 ploughs. In demesne are 3 ploughs and 3 serfs, and there are 23 villeins and 10 bordars with 9 ploughs. There is a mill paying 20 shillings and 250 eels, and there are 50 acres of meadow. There is woodland 3 leagues long and 2 wide. It was worth 5 shillings, now 11 pounds.

CHESHIRE

This same church [St Werburgh's, Chester] held and holds Shotwick. There is one hide liable to geld. There are 3 carucates of land. There are 4 villeins and 2 bordars with 1 carucate and 1 acre of meadow. T.R.E. it was valued at 16 shillings. Now at 13 shillings and 3 pence.

YORKSHIRE

In Leeds there are 10 carucates and 6 bovates of land for geld [8 bovates = 1 carucate]. There is land for 6 ploughs. T.R.E. 7 thegns held it for 7 manors. Now there are 27 villeins there and 4 socmen and 4 bordars have 14 ploughs. A priest is there, and a church, and a mill worth 4 shillings a year and 10 acres of meadow. It was worth 6 pounds: now 7 pounds.

LANCASHIRE

[There was no county of Lancashire in 1086. The area between the Ribble and the Mersey was tacked on to the Cheshire survey: the remainder was treated as part of Yorkshire.]

Four thegns held Bootle as 4 manors. There are 2 carucates of land. It was worth 64 pence. A priest had 1 carucate of land belonging to the church of Walton.

Every page of Domesday Book raises problems of interpretation. The commissioners' Latin equivalents for English, Danish, and Norse technical terms are often difficult to translate back again with certainty. Many of the chief landholders, referred to merely by their Christian name, cannot be identified, and the clerks' abbreviations and cryptic sentences sometimes cause ambiguities. *Car*, for example, has two meanings – *carucate*, a measure of land, and *caruca*, a plough team. Eight oxen constituted a plough team in East Anglia and Lincolnshire, but this did not necessarily apply elsewhere. If the carucate was a fixed measure throughout England, then the hide could not possibly have been, for in Cheshire *carucate* and *hide* were used interchangeably, but across the county border in Staffordshire a hide contained three carucates, and north of the Mersey six carucates. Norfolk, Suffolk, and some midland counties did not use the hide at all, and the people of Kent, as we have seen, preferred the sulung to either hide or carucate. Frequently the Domesday commissioners used these measures merely as assessment figures for the payment of geld, and too many writers, taking them at their face value, have equated each carucate with 8 bovates and eventually with 120 acres. The word *acre* often appears in Domesday Book, but it is as rash to

assume that it implies statute acre, based on the rod of 16 ft 6 ins.
as that *league* implies either the present 3 miles or the usual
medieval 1½ miles. Local usage determined the size of such
measurements before, during, and for many centuries after
Norman times. In Lancashire, to take but one example, there
were three very different acres – 24 ft, 22 ft 6 ins., and 21 ft to
the rod – in widespread use well into the nineteenth century,
and this good choice of measures did not prevent tiny pockets
of the county from working with acres peculiarly their own, and
varying in size from the statute acre to a massive acre calculated
from a 25½-ft rod. To add further to the confusion *acre* sometimes meant nothing more than a piece of arable land irrespective of size. It must also be remembered that many Domesday
measurements are only approximate. When the commissioners
recorded that at Oundle the woodland was 3 leagues long and
2 wide, they did not mean that there were exactly 6 square
leagues of woodland. The distances had probably been
measured by nothing more accurate than the mind's eye of the
witness who had given the information to the commissioners,
and all irregularities of shape had been ignored. Therefore many
of the neat calculations which have been based on Domesday
Book figures must be treated with caution, if not distrusted
altogether.

Yet, despite the many problems they raise, the Domesday
Survey manuscripts are as invaluable to historians, economic,
constitutional, or political, as they are to the place-name
scholars or the historical-geographers. They give them their
first detailed look at most parts of England, and in many areas
after 1086 they do not get more than an occasional glimpse for
at least another century. In Domesday's pages they can find
information about methods and varieties of farming, about the
proportions of arable, waste, and grasslands, and, with the help
of the geologist, the relationship of particular crops and herds
to the soil. They can study population figures, local traditions
and privileges, and the distribution of mills, and they can
estimate the importance of Norman England's infant industries.

There are many entries which refer to salt making, and to rents being partially paid in salted fish, chiefly for Lenten eating. Along the Sussex coast and in the estuaries of the rivers nearly 300 saltpans, each worth about 2s. 6d., were recorded. Here and elsewhere sea water was trapped and allowed to evaporate, but at Droitwich in Worcestershire and in the Cheshire 'wiches' the salt industry was much more efficiently managed. William I owned the Droitwich brine pits directly; in Cheshire he and the earl of Chester shared the profits, the king taking two thirds and the earl one.

Domesday Book describes in detail many towns in Norman England. Unfortunately, they do not include London, Winchester, or Bristol. How informing these descriptions can be may be judged from the following extracts from the entries for Southampton and York.

In the borough of Southampton, the king holds in demesne 76 men who pay a tax of 7 pounds on their land, and who used to pay the same tax T.R.E. Of these men 27 pay 8d. each, 2 pay 12d., and the others, 50 in number, pay 6d. each. [Note arithmetic. 76 in D.S. = 'quatuor 20 homines 4 minus'.]

The land which they held in the borough itself King Edward himself freed of taxes.

Odo of Winchester; Anschitil, the priest; Chetel, Fulghel, and Tostill, sons of Elric, had 16 acres of meadowland. Gerin, 18 acres. Cheping had 3 houses quit of tax: Ralph de Mortimer now holds these. Godwin also had 3 houses: these Bernard Pancevolt now holds.

Since King William came to England, 65 Frenchmen and 31 Englishmen have been accommodated in Southampton. These between them pay £4. 0s. 6d. for all accustomed dues.

The undernamed have houses in Southampton free of tax, by a grant of King William: G., the bishop, has one house, the Abbey of Cormelies, 1; the Abbey of Lire, 1; the Earl of York, 2; Ralph de Mortimer, 2; Gilbert de Breteville, 2; William, the son of Stur, 2; Ralph de Todeni, 1; Durand de Gloucester, 2; Hugh de Port, 1; Hugh de Grentemaisnil, 2; Earl Moritan, 5; Aiulf, the chamberlain, 5; Humphrey, his brother, 1; Osburn Gifard, 1; Nigel, the physician, 4; Richerius de Andeli, 4; Richard Pugnant, 1; Stephen

Stirman, 2; Turstin, the chamberlain, 2; Turstin, the engineer, 2; Anschitil, the son of Osmund, 3; and Rainald Crock, 1.

The Abbess of Wherwell has a fishery and a small parcel of ground. Formerly they were taxed at 100d., but now 10s.

T.R.E. in the city of York there were 6 shires as well as the arch-bishop's shire. One shire has been despoiled for castle building. In five shires there were 1,418 inhabited houses. Of one of these shires the archbishop has yet a third part . . . Of all the houses mentioned above there are now inhabited 391 great and small belonging to the king and rendering custom, and 400 other dwellings not inhabited which yield, the better ones 1d. and the others less. 540 houses are so empty that they yield nothing at all, and Frenchmen hold 145 houses. . . . In the shire of the archbishop there were T.R.E. 189 in-habited houses; now there are 100 inhabited houses both great and small as well as the court of the archbishop and the houses of the canons. In this shire the archbishop has as much custom as the king has in his shires.

In the geld of the city there are 84 carucates of land, and each of them rendered as much geld as 1 house of the city, and shared with the citizens the 3 works of the king. Of these the archbishop has 6 carucates, which 3 ploughs can plough. These are part of the farm [tenure] of his hall. This land was not built upon T.R.E. but the bur-gesses farmed [rented] parts of it: now it is the same. On this land the King's pool destroyed 2 new mills worth 20s., and fully 1 carucate of arable land, meadows, and gardens. T.R.E. it was worth 16s., now it is worth 3s.

Domesday Book often confirms and gives a sharper sense of reality to events recorded by the chroniclers. Several sources, as well as material remains examined by archaeologists, testify that the Norman conquerors rapidly built a network of motte and bailey castles from which they dominated England, but the matter-of-fact entries which the royal clerks made in Domesday Book about houses destroyed in York, Oxford, Norwich, Lincoln, Cambridge, and other centres to clear sites for castles are the best indication of the ruthless priority which William gave to castle building. Again, it is well known that the Normans' military efficiency did not save them from having to face several English revolts. No uprising was any fiercer than that in the north-east, which resulted in the defeat and death of the Norman earl, Robert, at Durham in 1068. Anglo-Saxon Chronicle D tells the story of the sequel to the revolt.

[1068] ... And soon afterwards Edgar the Atheling came with all the Northumbrians to York; and the townsmen made alliance with him. And King William surprised them from the south with an overwhelming force, and put them to flight, and slew those who could not escape, who were many hundreds, and plundered the town and defiled St Peter's monastery, and also pillaged and defiled the others. And the Atheling returned to Scotland ...

[1069] ... Soon afterwards there sailed into the Humber from Denmark three sons of King Swein, Earl Osbeorn and Earl Thurkil with 240 ships; and Edgar the Atheling came to greet them, and Earl Waltheof and Maerleswegen and Earl Gospatric with the Northumbrians, and all the people of the land, riding and marching with an immense host greatly rejoicing. And thus all marched on York together, and stormed and demolished the castle and seized countless treasure therein, and slew many hundreds of Frenchmen and led many captive to the ships. But before the men from the ships arrived, the Frenchmen had set fire to the town and had also despoiled and burnt the holy monastery of St Peter. When the king heard of this, he marched north with all the troops he could muster, and completely harried and laid waste the shire.

Anglo-Saxon Chronicle E, which records the same events without D's detail, concludes with the words, 'And King William marched into the shire and devastated it completely.'

Domesday Book clearly shows that the chroniclers were not speaking lightly when they used such words as *laid waste*, *devastated*, and *completely*. Nearly twenty years later the material damage caused by the harrying of the north was clearly visible to the commissioners. There are many entries, similar to the three following, which speak of waste.

In Pudsey Dunstan and Stainulf held 8 carucates of land for geld, where there is room for 4 ploughs. Ilbert [de Lacy] holds it now, but it is waste. T.R.E. it was worth 40 shillings. Woodland for pasture is half a league in length and half a league in breadth.

In Shipley Ravenchil held 3 carucates of land for geld, where there is room for 2 ploughs. Ilbert holds it now and it is waste. T.R.E. it was worth 10 shillings.

In Cleckheaton Dunstan and Ravenchil held 6 carucates of land for geld, where there is room for 3 ploughs. Ilbert holds it now, and it is waste. T.R.E. it was worth 20 shillings.

The contrast between the values and assessments for 1066 and those for 1086 tells its own story. In the West Riding the T.R.E. value of the Skyrack, Agbrigg, and Morley wapentakes were £97 5s. 0d., £108 10s. 8d., and £42 5s. 0d. respectively. In 1086 they were assessed at £32 5s. 4d., £12 16s. 0d., and £7 0s. 0d. The North Riding suffered even more because William's soldiers first ravaged the route between York and Durham. In Northallerton wapentake values plunged from £102 3s. 8d. to 29 shillings, and in the three divisions of the large Langbargh wapentake in the most northern part of the riding, the T.R.E. figures of £179 2s. 0d., £26 16s. 8d., and £109 16s. 4d. had sunk to £3 18s. 6d., £10 12s. 8d., and £15 1s. 8d. by 1086. There were no signs of real recovery from the devastation nearly a generation after the fighting. In the East Riding destruction was severe enough, but it did not ruin the countryside as completely as in some areas farther north. Driffield wapentake's value fell from £57 2s. 0d. to £3 10s. 0d., and Pocklington's from £129 6s. 0d. to £32 2s. 0d. In the extreme east, the southern half of Holderness which had been valued at £262 in 1066 was worth £55 6s. 0d. twenty years later.

In Domesday Survey Yorkshire covered a much wider territory than does the present county. It pushed into Durham and crossed the Pennines to include large areas of modern Lancashire, Westmorland, and southern Cumberland. Signs of devastation are not so striking in the north-west as they are in the north-east, except in the Fylde. There the commissioners quickly dispatched their responsibilities. They merely listed the 62 vills with their T.R.E. assessment – Ashton, 2 carucates; Lea, 1 carucate; Salwick, 1 carucate, etc. – and then added the significant words, 'Of these vills 16 are inhabited by a few people, but it is not known how many inhabitants there are. The rest are waste.' This might well be another piece of evidence of the severity of the Norman soldiers, but since the Fylde was Tostig territory, it is quite likely that at least part of this destruction occurred earlier at the hands of Harold's soldiers.

The reputation of Domesday Book grew steadily as the eleventh century gave way to the twelfth. Landholders used its authority to confirm titles to their land or to claim privileges and exemption from taxation. Inevitably it became out of date, but subsequent county or area surveys modernized sections of it by adding the names of later landholders and revising the spelling of place-names. Working copies were often amended with marginal notes. By the twelfth century it was looked upon as a charter, and in the *Dialogue of the Exchequer* (*Dialogus de Scaccario*) Richard fitz Nigel wrote, 'Metaphorically the book is called by the English, *Domesday*, the Day of Judgement. Just as the verdict of that strict and awful last account cannot be escaped by any skilful subterfuge, so when this book is quoted on those matters which it covers, its evidence cannot be suppressed or ignored with impunity.'

Bibliography of Eleventh-Century Documents

The most comprehensive and readily obtainable collection of later eleventh-century manuscripts translated into English is *English Historical Documents, 1042–1189* by D. C. Douglas and G. W. Greenaway. It contains a reproduction and explanation of the Bayeux Tapestry, a translation of the Anglo-Saxon Chronicle from 1042, extracts from Orderic, William of Poitiers, William of Jumièges, Domesday Book and its associated manuscripts, as well as many lesser documents not mentioned in this chapter.

Full texts, some in English and some in Latin, are published as follows:

The Ecclesiastical History of England and Normandy by Ordericus Vitalis, ed. T. Forester (1853).

Scriptores rerum gestarum Willelmi Conquestoris, ed. J. A. Giles (1845). (For text of William of Poitiers.)

Gesta Normannorum Ducum, ed. Jean Marx, published by the Historical Society of Normandy (1914). (For text of William of Jumièges.)

The Anglo-Saxon Chronicle: a revised translation, ed. D. Whitelock (1962).

Lives of Edward the Confessor, ed. H. R. Luard, Rolls Series (1858).

Domesday Book, ed. A. Furley, Record Commission (1783).

Inquisitio Comitatus Cantabrigiensis and Inquisitio Eliensis, ed. N.E.S.A. Hamilton (1876).

Exon Domesday is printed in Vol. III of the Record Commission's edition of Domesday Book (1816).

Translations of most of the Domesday Survey manuscripts will be found in the appropriate volumes of the Victoria County History. The latest authoritative discussion of the interpretation of Domesday Survey is V. H. Galbraith, *The Making of Domesday Book* (1961).

THE TWELFTH CENTURY

1. MONASTIC CHRONICLERS

Monasticism flourished throughout the twelfth century. In the reigns of William I and William II many Benedictine monks, fired by the enthusiasm of the Cluniac revival, had left monasteries in Normandy to found, or revive, in England religious houses which their soldier brothers had been eager to endow. During the first years of the twelfth century, other orders of monks built new monasteries. Both the Augustinian and the Premonstratensian canons attracted ardent members and wealthy patrons, and in 1131 Gilbert of Sempringham founded the first house of his English order in Lincolnshire. More important still, the Cistercians arrived in England in the late twenties. Their ideal of leading a simple, hard life in an undeveloped countryside drew scores of young men to such unpromising places as Rievaulx, Furness, and Tintern, so that before the end of the century these ardent pioneers and their successors had greatly enlarged the area of agricultural England as well as enriching Christendom with their ceaseless prayer and praise. To become a Cistercian monk was 'now both believed and declared to be the surest road to heaven', wrote William of Malmesbury soon after the first Cistercian communities had been established, but half a century later the Carthusians, who founded their first house at Witham in Somerset in 1173, were offering a still more exacting way of life to the Christian idealist.

In many English monasteries, especially the older, Benedictine houses, monks of the twelfth century continued the tradition of writing annals. Occasionally in the past these bare records had flowered into histories. Bede had set a remarkable example as early as the late seventh and early eighth centuries, and the various scribes who had kept the different versions of the Anglo-Saxon Chronicle going had followed uncertainly in his footsteps. The twelfth-century writers admired Bede, and preferred his Latin to the English of the Chronicle. A few approached his skill as a writer, but most failed to rise much above the chroniclers' level of ability. A surprising number wrote detailed manuscripts, and if most of their books cannot properly be called histories, they have long provided a rich, primary source of material for historians.

The work of the monastic chroniclers is so interlocked and interdependent that some of the tangles cannot be unravelled sufficiently to determine whose hand wrote which particular section. The chronicle generally attributed to Florence of Worcester seems to have been written by one author in the thirties and forties of the twelfth century, but it contains many pages copied from the Anglo-Saxon Chronicle, from the writings of Eadmer of Canterbury and Marianus Scotus, an Irish monk living in Mainz, from a previous biography of Bishop Wulstan of Worcester, and probably from other sources now lost. In the reign of Stephen, John of Hexham borrowed freely from his contemporary, Richard of Hexham, and added to the work of an older man, Simeon of Durham; and for the last hundred years scholars have examined and discussed a collection of St Albans histories and chronicles written during the late twelfth and early thirteenth centuries without being able to agree which parts were written by Roger of Wendover, which by Matthew Paris, and which by Walter of St Albans and Matthew of Westminster – if either of the last two ever wrote a single line. Our difficulty in identifying the work of different authors is due partly to the fact that used manuscripts became tattered and needed rewriting, and partly to wholesale plagiarism. This medieval habit was neither new nor wicked. Knowledge, medievalists believed, belonged to everyone, and anything which preserved it and made it more available was good. Twentieth-century textual criticism has enlarged our understanding of the Synoptic Gospels by showing which parts of their narratives the evangelists took from Q, M, proto-Luke, and other lost documents. In the same way it is possible, if not so profitable, to show how particular monastic chroniclers built the earlier parts of their stories from extracts from older writers. They chose what appealed to them, and often embellished it with imagination and fancy. The monk who wrote the chronicle at St Martin's Priory, Dover, has not set archaeologists digging with his story of Julius Caesar building a treasury tower on the cliffs, nor has Ailred of Rievaulx convinced genealogists by the way he traced the descent of Henry II from Adam. But the works of all the chroniclers tell us something of how twelfth-century minds worked. None could resist retailing a good story however much they doubted the truth of it, and all of them studied dreams, visions, and the effect of the stars and planets on the course of human affairs. William of Malmesbury, the best of the monastic writers of the first half of the century, told how in the tenth year of the reign of Rufus, 'a comet appeared for a fortnight, with its larger train turned to the east and its smaller to the south-west. Other stars also appeared, apparently darting at each other.' These unusual sights in the night sky he seriously associated with 'Anselm, the light of England, voluntarily escaping from the darkness of error' at Rufus's court and going to Rome. Florence of Worcester's account of the year 1132 included nothing but strange portents and disasters. It began back to front by recording the appearance of a comet in October, and then described how in Whitsun week a disastrous fire destroyed most of the city of London including 'the principal church of St Paul the apostle'. The remainder of the long entry in the chronicle concerns an eclipse of the sun in August and the alarming events associated with it.

King Henry went down to the shore about noon to take ship [across the Channel] surrounded by his guards, as is the custom of kings, when suddenly a cloud was seen in the sky. It could be seen in all parts of England, although it varied in apparent size: in some places the day only seemed to be dull, but in others the darkness compelled men to light candles to see what they were doing. The king and his attendants and many others walked about in great wonder, and looking upwards saw the sun shining like a new moon. But it did not keep the same shape for long. Sometimes it was broader, sometimes narrower, sometimes more curved, sometimes more upright, now steady as usual, and then moving, and quivering and liquid like quicksilver. Some say that the sun was eclipsed. If this is so, the sun was then in the head of the dragon, and the moon in its tail, or the sun in the tail and the moon in the head, in the fifth sign [of the Zodiac] and the seventeenth degree of that sign. The moon was then in her twenty-seventh day. On the same day, and at the same hour, many stars appeared.

Moreover, that very day, when the ships were anchored on the shore ready for the king's voyage and the sea was calm and the wind slight, the heavy anchors of one of the ships were suddenly pulled out of the ground as though by a violent shock. To the surprise of the many men who tried in vain to stop her, the ship got under way, collided with the ship next to her and in the end eight ships were damaged by this unknown force. It was also generally reported that on the same day and about the same hour, many churches in the province of York were seen to be sweating, as it were, great drops. . . . Also there were some who said that in the week following, on Monday, the sixth of the ides of the same month, when the moon was three days old, they saw her first as she generally appeared at that age, and in a while, in the evening of the same day, they saw her full, like a round, shining shield. Many also said that on the same occasion they saw two moons, separated from each other by about the length of a spear.

Today, historians use the chronicles chiefly for their description of contemporaries, and the record of events which the authors either witnessed or heard about at second or third hand. Most chroniclers, and certainly those who aspired to write histories, would have accepted Carlyle's definition of History as the biography of great men. They believed that men's lives showed how God rewarded good living and punished wickedness and sin. Therefore, to write the life of a saint or to explain the disasters of a reign by demonstrating the weak, immoral character of the king was to exemplify a moral truth and to deliver a warning to others. Like the Old Testament chroniclers, these twelfth-century monks were quick to denounce any who laid hands on the church. The slightest interference or curtailment of clerical privilege was to do evil in the sight of the Lord. The unknown author of *Gesta Stephani* (*The Deeds of Stephen*) takes Stephen's side against Matilda, but does not hesitate to condemn him for treating a bishop with insufficient reverence, or to point out that if his followers disregarded sanctuary, they were certain to suffer violent death or the agonies of incurable disease. William of Malmesbury too found sermons in the lives of men. In a lifetime of barely fifty years devoted chiefly to the time-consuming duties of the monastic round, he wrote an impressive number of biographies of saints. Dunstan, Patrick, and Wulstan of Worcester were probably his best studies. In his more general histories he occasionally wrote graphic impressions of prominent men, some of whom he had probably seen and some of whom he knew only as historical characters. It is obvious from the following two extracts from his *Gesta Regum* (*Deeds of the Kings*) that he much preferred Henry I to William Rufus, although he did his best to be fair to both.

No doubt he [William Rufus] would have been a prince without equal in our time, had not the greatness of his father overshadowed him and had not fate ended his life before his maturer years could correct the errors which sprang from licence granted by power and from youthful impetuosity. When his childhood was over, he spent his youth in military activities, in riding, dart-throwing, contending with his elders in obedience, with his contemporaries in action. He thought it impaired his reputation not to be the first to take up arms in combat, not to be the first to challenge the enemy, or, when challenged, to defeat him. He always obeyed his father, always strove hard in battle in his sight, always was by his side in peace . . . Greatness of soul was pre-eminent in the king, but, as time passed, he hid this virtue with his excessive severity. Indeed, so insensibly did vices creep into his bosom that he could not distinguish them from virtues. The world long doubted which way he would go, what direction his disposition would take. At first, so long as Archbishop Lanfranc lived, he abstained from all crime, so that there was good hope he would be the very mirror of kings. For a time after Lanfranc's death he showed himself so variable that vices and virtues were evenly

balanced. At last, however, in his later years, his desire to do good
grew cold, and evil ripened within him: his liberality became prodigality, his magnanimity pride, his austerity cruelty. May I be allowed
with the king's permission not to conceal the truth; he feared God
but little, man not at all. Anybody who says this is undiscerning will
not say wrongly, because wise men should obey this rule, 'God
ought to be feared at all times; man, according to circumstances'.
In public William affected a supercilious look. He looked threaten-
ingly at bystanders, and attacked those who spoke to him with an
assumed scowl and harsh voice . . . At home and at table with his intimates, he constantly laughed and joked. Habitually he poked fun at
anything he had done wrong, so that he might disarm criticism and
make it a joke. But I shall expand somewhat on that liberality with
which he deceived himself . . . [The chronicler here discusses at length
the vices of prodigality and the virtues of liberality, and then describes
some of the evil consequences of William's actions. After some pages
he gives us this description of the king.] . . . William was well set. He
had a ruddy face, fair hair, and an open countenance. Each of his eyes
had different-coloured glittering specks. Though he was rather short
and corpulent, he had astonishing strength. He did not speak eloquently, but was known for his stuttering especially when he was
angry.

Henry, the youngest son of William the Great . . . was early instructed in the liberal arts, and so thoroughly did he imbibe the sweets
of learning, that ever after neither the disturbance of war nor the
pressure of business could deprive his noble mind of them. Although
he never read much in public and sparingly displayed his attainments,
yet his learning, as I can truthfully say, though acquired in snatches,
helped him considerably in the science of governing according to
Plato's dictum, 'The commonwealth would be happy if philosophers
were kings or kings philosophers.' . . . He busied himself maintaining
the strength of his dominions. Firmly he defended them, though he
refrained from war as long as he could with honour. When he took
up arms he severely avenged his injuries and dispelled every danger
by his energy and courage. He was constant both in his enmities and
his general benevolence; in the one case he displayed too much anger,
in the other his royal magnanimity, for he reduced his enemies even
to ruin, and exalted his friends and dependants so that everyone

envied them. Does not philosophy teach us that the first and greatest concern of a good king should be 'to spare the suppliant and restrain the proud'? In his steady administration of justice, he ruled the people with moderation, and with dignity he restrained the nobility. Diligently he hunted down robbers and counterfeiters, and punished them smartly when caught. Nor did he neglect less important matters. When he heard that traders were refusing broken money though it was of good silver, he ordered that all coins should be broken or cut in pieces. He used the length of his own arm to correct the false ell of traders, and made it the standard throughout England. He instructed his courtiers and court officers, no matter on which of his estates he might be, concerning what things they should accept without payment from the country folk, and how much and at what price they should purchase. He punished those who disobeyed these instructions by a heavy fine or even by loss of life. At the beginning of his reign, that he might deter wrongdoers, he usually punished by mutilation, but later he used fines more often. Thus by virtue of the rectitude of his conduct, as is natural to man, he came to be respected by the magnates and beloved by the common people. If at any time the better men, forgetting their solemn oath, wandered from the path of loyalty, he immediately called them back to it by the wisdom of his constant exertions; he brought back the refractory to reason by the wounds he inflicted on their bodies. I cannot easily describe how closely he watched such people, and he allowed nothing which had injured his authority to go unpunished . . . He was of middle height, neither unduly short nor tall. His hair was black but thin at the front. His eyes were fairly bright, his chest brawny, and his body plump. He joked on appropriate occasions, and pressure of business did not cause him to be anything but pleasant in company. . . . He preferred to fight by diplomacy rather than by the sword . . . If he could, he made his conquests without bloodshed, but if that were unavoidable, with as little as possible. During the whole of his life he was free from lustful desire, for as we know from those who were well informed, he lay with women not for carnal satisfaction but from his desire for children. Thus he did not condescend to intercourse unless it might have that result: in this he was the master of his passions and not their slave. He ate plain food, seeking to satisfy his hunger rather than bloat himself with a multitude of delicacies. He drank to slake his thirst, deprecating in himself and others the least lapse into drunkenness. He slept heavily with much snoring. His eloquence was more natural than studied, more deliberate than fluent.

His piety towards God was praiseworthy for he built monasteries in England and in Normandy. But since he has not yet completed them, I should suspend my judgement for the present were it not that my affection for the brotherhood at Reading forbids my silence. He built this monastery between the rivers Kennet and Thames, on a site convenient for the reception of almost all who might have occasion to travel to the more populous towns of England .... [This leads William into a description of activities at Reading and into an explanation of investiture.]

Just as interesting as the 'profiles' of people are the chroniclers' occasional thumb-nail sketches of places. They may consist of a single phrase such as the description of Cricklade in *Gesta Stephani* – 'sited in a beautiful spot rich in all kinds of possessions' – or run to a short paragraph as do the same author's word pictures of Bristol and Oxford. The following twelfth-century descriptions of Bath and Rievaulx, the first from *Gesta Stephani* and the second from William Daniel's *Life of Ailred*, sound surprisingly modern.

Six miles from Bristol is a town, where, through concealed pipes, springs supply waters, heated not by human skill or art, from deep in the bowels of the earth to a basin beneath a vault of splendid arches, thus providing in the centre of the town baths which are pleasantly warm, healthy, and a pleasure to see. This town is called Bath, from a word peculiar to the English tongue meaning a washing place, because from all over England sick people come to wash away their infirmities in the healing waters, and the healthy come to gaze at the remarkable jets of hot water and bathe in them.

The site [where the first monks built their huts near Helmsley] was by the side of a rapidly-flowing stream called the Rie in a broad-bottomed valley. The name of their little settlement and of the place where it lies was taken from that of the stream and the valley – Rievaulx. High hills, covered with many kinds of trees, surround the valley and encircle it like a crown: the pleasant retreats of the monks safeguard the privacy of the valley and give them sylvan beauty reminiscent of paradise. From the highest rocks the waters swirl to the valley below, and while they rush through restricting banks and still narrower gorges and spread out in the wider reaches, they gently murmur soft sounds and together produce the sweet notes of a harmonious melody. When the branches of the beautiful trees move and sing together and leaves fall gently down, the happy listener's ears are increasingly gratified with the glad jubilee of pleasing sounds, as so many different things combine together so well to give him music in which every single note is equal to the others.

Some of the lesser chroniclers, such as Hugh Candidus who wrote a Peterborough chronicle and the monks who compiled the chronicle at Abingdon, were content to record purely local events. But even their accounts of the disputes which the abbot was waging with the neighbouring lord or bishop, and the tittle-tattle they related about triumphs and disasters inside the monastery have some historical value. Occasionally a local chronicler had most important happenings to record. Gervase of Canterbury described in dramatic detail how in 1174 the roof of Canterbury Cathedral was set on fire by sparks from burning houses and how the flames melted the lead, gutted the choir, and destroyed valued shrines. William of Sens, the master mason chosen to supervise the work of restoration, decided to clear away the broken columns and charred remains of the choir and make a fresh start. This led Gervase not only to record in detail how William and his successor planned the rebuilding and what a rush there was to get the choir ready for Easter 1180, but also to review the improvements made at Canterbury during the days of Lanfranc and Anselm, and to compare the architectural features of the new building with those of the old one. He reported a splendid achievement, and incidentally gave us details of medieval methods of building. These pages of his chronicle are a rich source for the student of medieval architecture.

To some extent all the monastic chroniclers tended to exaggerate the importance of local events, but the greater writers rose beyond this restricted interest and attempted to give us a history or contemporary account of events in the whole of England, seen of course, from their particular corner of the country and from their own political point of view. William of Malmesbury set out not to keep a diary-type chronicle, but to write histories, balanced authoritative accounts of both the distant and the recent past. However, even in his best works, *The Chronicle of the Kings of England* and *The Chronicle of the Bishops*, he fell short of what today we regard as the basic requirements of historical scholarship, for he was not critical enough of his sources, and too readily abandoned his narrative to point a moral lesson or merely to tell an interesting but unrelated story. On the other hand, before he began to write he studied all the manuscripts he could find, and he constantly revised his work as if never satisfied with it. William of Newburgh, an Augustinian canon from Yorkshire and a historian who wrote in the second half of the century, was perhaps the most discriminating of these twelfth-century writers. In the preface of his *History of England* he dismissed as fable the stories of King Arthur and Merlin, and resisted the temptation to push back his history into times for which he had no reliable sources. Book I begins in 1066, and Book V ends suddenly in 1198, probably a few months before his death. Throughout his work William tried to set down an impartial account of events even to the extent of putting aside his clerical interests and attempting to justify Henry II's treatment of Becket, but, like his contemporaries, he broke his narrative to tell stories of miracles and marvels, or to relate legends and superstitions.

We shall not find the truth about political events in the twelfth century by sticking to one or two of the chroniclers. We must read as many as are available, and weighing the probability of one contradictory manuscript against another, construct the best mosaic we can. Some chroniclers are better placed geographically to know particular aspects of events. Not surprisingly John of Hexham relates details of Prince Henry's movements, after he had met David of Scotland and Ranulf, earl of Chester, at Carlisle in 1149, which other chroniclers omit or confuse, but it is the author of *Gesta Stephani*, who obviously knew the Bristol area well, who gives us the best account of how Stephen failed to ambush the prince in Gloucestershire as he fled to the south-west in the hope of finding a ship for Normandy. Again, we must allow for every writer's natural bias and try and eliminate his preconceived judgements. This is not easy especially with topics such as the quarrel between Henry II and Becket or the character of Richard I, upon which it is still possible to hold two informed but opposite opinions. *Gesta Stephani* and *Historia Novella* both tell the story of Stephen's reign, the one from Stephen's point of view, the other from Matilda's. Neither author is guilty of deliberate falsehood – indeed both make conscious efforts to be fair – but they succeed in giving us entirely contradictory opinions of the merits of Stephen's claim to the throne.

The author of *Gesta Stephani* began by bewailing and probably exaggerating the chaos which followed Henry I's death. Men, he wrote, disregarded the law, indulged in private war and pillaging, committed robberies, and slaughtered wild animals so indiscriminately that they were soon in danger of extinction.

Meanwhile, while the English were living so disorderly and disastrously, relaxing the bridle of justice and freely committing all kind of sins, Stephen Count of Boulogne, a man made famous by his illustrious descent, landed in England with a few attendants. To King Henry the peacemaker this very man was the dearest one of all his nephews, not only because he was closely bound to him by blood, but also because he was particularly distinguished for many shining virtues. Indeed he was what is acknowledged to be most rare among the rich these days, wealthy yet modest, generous and approachable, and furthermore, in all battles and sieges of the enemy, bold and brave, discerning and patient. As soon as he heard the report that King Henry had died, this man, like famous Saul, devised a great plan, and since he was across the water, he moved to the coast. By good chance he found the wind favourable, and he turned his attention and his ship towards England. After he had disembarked with his few attendants, as already stated, he rode quickly to London, the capital and the queen of the whole country.

London received Stephen with open arms, and a council, summoned by 'the elders and experienced counsellors', agreed unanimously to choose a king. No one but a king, they argued, could re-establish peace and respect for the law. Besides it was their right and privilege to appoint a successor to Henry, and they accepted Stephen, virtuous and nobly born, as sent by heaven. But William, archbishop of Canterbury, protested that he could not lightly agree to anoint Stephen. He argued

that King Henry had bound leading men from every part of the kingdom by a most solemn oath that after his death they would accept as sovereign no one but his daughter, whom he had given in marriage to the count of Anjou, or her heir, if heir she had. Therefore, he said it was going too far to wish for anything contrary to this, especially as Henry's daughter was living and had not been denied the blessing of children. The king's supporters resolutely answered these words. 'It is true and undeniable', they said, 'that King Henry arranged a shrewd marriage for his daughter, that he might make peace more surely and firmly between the Normans and the Angevins, who had often unsettled each other with quarrelling. Also with that authoritative voice like thunder that nobody could question, he forced rather than bade the leaders of the whole kingdom to swear to recognize her as his heir. And although he knew that they would take the oath against their will and would not keep it, yet he wished, as Ezekiel did, to insure peace in his own time and by one woman's marriage to hold together many thousands of men in friendship. And in order that we might clearly realize that he did not wish that which he had approved for a definite purpose in his lifetime to remain binding after his death, on his death-bed, with very many people present listening to his truthful confession of the wrongs he had done, he clearly showed that he repented for forcing the oath on his barons. Wherefore, since all agree that to force an oath on anyone makes it impossible for him to commit perjury by breaking it, it was wise and obviously expedient gladly to acknowledge as king one whom London, the capital of the whole kingdom, had accepted without scruple, and who, moreover, was a strong claimant by the right of descent. . . .'

These and other arguments won over the archbishop, and he, in the presence of other bishops and many clergy, anointed Stephen king. Almost all the barons approved the choice, and once Stephen had rewarded them with gifts and new estates, they freely took the oath to be faithful to him.

William of Malmesbury, the author of *Historia Novella* (*A History of Recent Events*), made a hero of Robert of Gloucester, who after temporarily accepting Stephen, championed Matilda, his step-sister. Naturally, William viewed the coming of Stephen very differently from the author of *Gesta Stephani*. He laid stress not upon the expediency of appointing a king, but upon the solemnity of the oath taken by the barons. After explaining in detail Henry's dilemma in not having a son to succeed him, he related how in 1126 his council had sworn to acknowledge Matilda as queen.

In the twenty-seventh year of his reign King Henry came to England in September bringing his daughter with him. Next Christmas, after he had summoned a large number of the clergy and baronage to London, he endowed his wife (the duke of Louvain's daughter whom he had married after Matilda's death) with the earldom of Shrewsbury. Clearly he grieved that the woman did not conceive and feared that she would always be barren. With every reason to do so, he thought anxiously about his successor to the throne. After he had discussed this matter earnestly and long, at this same council, he bound and with an oath obliged the barons of all England, as well as the bishops and abbots, that, if he died without a male heir, they would immediately and unhesitatingly accept his daughter, one-time empress, Matilda, as their sovereign.

Matilda, her father insisted, was most nobly born. Her grandfather, uncle, and father had in turn sat on the English throne, and her descent on her mother's side went back through fourteen kings to Egbert, king of Wessex.

Therefore everyone of importance in that council swore the oath, first William, archbishop of Canterbury, followed closely by other bishops and abbots. First of the laity swore David, king of the Scots, uncle to the empress. Next came Stephen, count of Mortain and

Boulogne, King Henry's nephew by his sister, Adela: then Robert, the king's son, to whom he had given recognition before he came to the throne and had made earl of Gloucester . . . It is said that there was a remarkable struggle between Robert and Stephen, two rivals who each contended for the distinction of being the first to take the oath. The one claimed a son's privilege, the other the precedence of a nephew . . .

William of Malmesbury next described the death of Henry I in Normandy, and told how Stephen, 'the first of the laity, after the king of Scots, who had bound himself in faith to the empress', hastened to England.

It is soberly agreed that on the day Stephen sailed to England, there occurred at dawn, quite contrary to winter's habit in our area, a frightening peal of thunder with terrifying lightning, so that men almost thought the earth was breaking. By being accepted as king by the people of London and Winchester, Stephen won over Roger, bishop of Salisbury, and William de Pont de l'Arche, the custodians of the royal treasure. However, lest the truth be hidden from posterity, all his efforts would have been useless had not his brother Henry, bishop of Winchester, who now is papal legate in England, given him ready approval. Of course he was enticed to do this by the strongest hopes that Stephen would rule the country as his grandfather William had done, especially with strict uprightness in church affairs . . .

We cannot discount the historical value of these two conflicting versions in *Gesta Stephani* and *Historia Novella* as much as today we would discredit election-minded propaganda. There was, it is true, a genuine difference of opinion, nurtured by self-interest, throughout the baronage, and, like political pamphleteers, one author looked at events through the eyes of a strong supporter of Stephen, and the other through those of his opponent, Gloucester. But, unlike most pamphleteers, neither author was blind to the faults of his own side nor to the merits of his opponents. William of Malmesbury admired Stephen for his energy, courage, leniency, and courtesy to all he met, though he thought he had little judgement and felt that one could not trust him to fulfil his promises. In one chapter he came near to admitting that there might have been some moral justification for men not keeping the oath they had made to support Matilda. Similarly, the author of *Gesta Stephani* praised the ability and wisdom of Robert of Gloucester, but explained that since he had offended God by initiating civil war in England, he inevitably suffered sudden death without a chance to repent. Stephen was no Galahad to this writer. In particular he realized what misery the long war was creating, and apologetically attempted to justify Stephen's policy by the argument, used later by Cromwell at Drogheda and by the allies at Hiroshima and Nagasaki, that it was kindest to strike the enemy without mercy and inflict grievous harm on the innocent if such actions were likely to end the war more quickly:

... it seemed to him right and just to attack his enemies everywhere, plunder and destroy all they possessed, fire crops and everything else that supported human lives and let nothing remain anywhere, so that, deprived in this way and reduced to starvation they might at length be forced to yield and surrender. He knew that in truth it was evil to destroy that which God had provided for the maintenance of human life, but he considered it much worse for the kingdom to be constantly disrupted by enemy raids and violated by daily marauding ...

William of Malmesbury also deplored the results of the war, especially the plundering of churches and church property. But he did not lay all the blame, as we might have expected, on Stephen. He believed that this 'very kindly man' had listened to the siren voices of the ill-disposed, and that they had urged him not to let his cause founder for lack of money so long as he could extract it from the church.

In the second half of the century the writings of three literary commentators and men of letters, John of Salisbury, Gerald of Wales, and Walter Map, coupled with the manuscripts written by more traditional chroniclers such as Ralph de Diceto, William of Newburgh, and the author of *Gesta Henrici Secundi* (*The Deeds of King Henry II*), have given historians exceptionally full contemporary comment upon the events and personalities

of the reigns of Henry II and Richard I. John, Gerald, and
Walter were all secular, not regular, clergy: they lived at court
and occasionally in the parish, but, with the exception of three
years by John as a young man, never in the cloister or the cell.
All three had benefited from the widespread enthusiasm for
education and learning in the twelfth century, and their work
graced the literary–artistic movement, which is often termed
by historians 'the twelfth-century renaissance'. None of them
were historians in the Bede or William of Malmesbury tradition, but all spoke eloquently of the age in which they lived.
Moreover, all had exceptional opportunities for witnessing
many dramatic incidents and for intimate knowledge of leading
personalities. As confidential secretary and emissary of Thomas
Becket, John of Salisbury was at the heart of political and ecclesiastical affairs in England, and his frequent diplomatic
errands into western Europe and across the Alps gave him a
wide knowledge of Europe. Gerald of Wales served Henry II
as chaplain, and, in 1185 and 1188 respectively, Henry sent him
on missions to Ireland and Wales, which prompted him to
write *Topographia Hibernica* (*The Irish Landscape*) and *Itinera-
rium Cambriae* (*Journey into Wales*) and, later, *Expugnatio
Hibernica* (*The Irish Invasion*) and *Descriptio Cambriae*
(*Portrait of Wales*). Walter Map was another member of
Henry II's household. He served for a time as a justice in eyre,
and, on one occasion at least, crossed the Channel on royal
business. He held a canonry at St Paul's along with a few minor
ecclesiastical appointments, and in 1196 was appointed archdeacon of Oxford. Just as Gerald suffered bitter disappointment
by not being elected bishop of St Davids, so Walter Map,
despite his efforts, failed to crown his career by being elected
bishop of Hereford.

The historical value of Gerald's topographical descriptions
and journalistic accounts is as obvious as that of the hundreds of
John of Salisbury's letters which have survived, and of his flattering but well-informed account of Becket's life. Our knowledge
of events in twelfth-century England would be much poorer

without them, but our understanding of twelfth-century thought and values, and our insight into life at Henry II's court, would be even more deprived had not John written *Policraticus* (*The Statesman's Book*), Gerald *Liber de Principis Instructione* (*the Book concerning the instruction of a Prince*), and Walter Map *De Nugis Curialium* (*Concerning Courtiers' Trifles*). There is something of a logical arrangement in the first two works – John set out to discuss morality and to attack the widespread belief in magic and portents, Gerald to demonstrate the characteristics of good and bad kings – but all three books contain many personal and miscellaneous observations on people, institutions, and ways of life. All are critical of Henry II. Gerald admitted his great energy, skill, wit, almsgiving, and good manners, but he attacked him bitterly for dilatoriness in administering justice, for attempting to turn everything to his own profit, and, above all, for 'his detestable usurpations in matters belonging to God'. He deplored the king's neglect of church services: 'as a son of the Church, whence he received the sceptre of royalty, he either failed to remember his sacramental anointing or ignored his receiving it; he spared but an hour for the divine mysteries of the sacred Host, and, perhaps because of state affairs, he would spend that time oftener in listening to his advisers and in discussion rather than in his devotions'. Apart from his championing of Becket against the crown, John of Salisbury's criticism was more indirect. He pointed it at the court and the age rather than at Henry himself. Walter was more subtle still in his delightful and diverting account of the court, but in his survey of English kings towards the end of his book he gave us a character sketch of Henry II, which reinforces much that Gerald of Wales had to say. The following extracts are taken from the excellent translation of Map's book made by M. R. James.

Henry himself was about twenty years old when he began to reign, and he reigned thirty-six years unconquered and undismayed, save by the sorrows which his sons occasioned him, and these, they say, he could not bear with patience, and died of the rancour they caused him. . . . I saw the beginning of his reign and his subsequent life, which in many respects was commendable. He was a little taller than the tallest men of middle height, and was blessed with soundness of limb and comeliness of face, one, in fact, whom men flocked to gaze upon, though they had scrutinized him a thousand times already. In agility of limb he was second to none, failing in no feat which anyone else could perform: with no polite accomplishment was he unacquainted; he had skill of letters as far as was fitting or practically useful, and he had a knowledge of all the tongues used from the French sea to the Jordan, but spoke only Latin and French. He had discretion in the making of laws and the ordering of all his government, and was a clever deviser of decisions in unusual and dark cases: affable, sober, and modest: tolerant of the discomforts of dust and mud: when oppressed by importunate complaints or provoked by abuse, bearing it all in silence. On the other hand, he was always on the move, travelling in unbearably long stages, like a post, and in this respect merciless beyond measure to the household that accompanied him: a great connoisseur of hounds and hawks, and most greedy of that vain sport: perpetually wakeful and at work. When troubled by erotic dreams he would curse his body which neither toil nor abstinence could avail to tame or reduce. From that time we used to ascribe his exertions, not to fickleness, but to his fear of growing too fat.

I have heard that his mother's teaching was to this effect, that he should spin out all the affairs of every one, hold long in his own hand all posts that fell in, take the revenues of them, and keep the aspirants to them hanging on in hope: and she supported this advice by this unkind parable: an unruly hawk, if meat is often offered to it and then snatched away or hid, becomes keener and more inclinably obedient and attentive. He ought also to be much in his chamber and little in public: he should never confer anything on anyone at the recommendation of any person, unless he had seen or learnt about it: with much more of the worst kind. And I confidently impute to this teaching all the points in which the king was vexatious. . . .

. . . King Henry II was distinguished by many good traits and blemished by some few faults. There is a fault which, as I have already said, he contracted from his mother's teaching: he is wasteful of time over the affairs of his people, and so it comes about that many die before they get their matters settled, or leave the court depressed and penniless, driven by hunger. Another fault is that when he makes a stay anywhere (away from home), which rarely occurs, he does not allow himself to be seen as honest men would have him do, but shuts himself up within, and is only accessible to those who seem unworthy of such ready access. There is a third fault, that he is intolerant of quiet and does not in pity refrain from troubling almost the half of Christendom. In these three ways he goes wrong: in other respects he is very good, and in all amiable . . .

Right at the end of the twelfth century – or it may have been during the first year of the thirteenth – was born Matthew Paris, whom the later Middle Ages and some distinguished modern historians have deemed the greatest of medieval chroniclers. He wrote in the cloisters of the Benedictine abbey of St Albans. He had not the same opportunities as John of Salisbury or Gerald of Wales to go into the world, but in the shape of messengers, judges, royal officials, bishops, barons, and even kings, the world sooner or later came to St Albans. From these visitors, some of whom stayed a few hours and some several days or weeks, Matthew gained most of the information he recorded in his *Chronica Majora* (*Greater Chronicle*) and his part of *Flores Historiarum* (literally, *Flowers of Histories*). But occasionally he witnessed an important event himself; he was present at Westminster, for example, for the marriage of Henry III and Queen Eleanor in 1236. He made no secret about his nose for news, and in October 1247, at the Westminster celebrations of the feast of St Edward, Henry III granted him a 'press seat' at the foot of the throne so that he could see all that went on. 'I beg you', so Matthew records the king as saying, 'to write an accurate and full account of all these events . . . lest in the future their remembrance should be lost in any way to posterity'.

Matthew proved worthy of the trust that Henry and others put in him. He wrote busily, recording news which came from as near as his own cloister or Westminster, and from as far away as Scandinavia, Spain, Italy, or the Near East. He has left for us pen pictures of contemporaries such as Henry III, Emperor Frederick II, Grosseteste, and Hubert de Burgh, details of prices and overseas trade, and his comments on many different aspects of medieval life. But he was far from being the perfect chronicler. He indulged his strong prejudices, and displayed a schoolboy's loyalty for St Albans above all other religious houses, for Benedictines above all other orders, and for monks when they were in dispute with abbots or in conflict with friars or seculars. He welcomed rumour, portents, and prodigies, and was not above inventing stories to illustrate his arguments. None the less, Matthew Paris was a likeable, energetic monk, as famous for his work as illuminator, goldsmith, and cartographer as he is for his chronicles.

2. ADMINISTRATIVE DOCUMENTS

William I neither ignored nor abandoned the English kings' method of governing, but so steadily did he and his successors experiment and make changes that well within a century after the Conquest they had revolutionized the machinery of English government. From the beginning William rode his tenants-in-chief on a tighter rein than the English kings had ridden their noblemen. He insisted upon homage and regular military service from all who held estates directly from the crown. He used the sheriff to safeguard his interests in the shires, and, through this officer whose authority rapidly increased, he and his sons extracted from rents and taxes a formidable income. In the twelfth century Henry I and Henry II continued to experiment. Changing conditions challenged them to find practical solutions to new problems, and as they did so they determined the way government and legal practice would evolve in England in the future. Norman government in England was *feudal*, but it was too sensitive to new situations and requirements ever to be considered a *system*.

A number of extant manuscripts give us official versions of the relationship between crown and baronage, and of innovations introduced into the government. Anglo-Saxon Chronicle E related how, at the Salisbury Council of August 1086, William required all the important tenants-in-chief to do him homage and swear that they would faithfully support him against all other men. An early twelfth-century manuscript has preserved a few laws which William made in consultation with his tenants-in-chief after the Conquest, and the charters, which Henry I and Stephen issued when they first came to the throne, declared the new kings' good intentions. Henry I was anxious to assure the church and the barons that he would not abuse their rights and privileges as Rufus had done:

... for reverence of God and for the love which I have for you all, I make the holy Church of God free. Thus I shall neither sell nor lease its property, nor shall I take anything from the Church's demesne on the death of an archbishop, bishop, or abbot, or from its vassals while a successor is being found. I immediately remove all the evil customs by which the kingdom of England has been unjustly oppressed ...

If any baron or earl of mine or anyone else who holds from me directly shall die, his heir shall not redeem his land as he would have done in my brother's day, but he will redeem it by a just and lawful payment ...

To knights who hold their land by military service, I grant as my own gift that their land shall be quit of all gelds and all labour requirements, so that, relieved of so heavy a burden, they may equip themselves well with horses and arms to be ready and able to serve me and to defend my realm ...

I restore to you the law of King Edward, together with all those amendments which my father made to it with the advice of his barons. ...

Stephen was just as determined as Henry to earn the blessing of the Church and the support of the barons by recognizing their traditional rights. He spoke with dignity and considerable kingly authority, but clearly he intended to show his subjects that he would consider himself bound by custom and law:

... I promise that I will neither do nor allow to be done anything which smacks of simony in the church or in church affairs. I declare and confirm that jurisdiction and authority over ecclesiastics and all clerks and their possessions as well as over the distribution of church

lands shall be in the hands of the bishops . . . I declare that all possessions and tenures, which the church held on the day King William,
my grandfather, died, shall be free and absolute and not affected by
the claims of any impostor. If in the future the church shall seek to
recover lands which it held before the death of this same king and
which it has now lost, I reserve to my own pleasure and judgement
either the restitution of the property or the discussion of the claim . . .

. . . I will observe good laws and traditional and lawful customs
concerning murder fines, and pleas, and all other matters, and I order
that the same be observed and recognized . . .

In the same formal type of document are recorded the major
judicial changes initiated during the reign of Henry II. There is
no gainsaying their supreme importance for the understanding
of twelfth-century government. They set down decisions
arrived at by the king's government, confirming or rejecting
experiments that have been tried out or changes that have crept
into judicial procedure. They give us the new law, but leave us
to find out, partly by inference and partly from other documents, how decisions were reached and how the law worked
out in practice. The Assize of Clarendon, issued by Henry II
'with the assent of the archbishops, bishops, abbots, earls, and
barons of all England' in 1166, decreed that in each hundred
and vill local men should be given the responsibility of bringing
suspected criminals before the king's justices and sheriffs:

. . . inquiry shall be made throughout each county and throughout
each hundred, through twelve of the more law-abiding men of the
hundred and through four of the more law-abiding men of each vill,
on oath that they will tell the truth, if in their hundred or their vill
there is any man who is accused or suspected of being a robber or
murderer or thief, or anyone who has sheltered robbers, murderers,
or thieves since the lord king has been king . . .

But these juries of presentment, forerunners of the grand juries,
were nothing new in 1166: at Clarendon the king merely confirmed and made regular a practice that had been tried and
found successful. From what the Assize assumed rather than
from what it initiated we can see how established the system of

itinerant justices had become since Henry I had first experimented with it, and also how, in his bid to improve law and order, Henry II was making widespread use of the system of frankpledge, by which groups of ten or twelve men were held corporately responsible for the good behaviour of their fellows. Two years previously, in much the same way, the Constitutions of Clarendon had formally proclaimed 'the acknowledged customs and privileges' which Henry II had been willing to accept as traditionally governing relations between the jurisdictions of church and crown, and from the terms of the Assize of Northampton, which revised the Assize of Clarendon in 1176, we can imply that in 1170 the Inquest of Sheriffs had presented the king with evidence which caused him to reduce the sheriffs' judicial authority and increase that of the itinerant justices.

Fortunately we can supplement these formal enactments from two other types of documents. First, there have survived three long manuscripts which give us detailed accounts of how Henry I's court was organized, how the exchequer functioned in the middle decades of the century, and how Henry II's judicial reforms were working out in practice at the end of his reign. None of these three documents are enactments. They are factual descriptions, most probably written to enlighten and guide administrators recently installed in office. Secondly there are the day-to-day records of the administrative departments of government. They were not plentiful in the twelfth century, but from John's reign they grew steadily in volume and became a rich source of exact, detailed information.

The first of the long manuscripts, *Constitutio domus regis* (*The Establishment of the King's Household*), was written about 1136. Its author is unknown, but it might well have been Nigel, bishop of Ely and treasurer at the close of Henry I's reign. It described how the peripatetic Norman court was divided into four divisions, each with its own hierarchy of officials and servants. The chancellor took charge of the secretariat and the chapel; the steward and the butler superintended the buying of food and drink and the preparation and provision of meals; the chamberlain and the treasurer looked after the king's most private needs, including his bed, his clothing, and his purse; and the constable and marshal cared for the horses and the dogs and protected the travelling court from marauders and thieves. At this period household and government administrations were one. The chancellor served the king as his secretary in both national and domestic affairs, and out of the same treasury came the money to pay household servants or to meet the cost of war. Therefore the most powerful of the barons did not scorn appointments in the royal household, though they pushed the more routine work on to their deputies. In *English Society in the Early Middle Ages*, the third volume of *The Pelican History of England*, Lady Stenton has quoted from this manuscript many details concerning the departments managed by the chancellor, the steward, and the chamberlain. In the staccato fashion of the whole document, the following extract recounts the details of the staff of the fourth department of the household.

The constables have allowances similar to the stewards and in the same manner. William, son of Odo, one simnel loaf of better quality, and one measure [sextary] of clear wine, and one wax candle, and twenty-four candle-ends. Henry de la Pomerai, if he resides outside the household, two shillings a day, and one salted simnel loaf, and one sextary of ordinary wine, and one candle, and twenty-four candle-ends. If he is resident in the household, fourteen pence, half a sextary of ordinary wine, and a candle if necessary. The same applies to Roger de Oyli.

The master-marshal, that is, John, shall be treated similarly. And in addition he ought to have tallies for the gifts and allowances which are made from the king's treasury and chamber; and he ought to have tallies against all the royal officials as a witness to all these things. The four marshals, who accompany such royal servants as clerks, knights, and serjeants when they are arranging billets or are otherwise engaged outside the court on the king's business, eightpence a day, one gallon of ordinary wine, and twelve candle-ends. If employed within the household, threepence a day for their men and a candle if necessary. But if any marshal shall be sent on the king's business, eightpence a day only. The serjeants of the marshals if they shall be sent on the king's business threepence each a day; but if not they shall mess in the household. The ushers, those who are knights, shall themselves mess in the household, and receive three halfpence a day for each of their men and eight candle-ends. Gilbert Goodman and Ranulf shall mess in the household, and receive three halfpence a day for their men. Other ushers who are not knights shall mess in the household without other allowances. The watchmen shall have double rations, three halfpence a day for their men and four candles; and in addition, in the morning, each is to have two loaves, and one portion of meat, and one gallon of ale. The stoker shall always live in the household, and from Michaelmas to Easter have fourpence a day for the fire. The usher of the chamber shall have fourpence for the king's bed every day the king is travelling. The tent-keeper shall live in the household, and when he has the tents moved, he has allowances for one man and one pack-horse.

Each of four hornblowers threepence a day. Twenty servants each a penny a day. Those who keep the greyhounds threepence each a day, and twopence for their men and a halfpenny for each greyhound. The royal keeper of hounds eightpence a day. Huntsmen who are knights eightpence each a day. Other huntsmen fivepence each. The handler of the blood-hound [*liemarius, cf.* French *limier*: blood-hound or staghound] one penny, and the blood-hound a halfpenny. The feeder of the hounds threepence a day. Huntsmen of the pack threepence each a day; every four [hounds] of the large pack [*magni harred*] ought to have one penny, every six of the lesser packs one penny. For the large packs [*magnos harrede*] two men, each receiving one penny a day, and for the lesser packs two men, each receiving one penny a day. Keepers of the small hounds [*braconarii*], each threepence a day. Wolf-hunters, twenty pence a day for horses, men, and hounds, and they ought to keep twenty-four running hounds [*canes currentes*] and eight greyhounds, and six pounds a year for buying horses; but they say eight pounds. Of the archers who carry the king's bow, each fivepence a day, and the other archers as much. Bernard, Ralph le Robeur and their associates threepence a day.

The second of the three twelfth-century manuals, *Dialogus de Scaccario* (*The Dialogue of the Exchequer*) is much more detailed than the *Constitutio*. It was written late in Henry II's reign, probably about 1179, and almost certainly by Richard, the son of Bishop Nigel of Ely. By that stage of the twelfth century it had long been clear to the king and his counsellors that a peripatetic court had serious disadvantages not only for those who were seeking justice, but also for sheriffs, reeves, and all who needed to pay the king the rents and taxes they had collected for him. Frequent royal visits to domains across the Channel made administration even more difficult. Rufus had tried to solve this problem by using Ranulf Flambard as his deputy when he himself was out of England. Henry I followed this precedent, and it was Roger, bishop of Salisbury, his deputy or justiciar in the twenties, who experimented with a permanent exchequer: 'This wise man, far-seeing in counsel, eloquent in debate . . .', wrote Richard fitz Nigel, his great-nephew, in the *Dialogus*, 'had the most profound knowledge of the exchequer, so profound that it is apparent beyond doubt from the rolls themselves that it developed strongly under his direction.' It continued to grow, and half a century later fitz Nigel was able to paint a picture of an important department of royal administration, which, though in theory still part of the court, had set up its own complicated machinery, established its own precedents, and was employing its own staff at its permanent home in Westminster. Richard fitz Nigel became treasurer at the end of the fifties, so that when he wrote the *Dialogus* he had had long experience of exchequer work and had probably helped to shape and prune the administration. He spoke of two exchequers: the upper, the policy-making body, concerned with supervision and acting as an appeal court; the lower, responsible for the daily task of receiving and spending money. The *Dialogus*, written in the form of questions and answers by a pupil and master, described in detail how each exchequer was staffed, how it worked, and what wages it paid. It is far too long a document to be quoted in full here, but the following short extract gives Richard's explanation of the name.

PUPIL: What is the exchequer?

MASTER: The exchequer is a rectangular board, about ten feet in length and five in width, used as a table by those who sit at it. A rim, about four fingers deep, runs round it to prevent anything which is placed on it from falling off. Over the board is spread a cloth, bought at the end of Easter. It is not an ordinary cloth, but a black one marked with stripes, a foot or a hand-span apart. Between the stripes counters are placed in their order, as will be explained below. But though such a board is called an exchequer, the name is also given to the court which sits at the board.

PUPIL: What is the reason for this name?

MASTER: At the moment I can think of no truer reason than because it is marked like a chess-board.

PUPIL: Did ancient wisdom give it that name merely because of its markings? For an equally sound reason it might have been called a draught-board.

MASTER: I was right when I called you meticulous. There is another deeper reason, for just as in the game of chess there are different classes of chessmen, which move or stand still by strict rules or within certain limits, some being more important and some being placed at the front, so in the exchequer some men preside, others are present by virtue of their office, and no one is free to go beyond the established rules, as will be clear from what follows. Again, just as in chess the battle is fought between kings, here the struggle takes place and the battle is fought mainly between two men, namely, the treasurer and the sheriff who sits with his account before him while the others sit like judges to watch and make decisions...

The last of the three major commentaries concerns legal administration. Historians have traditionally regarded it as the work of Ranulf de Glanvill, justiciar during the last decade of Henry II's reign, but there is no proof that he wrote it. It is a long work entitled *Concerning the Laws and Customs of the kingdom of England*. In his first thirteen sections or 'books', Glanvill discussed chiefly civil procedures. He distinguished pleas of the crown, such as those concerned with baronies, advowson, or dowries, from lesser pleas which could be heard by the sheriff. To guide new clerks and administrators, he wrote out specimen writs for use in specified circumstances, and carefully explained the details of procedure in the different

courts. A dispute about the possession of land could be settled
either by a duel or by pleading before the grand assize. The
plaintiff had to be ready to fight for his claim either in his own
person or through a champion, a so-called witness of the truth;
the defendant had the choice of either accepting the challenge,
or, from about 1180, submitting his case to a jury of twelve
knights, who had been nominated for the work by four other
knights chosen by the sheriff. This new grand assize method
quickly became popular, and Glanvill sang its praises. He was in
no doubt that the assize achieved justice better than the duel.

The grand assize is a royal benefit granted to the people through the
clemency of the king on the advice of his council, by which men may
advantageously preserve their lives and social status by legally re-
taining possession of their freeholds and being able to avoid the
doubtful decision of a duel. Also by means of the assize men are able
to escape the ultimate penalty of sudden and premature death, or at
least avoid the everlasting disgrace and infamy of that hateful and
shameful word which to his dishonour the defeated champion must
utter. [He had publicly to admit he was a coward.]

This legal institution is characterized by the greatest degree of
equity, for through it justice, which after many and long delays is
scarcely ever demonstrated by the duel, is hereby procured more
suitably and more speedily. For, as will appear from what follows, the
assize does not tolerate so many essoins [excuses] as the duel, and by
this both man's labour and the poor's substance are spared. Moreover,
just as in court the evidence of many reliable witnesses is more valuable
than the evidence of a single witness, so the assize is based on greater
equity than the duel. For whereas the duel arises from the evidence of
one juror, this institution demands the oaths of at least twelve men . . .

Ordeal by combat for knights, by fire for freemen, and by
water for villeins and serfs still remained the official way of
proving guilt or innocence in criminal trials, but by the end of
the twelfth century men had not the same faith in ordeals as
they used to have. Judicial inquiry, evidence brought before
the court, and the previous record of the accused, were all
carrying more weight than the simple verdict of sword, fire, or

water. Evidence on his behalf could sometimes save the accused from ever facing the ordeal. On the other hand surmounting an ordeal would not necessarily protect a heavily suspected prisoner from further punishment. In 1166 the Assize of Clarendon formally laid it down, and ten years later the Assize of Northampton confirmed, that such a prisoner, despite the supposed verdict of God in the ordeal, could be exiled.

Also the lord king ordains that those who shall be tried by his law and acquitted by law [i.e. by ordeal], if they have a bad character and have been publicly denounced by many law-abiding men, shall swear to leave the king's lands, so that within eight days, unless winds prevent them, they shall cross the sea, and [if contrary winds do delay them] they shall cross the sea by the first favourable wind they shall have afterwards, and, except by the mercy of the lord king, they shall not again set foot in England. There let them be outlawed; and if they return let them be arrested as outlaws.

Assize of Clarendon, clause 14.

If anyone has appeared before the lord king's justices on a charge of murder, theft, robbery, or of sheltering men who commit such crimes, or of forgery or arson on the sworn evidence of twelve knights of the hundred or, if knights are not available, on that of twelve freemen and that of four men from each vill in the hundred, let him undergo the ordeal of water . . . And if he shall be absolved at the water, let him find sureties and remain in the kingdom, unless he has been accused of murder or some other serious offence by the general opinion of the county and of the lawful knights of the land. If he has been accused in this way, although he may have been absolved at the water, nevertheless let him leave the kingdom within forty days, and let him take his belongings with him so long as he safeguards the rights of his lords, and let him swear to remain in exile at the mercy of the lord king . . .

Assize of Northampton, clause 1.

Yet, despite the discredit it was earning in legal circles, the ordeal continued to be used to determine guilt or innocence in criminal cases until the end of John's reign. In the last section of his treatise Glanvill explained how important it still remained notwithstanding the Assizes of Clarendon and Northampton.

Therefore when anyone is accused of regicide or of having incited men to rebellion in the realm or in the king's army, either an individual accuser will come forward or not. If the accused stands charged by rumour only, he shall be safely held by sureties or committed to prison. The charge shall then be investigated before the justices by means of many questions and cross-examination. The background of the case, as well as every opinion for or against the accused, shall be carefully considered.

The accused must clear himself by ordeal, or show that he is quite innocent of the crime of which he is accused. But if the ordeal proves a man guilty of a capital crime, then sentence will be pronounced on his life and body, which, as in other cases of felony, will be subject to the king's mercy.

But if from the first there be an individual accuser, he shall be bound by sureties (if he can provide them) that he will prosecute. . . The accused is usually held by satisfactory sureties, or, if he cannot provide them, he is committed to prison. An accused man is normally allowed to offer sureties in all cases of felony except murder . . .

On the day appointed the accuser will prefer his charges, that he has seen, or known for certain by other recognized means, that the accused has conspired against or otherwise endangered the king's life, or that he has spoken seditious words either in the realm or in the king's army, or has approved or counselled any such action, or ordered someone to do such things. He must agree to prove his accusations in whatever way the court should direct.

If in court the accused shall duly deny all the accusations, the case is usually decided by duel. In such cases neither of the parties, from the moment the duel is offered, may add anything to or withdraw anything from the statements made at the time of challenging without being declared vanquished and made liable to the penalties of the law. Nor may the two parties become reconciled to each other except by permission of the king or his justices. But if the accuser is defeated he shall be placed at the king's mercy. The other penalties and humiliations he shall suffer [fine and inability to raise the matter again] have already been described. Also the penalties the accused shall suffer if he is defeated have been previously stated. There should be added the confiscation of all his goods and the disinheritance of his heirs for ever.

Just as the writings of fitz Nigel and Glanvill help historians to interpret and assess the effectiveness of formal edicts and charters, so the humble day-to-day accounts of royal officers enable them to see law and administration in action. A single section of an account roll often seems too drab and trivial to enlighten the past, but a series of accounts is capable of painting a clear picture of procedure. The earliest accounts that have survived are the pipe rolls, on which every Michaelmas the exchequer clerks recorded the sums of money which the sheriffs paid into the royal treasury, i.e. the lower exchequer, that year. Pipe rolls acquired their unusual name because, when rolled up, the pieces of parchment, clipped together at the top, reminded men of pipes. The pipe roll for 1129–30 is the oldest one extant; from 1155 onwards they have survived in continuous succession and can be studied in the Public Record Office or from the publications of the Pipe Roll Society.

The local historian is particularly grateful for the early pipe rolls of his area, because they help to fill some of the nasty gaps which usually exist in his knowledge of events between Domesday Survey and the end of the twelfth century. From them he can distil details of succession to estates, of the transfer and value of land, and of royal grants and penalties. Occasionally an entry explains facts he has found elsewhere, or an unusual item disturbs the conventional pattern into which entries on the pipe roll quickly hardened. The following extract from the pipe roll of 28 Henry II, written in September 1182, is historically important because for the first time the exchequer treated Lancashire as a separate shire and not as part of Yorkshire or Northumberland. The heading reads strangely, 'Lancaster because there was not a place for it in Northumberland'. A dozen years later, King Richard gave the new shire full recognition when he declared that both 'the honour and county of Lancaster' were to be brought under direct royal control.

Ralph fitz Bernard renders account for £200 by tale for the farm of Lancaster. He has paid into the treasury £150 15s. 7d. And he has paid in lands granted to William of Valoines in Culpho £10 [Culpho is in Suffolk but was part of the honour of Lancaster]; to William fitz Walkeline in Stainsby £9; to Nigel of Gresley in Drakelow £4 16s. 0d; and to Engeran the porter and to Roger of St Aubin in Croxton £20.

And he has paid Warin the hunter on the king's writ 25s. 1d.; James on the same writ 50s. 1d.; Gibbe on the same writ 26s. 3½d.; and Peter fitz Bernard on the same writ 7s. 2d. And he is quit. [The farm of £200 was the fixed annual sum required from the honour of Lancaster. The sheriff subtracted from it rents of lands which the king had given away, and any special payments which he had made on the king's orders. He paid the balance into the treasury in cash, and it will be seen that in this particular year the crown was 2½d. to the good.]

The same Ralph renders account for £6 for an increment [to the farm] paid by Preston, and for 6s. for the farm of Marton this year. He paid this into the treasury by means of 2 tallies. And he is quit. [A tally was half a notched stick given to the sheriff as a receipt for money paid into the lower exchequer at Easter. The exchequer clerks split the whole stick from top to bottom and kept the other half as their own record.]

Gilbert fitz Waldeve renders account for £33 15s. 6d. in order that the king might remit his sentence of outlawry. He paid into the treasury £29 4s. 8d., and owes £4 10s. 10d.

The same Ralph owes 4s. 8d. of the aid from Preston. Robert, archdeacon of Chester, owes 100s. fine for a forest offence. Ralph fitz Bernard owes half a mark of Lancaster's aid.

Concerning payments made to the crown (*curia regis*):

The men of Preston render account for £30 for having a royal charter, so that they might enjoy the liberties which the men of Newcastle [under Lyme] enjoy. They have paid this into the treasury and are quit. [The king issued the Preston charter in 1179.]

Richard fitz Roger renders account for £73 7s. 0d., the fine he suffered for giving land to his daughter and heiress without the king's licence. He has paid into the treasury £20. He owes £53 3s. 0d. [*sic*].

The same Ralph renders account for £78 3s. 8d. for the county of Lancaster [*de Comitatu Lancastra*] so that they [i.e. those who dwelt within the forest boundaries in Lancashire] might be free of the pleas of the forest. He has paid £71 11s. 11d. into the treasury and owes £6 11s. 9d.

Richard fitz Waldeve renders account for 100s. for a writ against his men [villeins], who without right were making themselves free. He paid into the treasury 5 marks, and owes 2½ marks.

Richard of Molyneux renders account for 20s. for a licence to make concord with the men of Singleton concerning a certain new assize. He has paid this into the treasury, and is quit.

Agnes Bonetable owes 3 marks for recognition of her rights in half a knight's fee in Appleton.

Dean Adam [of Kirkham] renders account for £26 0s. 4d. for the wardship of his nephew with half a carucate of land and for the marriage of the mother. He has paid this into the treasury and is quit.

To supplement such detailed but fragmentary information, the local historian can examine any charters and fines that may still exist for his area. Charters, granted by the king, an important nobleman, or a comparatively humble landowner, vary from the foundation charters of a monastery or borough to a small gift of land made to a relative or dependant: the fines, sometimes called feet of fines because the third copy preserved in the Public Record Office was written at the foot of the original tripartite document, recorded legal settlements or final agreements made about large estates or small plots of land. They might be the outcome of a serious dispute in the courts between two contestants, or the means used by a landholder to secure an incontrovertible title deed to his lands, but in either case they contain a date, the names of the principals and witnesses, as well as useful detail about the land itself. With the help of such auxiliary records the historian is able to give more life and significance to certain items in the pipe roll fragment quoted above. For example, the special payments made to Warin the hunter, James, Gibbe, and Peter, were probably connected with the progress which Henry II made through northern England during the summer of 1181; the £6 increment paid by the people of Preston was originally an inducement to the crown to grant them a borough charter, but rapidly became a permanent addition to the farm of Lancashire; and the large annual payment made by those who lived within the

metes of the forest eventually led to King John accepting two
lump sums of £500 and £200 to make their privileges permanent. But even without other documents to support them
the pipe rolls tell us much about the outlook and sense of proportion of twelfth-century Englishmen. Even from this short
extract from the 1181–2 roll, it is apparent how burdensome
were the forest laws, how seriously the king's government
viewed offences against feudal rights, and what a large sum
was necessary to purchase the wardship of the heir of a small
estate.

3. BOROUGH CHARTERS

The Norman kings and Henry II granted very few borough
charters, but both Richard I and John seem to have been willing
to seal a charter for any town that applied and had the money
to pay for it. To boast a royal charter was usually to enjoy
limited independence from the sheriff, and to be privileged to
manage town affairs through aldermen and gild officers. The
civic council made regulations and held a court, the powers of
which – 'sac and soc, toll and theam, infangenthief' – the charter
often defined in detail: the gild supervised the tradesmen and
organized a market once or twice a week and a fair once or
twice a year. The burgesses were free men. They rented their
burgage or small-holding in the heart of the town, farmed
strips in the open fields, and sold their goods in the market and
fair without paying the customs and tolls that were charged
to all outsiders. A royal borough was usually free to tax itself.
The exchequer assessed it as a single unit; the civic head – mayor,
bailiff, reeve, or provost – then divided the assessment among
the burghers, arranged for the collection of the tax, and saw
that the money was paid into the exchequer.

In the late twelfth and early thirteenth centuries an increasing number of boroughs enjoyed independence on the strength
of a charter granted by the local landholder. These were the
seigniorial boroughs, and the authority of their charter varied

according to the status of the landholder who sealed it. Chester could feel reasonably safe sheltering behind the charter granted by its powerful earl, and no doubt Bury St Edmunds considered itself fortunate to be granted a charter by the abbot as early as the reign of Henry I. But time proved that those boroughs which could display a royal charter were the favoured ones, chiefly because in the more exacting days of the three Edwards they were better able to satisfy the *quo warranto* commissioners and keep their status and privileges. Especially in the north-west, many infant boroughs failed to reach full stature. Ulverston achieved a seigniorial charter as early as 1200, but never enjoyed real independence. Warrington lost in Edward I's reign the benefits of a charter it had won from the William le Boteler who was lord of the manor from 1176 to 1233, and Manchester, which was described as a borough in the thirteenth century and received a charter from Thomas Grelley in 1301, the royal commissioners reduced to the status of a market town in 1359.

Some early charters became models for the charters of other boroughs. Thus in Henry I's reign the archbishop of York granted Beverley the privileges which he recognized the citizens of York possessed; Henry II allowed the burgesses of Gloucester 'the same customs and liberties throughout all my land in respect of toll and all other things, as well as the citizens of London and Winchester ever had them in the time of King Henry, my grandfather', and the burgesses of Preston 'all the same liberties and free customs, which I have given to my burgesses of Newcastle-under-Lyme'. Using some charters as 'controls' in this way – and the habit developed during the reign of John, the most prolific of chartermongers – gave a degree of uniformity to the rights and privileges which borough charters authorized. Nevertheless no two boroughs were exactly alike in their degree of independence, for whereas some were strong enough to deny or buy out the claims of the lord of the manor, others had to smart under irritating manorial interference throughout the Middle Ages, and whereas some enjoyed the profit and prestige of fairs and markets which attracted merchants from many quarters of England and western Europe, others never possessed anything more than a local market. To establish the true status of a particular medieval borough, it is necessary not only to read the honeyed words of the charter, but also to study the later history of the town and discover if the burgesses succeeded in holding out against the hostile pressures of sheriff, lord of the manor, and, from the second half of the fourteenth century, justices of the peace.

To grant a privilege to one body was to run the risk of placing a restriction on another. Two charters could easily cancel each other out or contradict one another. Richard I granted the burgesses of Colchester 'throughout the whole of England and the ports freedom from tolls, lastage [lading charges], passage [tolls upon passengers or goods], pontage [bridge tolls], and all other customs'. He granted similar rights to Winchester, Lincoln, and other boroughs, and they were a common ingredient of the many borough charters granted by John. Therefore, when merchants from one borough attended the fair or market of another, the claims of the visitors to be free of all tolls throughout England often clashed with the insistence of the host town that its charter empowered it to impose charges on all outsiders trading within its boundaries. Occasionally disputes of this kind were taken before the king's justices. In 1221 the burgesses of Bridgnorth indicted the burgesses of Shrewsbury for preventing them from buying untanned hides and undyed cloth in the town. In the same year Worcester was accused both of imposing tolls, in accordance with its charter, on sheep and pigs from Evesham whereas tradition only warranted tolls on oxen and horses, and of preventing the men of Droitwich from buying and selling freely in Worcester, despite the terms of Droitwich's new charter, which granted 'that they might buy and sell throughout England, within or without the cities, all kinds of merchandise'.

Bristol was one of the few boroughs fortunate enough to

acquire a charter from Henry II. In 1155 he granted 'my burgesses of Bristol that they should be quit of toll and passage and every custom throughout the whole of my land of England, Normandy, and Wales, wherever they or their goods shall come'. This charter was couched in sweeping, general terms, and though Henry granted two further charters to Bristol, they were of minor and partial significance. A later generation of burgesses wisely determined to have their liberties much more closely defined. Accordingly in 1189 they bought from John, at that time count of Mortain but ten years later to be king, a new charter which stated their rights in detail. In 1930 Miss N. D. Harding translated it for the Bristol Record Society, and in *English Historical Documents, 1042–1189*, D. C. Douglas and G. W. Greenaway improved that translation.

John, count of Mortain, to all men and to his friends, French and English, Welsh and Irish, present and to come, greeting.

Know that I have granted and by this present charter confirmed to my burgesses of Bristol dwelling within the walls and outside the walls, up to the boundaries of the town, to wit, between Sandbrook and Bewell and Brightneebridge and the spring in the road near Aldebury by Knowle, all their liberties and free customs as well, freely and entirely, as ever they had them in my time or in the time of any of my predecessors.

The liberties thus granted to them are these. That no burgess of Bristol shall plead outside the walls of the town concerning any plea excepting those relating to exterior holdings which do not pertain to the Hundred of the town. And they shall be quit of the murder-fine within the boundaries of the town. And no burgess shall be forced to accept trial by battle unless he has been accused concerning the death of a stranger not belonging to the town who has been killed within the town. And no one shall take a dwelling within the walls by assize, or by livery of the marshals, against the will of the burgesses.

And they shall be quit of toll and lastage and passage and pontage and of all other customs throughout all my land and power.

And none shall be judged to be in mercy as to his money except according to the law of the Hundred, to wit, by forfeiture of 40 shillings. And the Hundred court shall be held only once a week. And in no plea shall any be able to sue by 'miskenning' [verbal error in formally protesting one's innocence]. And they shall have justly their lands and their tenures and their pledges and their debts throughout all my land whoever be their debtors. And right shall be done to them, according to the custom of the town, concerning all lands and tenures which are within the town. And pleas shall be held within the town, according to its custom, concerning debts and pledges which have been contracted in Bristol.

And if anyone anywhere in my land shall take toll of the men of Bristol, and after having been required to restore it shall fail to do so, then the reeve of Bristol shall take a distress at Bristol in respect of it, and shall continue to distrain until it be restored.

And no merchant from outside the town shall buy within the town hides or corn or wool from any stranger but only from the burgesses. And no stranger shall keep a tavern except on board a ship, nor shall he sell cloths for cutting except in the fair. And no stranger shall tarry in the town with his wares longer than 40 days in order to sell his goods.

And no burgess shall be attached or distrained anywhere in my land for any debt except he himself be debtor or pledge. And they shall be permitted to marry, and to give their sons and daughters and widows in marriage without licence from their lords. And none of their lords shall have the wardship of their sons, daughters, or widows, or be permitted to bestow these in marriage because of lands which the burgesses may hold outside the town: their lords shall only have custody of such holdings as are of their fiefs until such time as the wards come of age. And there shall be no recognition in the town. And no one shall take 'tine' in the town except for the use of the lord count [tine was the right to take a vat of 24 gallons of ale], and that only according to the custom of the town. And they shall be able to grind their corn wherever they wish.

And they shall have all their legitimate gilds as well as they had them in the time of Robert and William, his son, earls of Gloucester. [John, count of Mortain, was also earl of Gloucester.] And no burgess shall be compelled against his will to redeem anyone by surety although he be dwelling on his own land.

I have granted also to them all their tenures within the walls and outside the walls, as far as the aforesaid boundaries, in messuages, in gardens, in buildings by the waterside, and everywhere else in the town to hold in free burgage: that is to say, by payment of a ground rent which they shall pay within the walls. I have granted also that everyone of them shall be allowed to erect or improve buildings any-where on the waterfront or elsewhere, provided this be done without damage to the borough and the town. And they shall be allowed at their pleasure to build on any land or empty spaces which they have and hold within the aforesaid boundaries.

Wherefore, I will and firmly command that my aforesaid burgesses of Bristol and their heirs shall have and hold all their aforesaid liberties and free customs as are written down above, from me and my heirs as well and fully as ever they had them at any time they have been in operation. . . .

This seigniorial charter continued to be Bristol's authority for her independence until 1252, when Henry III confirmed 'for us and our heirs certain liberties granted to our burgesses of Bristol and to their heirs for ever by Lord John, the King our father, while he was count of Mortain'.

In 1193 John of Mortain used the Bristol charter quoted above as the basis for one he granted to Lancaster: '. . . know that I have granted and confirmed to my burgesses of Lancaster all the liberties which I have granted to the burgesses of Bristol'. In October 1199, six months after the death of Richard, Lancaster, apparently more apprehensive than Bristol, pur-chased a second charter from the new king. This made no mention of Bristol: instead John granted to the people of Lancaster all the liberties which 'the burgesses of Northampton had on the day when King Henry our father died'. Later in John's reign, Lancaster strengthened its independence by com-pounding all the rights due to the king for a fixed rent, the fee farm, of twenty marks a year.

Even the most detailed borough charter did no more than sketch the method by which the burgesses should govern their town. This problem they had to thrash out themselves by following custom where it existed, and by experimenting or copying the practice of other boroughs where it did not. Even-tually a body of rules and regulations gained the approval of

leading burgesses, and then hardened into an unyielding tradition. Some boroughs have in their archives written medieval
constitutions. Lincoln's is a good example, although the original
document of *c.* 1300 has disappeared and now exists only in an
eighteenth-century translation. It is quoted in full as Appendix
VII in J. W. F. Hill's *Medieval Lincoln*. The following brief
extracts indicate the substance of such constitutions.

These are provisions made together with the underwritten articles
by the mayor and whole commonalty of the city of Lincoln for keeping the peace of our Lord the King and for the perpetual observance
of the liberties and improvements hereunder mentioned (that is to say):

That the commonalty shall by their common council elect a mayor
from year to year of their own election; and that no mayor shall be
elected unless he shall before be assessed to the public taxes, with other
citizens of the said city; and that the mayor shall remain in his mayor-
alty so long as it pleases him and the commonalty . . .

And further it is provided that the commonalty with the advice of
the mayor shall choose twelve fit and discreet men to be judges of the
said city . . .

And it is further provided that the said citizens shall have bailiffs
every year of their own election, and that those bailiffs shall faithfully
discharge the fee farm rent of our Lord the King at the end of the
year . . .

And there shall be no weigher of goods unless he is elected by the
common council . . .

And . . . four men worthy of trust shall be elected from amongst
the citizens by a free election at the feast of St Michael to keep an
account of outgoings, tallages, and arrears belonging to the city; and
that they have one chest and four keys; and that they shall render up
their accounts to the city at the end of the year;

Also it is provided for the keeping the peace of our Lord the
King that they who ought shall appoint two men out of each parish
of the city worthy of trust to search their own parishes once a month;
And that no person shall lodge a stranger more than one night unless
he shall bring him forth to public view on the morrow if it shall be
necessary . . .

And if any person of the city shall oppose the mayor and commonalty concerning any matter of a public nature by them enacted, he

shall be in the mercy of the city; and it shall be lawful for the mayor and citizens to distrain him for his amercement until he shall make them satisfaction . . .

Also it is provided that no foreign merchant shall remain in the city more than 40 days for selling his merchandises, unless he shall have licence of the mayor and commonalty . . . no foreign merchant of any kind of merchandise ought to be admitted to sell it within the city by retail . . .

Also it is forbidden that anyone do go out of the gates of the city to buy anything that is coming towards it . . .

Also it is forbidden that anyone shall exercise his right of common in the common pastures but in a reasonable degree as he ought; and that any hog shall be suffered to enter thereon to the injury of the pasture;

And it is provided . . . that no weaver or dyer shall dye the wool or cloths of foreigners, nor fuller full the same against the liberties of the city . . . and that no merchant of the city shall buy cloth made out of the city to dye within the same . . .

And also that no regrator [to 'regrate' is to buy with the intention of selling retail] of flesh or fish shall buy any flesh or fish to sell which the Church of Lincoln refused before it was offered to the mayor . . .

And it is provided that no fisherman ought to fish in the free waters of the city, unless with nets provided and made by the consent of honest men of the commonalty . . .

Although London was so much bigger, richer, and more important to the king than York, Lincoln, Winchester, Bristol, or any other city in his realm, it cannot really be said that the crown gave the capital generous consideration. It is true that William I formally, though apparently grudgingly, recognized its unique position, but it was not until the last years of Henry I's reign that London received a detailed charter, defining and confirming its privileges. This allowed the citizens to appoint their own sheriff and justiciar, to be free from the jurisdiction of outside courts and from the necessity of submitting to trial by battle, and, in exchange for a farm or payment of £300 a year, to collect rents and dues throughout Middlesex. But Stephen eventually reduced this independence

and in 1155 Henry II issued a new charter which, by simply
failing to mention them, took away the Londoners' right to
elect their own sheriff and their privilege of collecting taxes in
Middlesex for £300 a year. Not until 1190 did the Londoners
recover these advantages, and then during the easier days of
Richard and John they purchased royal charters, which both
guaranteed all their ancient rights and privileges and gave the
city an effective administration free from outside interference.

All historians must regret that the Domesday Book description of London has never been found, but they have some compensation in the picture of late twelfth-century London, which
William fitz Stephen, one of Henry II's sheriffs and itinerant
justices, embodied in his biography of Thomas of Canterbury.
It is a most enthusiastic description of the city, which it announces Brutus founded before Romulus and Remus founded
Rome, but the accuracy of many of its details have been checked
from other sources. The following extract describes the topography of London. The whole document is available in translation in *Norman London*, Historical Association leaflets 93–4,
and in *English Historical Documents, 1042–1189*.

On the east stands the Palatine castle [Tower of London], very big
and strong: the walls and keep rise from very deep foundations and
are secured with a mortar mixed with beasts' blood. On the west stand
two strongly fortified castles [Baynard's and Montfichet castles], from
which runs a continuous massive and high wall, with seven double
gates and with towers at intervals along the north sides. London was
once similarly walled and towered along the south, but the mighty
river Thames, so full of fish, flowing on that side, has with the tide's
ebb and flow steadily washed against those defences, undermined
them and destroyed them. To the west the royal palace [of West-
minster] rises prominently above the river. With its ramparts and
bastions it is a building without compare. It is some two miles up
stream and is joined to the city by a populous suburb.

Everywhere outside the houses of those citizens who live in the
suburbs are their fine, large gardens, adjacent to one another and
planted with trees. On the north there are pastures and pleasant
meadows through which flow streams which turn cheerful-sounding

mill-wheels. Near at hand there is an extensive forest with woodland grazing and the lairs of wild animals, red and fallow deer, wild boars and bulls. The city's tillage is not barren soil but rich Asian plain which yields bountiful crops and fills the farmers' barns with Ceres' sheaves.

Also in the northern suburbs outside London are excellent wells, with sweet, clear drinking water that ripples over the bright stones. Among them are three celebrated ones, Holywell, Clerkenwell, and St Clement's Well. These are visited by greater crowds, and more students from the schools and more young men of the city go to them when they are seeking fresh air on summer evenings. London is indeed a good city when it has a good lord!

The three principal churches in London – the espiscopal church of St Paul, the church of the Holy Trinity, and the church of St Martin – have famous schools by privilege and by virtue of their venerable dignity. But by the favour of some influential person, or because of the presence of well-known scholars and eminent philosophers there are other schools licensed by special grace . . .

Immediately outside one of the gates is a field which is smooth both in fact and in name [Smithfield]. Every sixth day of the week, unless it be a major feast-day on which religious services are held, there takes place there a well-attended show of splendid horses for sale. To it come all the earls, barons, and knights who are in the city as well as many citizens either to be spectators or to buy . . . By themselves in a separate part of the field are the goods of the countryfolk – agricultural implements, long-flanked pigs, cows with full udders, mighty oxen and fleecy sheep. Also there are mares suitable for ploughing, or drawing sledges and two-horsed carts. Some are big with foal; close to others skip brisk young foals.

Merchants from every nation on earth delight to bring their trade to this city . . .

Obviously William fitz Stephen himself delighted in London. For him as for us, it was a re-built city, because in the first days of Stephen's reign fire had destroyed a vast area of it. Towards the end of the twelfth century, the fine new buildings and the greater degree of self-government could hardly help but engender a civic pride in the hearts of most of its citizens. This was the city whose mayor the Great Charter recognized as one of the twenty-five leading *barons* of England.

Bibliography of Twelfth-Century Documents

English Historical Documents, 1042–1189 by D. C. Douglas and G. W. Greenaway covers the bulk of the century, and contains translations of the whole or part of most documents quoted from or referred to in this chapter.

Full texts, some in English and some in Latin, are published as follows:

Chronicon ex chronicis (Florence of Worcester), ed. B. Thorpe, published by the English Historical Society (1848–9).

The Chronicle of Florence of Worcester, ed. and trans. T. Forester (1854).

Historia Regum, William of Malmesbury, ed. W. Stubbs (1887–9).

Gesta Pontificum, William of Malmesbury, ed. N. E. S. A. Hamilton (1870).

Historia Novella, William of Malmesbury, ed. and trans. by K. R. Potter, Nelson's Medieval Texts.

William of Malmesbury's Chronicle of the Kings of England, ed. and trans. J. A. Giles (1889).

Gesta Stephani, ed. and trans. by K. R. Potter, Nelson's Medieval Texts.

The Life of Ailred of Rievaulx, Walter Daniel, ed. and trans. by F. M. Powicke, Nelson's Medieval Texts.

Historical Works, Gervase of Canterbury, ed. W. Stubbs (1879–80).

Policraticus sive De Nugis Curialium et Vestigiis Philosophorum, John of Salisbury, ed. C. Webb (1909).

Opera, Gerald of Wales, 8 vols., Rolls Series (1861–91).

The Historical Works, Gerald of Wales, ed. and trans. T. Wright (1905).

De Nugis Curialium, Walter Map, ed. and trans. M. R. James, Cymmrodorion Record Series (1923).

Dialogus de Scaccario, Richard fitz Nigel, ed. and trans. C. Johnson. This volume also contains a translation of *Constitutio domus regis*. Nelson's Medieval Texts.

De Legibus et Consuetudinibus Regni Angliae, Ranulf de Glanvill, ed. G. E. Woodbine (1932).

The text of the Assizes of Clarendon and Northampton are to be found in Latin in W. Stubbs, *Select Charters*, revised edition (1913), and in English in G. B. Adams and H. M. Stephens, *Select Documents of English Constitutional History* (1901). See *The Governance of Medieval England* (Appendix IV), H. G. Richardson and G. O. Sayles for a discussion on these texts.

Pipe Roll Society Publications (1884–present).

Description of the City of London, William fitz Stephen, in *Norman London*, F. M. Stenton, Historical Association pamphlet (1934).

Bristol Charters, N. D. Harding, Bristol Record Society (1930).

Medieval Lincoln (quoting Lincoln Gild Documents), J. W. F. Hill (1948).

Useful commentaries upon and explanations of twelfth-century monastic chronicles are to be found in:

Descriptive Catalogue of Materials relating to the History of Great Britain and Ireland, T. D. Hardy, Vol. II (1865).

The Monastic Chronicler, C. Jenkins (1922).

Chronicles and Annals, R. L. Poole (1926).

THE THIRTEENTH CENTURY

I. JUDICIAL RECORDS

When today at Westminster lords and commons present for the monarch's approval a bill which has passed both houses, they are using a modified form of procedure which is far older than Parliament itself. From Anglo-Saxon days, men have sought a grant of liberties or privileges or the recognition of rights by bringing to the monarch a petition beseeching that he would concede their requests. The crown has shown its approval in different ways. Early Anglo-Saxon kings gave some of their petitioners a piece of turf, a bow, or other symbolic gift, and it has long been parliamentary practice for the monarch to accept a public bill with the Norman French formula *Le Roy (La Reyne) le veult*, and a private bill with *Soit fait comme il est desiré*. But most petitions presented to the crown in times past have been answered in writing, usually in the form of a letter: 'William, by the grace of God king of the English, to Ralph Bainard, Geoffrey of Manneville, and Peter Valognes, and to all his other liegemen in Essex, Hertfordshire, and Middlesex, greeting: Let it be known . . . ' Norman kings tended to use the same form of answer whether the petition came from a corporation such as a borough or monastery or from an individual, whether it asked for a permanent or temporary concession, and whether it concerned a matter of major or minor importance. But from the first years of the thirteenth century distinctions began to be maintained between charters which granted rights and liberties in perpetuity, and letters patent and letters close, both of which, when they were concerned with grants and not instructions, usually limited them to the lifetime of the petitioner. The general purpose of all three documents was the same, namely to convey, either to all it might concern, or, in the case of the letters close, to the individual petitioner, the crown's answer to a petition, and to provide the successful petitioner with written proof of his right to enjoy the benefactions bestowed upon him. Only in form did the three types of documents differ.

Hubert Walter's tidy efficiency is the source of these administrative distinctions, just as it is the reason why so many thirteenth-century administrative documents have been preserved. When he was Richard I's justiciar from 1193 to 1198, Walter began the systematic recording of pleas and final concords, and when he became chancellor during the first six years of John's reign, he began the filing of copies of charters, fines, letters patent, and letters close. His successors followed the precedents he had set, so that within a few years hundreds of parchments had already been preserved and the archives were constantly receiving further supplies. A mountain of records now confronts the historian. Fortunately many of these documents, stored in the Public Record Office, are available in print, either in full or in summary form. The Selden Society has published more than fifty volumes of judicial records of the thirteenth and fourteenth centuries; many county record societies have printed local selections from all types of early, administrative documents, and, above all, the Public Record Office itself has produced calendars of charters, letters patent, letters close, and inquisitions *post mortem* from the twelfth or thirteenth to the sixteenth centuries. Calendars do not quote the full texts, but they give the essential facts in each document, and since the form and style of documents quickly became stereotyped, they are usually sufficient for a researcher unless the names of witnesses are important in his work. Even when it is necessary to see the documents themselves, a calendar is a most useful guide and time-saver.

The main intention of the judicial record is to state the charges preferred against accused persons, the complaints made by plaintiffs against defendants, the courts' verdicts, and the punishments inflicted. These details help the historian to understand the age he is studying, especially if he can get behind the bare recital of facts and glimpse the philosophy and outlook of the men involved. But often the casual, incidental details help him more. The early records reveal widespread violence and poverty, as well as the sufferings caused to the innocent by wars and revolts, which romantic historians and many novelists clothe in dramatic and colourful pageantry. They refute the belief that the thirteenth century was a golden age, and answer those who assert that times past were never as lawless as the present. They demonstrate the personal conflicts occasioned by such changes as the extension of the area of ploughed land in a village or the granting of new rights under a charter. In these records humble people rub shoulders with the rich and powerful, and some men stand out either as persistent trouble-makers or active officials. They all contribute to historical understanding: even their names – English, Celtic, Danish, and Norse – as well as the spelling of the names of towns, villages, and fields can cause academic excitement. For historians waste less of early documents than butchers do of a pig's carcass. Not even the squeal escapes them.

Royal justice may have been one and indivisible, but it manifested itself in several different guises. The king himself, especially John and Henry III, frequently sat in court either at Westminster or at some provincial centre. When he did so that court heard all manner of suits and delivered judgements against which there could be no appeal. The justices of the bench, the most impressive of the crown's judicial deputies, generally sat at Westminster. During the thirteenth century the bench crystallized into two regular courts in which the king rarely, and later never, appeared – the court of common pleas which heard civil cases, and the king's bench, which in addition to being a criminal court both of first instance and of appeal, superintended the work of and heard complaints against royal officers. Associated with these two permanent courts was the exchequer court, half administrative body, half court of law, with its prescribed task of collecting the royal revenue. Outside Westminster worked the itinerant justices.

The king appointed them to serve as his deputies in the shires, but he strictly defined their purpose and authority. For each new circuit he issued a new commission, and by the beginning of the thirteenth century it was usually either a commission in eyre or a commission of assize. Justices in eyre were competent to hear all kinds of cases, but they were required to have present all the freeholders of the county as well as representatives from every hundred and township. Wherever they went they caused a big disturbance and poked their unwelcome nose into many affairs. Not unnaturally they grew more and more unpopular, and though there were eyres throughout the thirteenth century, they became less frequent and disappeared altogether in Edward III's reign. Justices of assize, who date from that rich period of judicial reform in the second half of the twelfth century, made far less fuss in the counties. But their authority was limited at first to cases of novel disseisin (recent dispossession) mort d'ancestor (claim to be the heir of the previous holder), and darrein presentment (to determine the right of advowson), all concerned with the right of holding land or of presenting to a benefice. In practice these judges, who used a jury to advise them on local opinion and knowledge, interpreted their commission quite widely. They visited the counties much more frequently than the justices in eyre, and, particularly after the Statute of Westminster of 1285, enjoyed increasing authority. Judges occasionally arrived at the county town charged by the king with gaol delivery, that is the trying of all prisoners waiting to have their cases heard. And later, when commissions of eyre were being issued less frequently, the king empowered other justices to hear all charges of felony in the country. Their authority was a commission of oyer and terminer.

But whatever the court or commission, its records reveal how ineffective criminal justice was in the thirteenth century. They show that each session the judges had to set aside a good number of cases because the crime had been committed by people unknown or by suspected persons who had fled. If he were brought into court to face heavy evidence against him, the accused could frequently turn the tables on the plaintiff by showing that he had not observed a technicality or had presented evidence that was not legally watertight. Even when the accused was considered guilty, his guilt, up to the end of John's reign, was often put to the further test of ordeal by water or fire, and in both these ordeals success was more frequent than failure. The following pleas of the crown, typical of scores of recorded cases heard by the king's justices, illustrate the value of this primary material for the social and general historian.

Two cases heard before justices in eyre, the one in Cornwall in 1201 and the other in Lincolnshire in 1202, seem to have been decided by strange reasoning. The knights of four Cornish hundreds gave evidence that they suspected Osbert of the death of Roland, son of Reginald of Kennel. Reginald and his son-in-law, Arkald, formally accused Osbert of murder. The court ordered Osbert to purge himself by water, and since the water declared him not guilty, he went free. But

Reginald is in mercy [liable to be punished] because he does not claim to have seen or heard the crime, and because he has himself withdrawn and in his place appointed another man [Arkald], who neither saw nor heard [the crime] and yet offered to prove it. So let both Reginald and Arkald be in mercy.

In the Lincolnshire case Thomas, son of Leofwin, accused Alan Harvester of assaulting and dismembering him. He gave evidence that Alan seized him on the highway, carried him to his house, stole his cape and knife, struck him so that he broke a bone in his arm, held him while two others cut off his testicles, and then carried him back to the road and dumped him there. Thomas further declared that he reported this crime as soon as he could, and claimed that the king's sergeant went to Alan's house and found there the cape and knife. In court the sergeant said

that he came to Alan's house and found there the knife and the testicles in a certain little bowl but not the cape. And the whole county testifies that before this hearing Thomas never accused Alan of breaking a bone. And therefore the accusation is considered to be null and Thomas is in mercy . . .

Clearly the wronged always ran grave risk of suffering twice over if he appealed to the law, and the criminal stood a sporting chance of escape especially if the court decided to use an ordeal. William Smallwood must have bitterly regretted taking legal action in Essex in 1220, but in his case one cannot feel any sympathy for him. He accused Hugh Large of Walthamstow, Nicholas of Trumpington, and others of stealing from him horses, which he admitted he had stolen from others. He also accused John and Adam, the priest's sons, of being associated with him in murder and further robbery. When this case of blackguards falling out came before the judges of the bench, the sheriff of Essex gave evidence that the plaintiff and the accused were all men of bad reputation. The judges granted William's request that he should be allowed to establish the truth of his accusations by ordeal by battle against Adam.

They prepare to fight. Adam is committed to the custody of Hugh of Eleigh, Adam of Eleigh, and Roger, serjeant of Waltham, who must answer for his body on Tuesday, and then he must come armed. John is committed in the same way to the same men.

William Smallwood is defeated and hanged, and Adam and John are discharged on pledges. The said Hugh, Adam, and Roger go surety for them, and they must find other pledges before the sheriff of the county.

The people of Essex must have been relieved that William Smallwood would trouble them no more, but must have speculated apprehensively upon what Adam and John, freed and somewhat encouraged, might try and do next.

One has only to leaf through the printed judicial records to get the impression that ordinary men and women in thirteenth-century England lived in continual fear and danger of violence, and that their lives were always poor and often 'nasty, brutish, and short'. Further study of the records merely strengthens one's first impressions. At Worcester in 1221, for example, the king's justices heard almost 200 cases of death or homicide, most of which were associated with robbery. These are four characteristic examples.

Ingrith of Comberton, William of Henwick, Richard of Powick, Alexander Percehaie, and Geoffrey son of Alice were killed in Ingrith's house by thieves. No one knows by whom. Englishry has not been presented, and therefore it is to be regarded as murder.

Roger of Severn Stoke was killed in his house by robbers at night. No particular person is under suspicion. Englishry was presented by Oliver of the Cross and William of the Vineyard and they are dead. One of the robbers was killed by his fellows and he is unknown. The verdict is murder. And since the manor of Severn Stoke is separately represented, let it answer for the murder fine by itself independently from the hundred.

Criminals came by night to the home of Alice of Stoke Prior. Richard de Strech killed one, cut off another's head, and held the third man, who was afterwards hanged at London. Therefore, Richard and Alice go free. William le Hore, the receiver of the criminals, has fled and is under suspicion. Therefore let him be questioned and out-lawed. His chattels were worth two shillings for which the sheriff shall answer, and he was in the frankpledge of Rannulf, son of Ailmar of Stoke Prior, which is therefore in mercy.

Nicholas Bricun of Ombersley killed Hugh Mac as they came from an ale-drinking session at Ombersley. Cecily, Hugh's wife, sued in the shire until Nicholas was outlawed. He was in Robert Culivert's frankpledge which is therefore in mercy. His chattels were worth ten shillings for which the sheriff shall answer. Englishry was presented.

Three of these cases mention 'Englishry'. It was customary from the Norman Conquest to the middle of the fourteenth century to state if a murdered man was Norman or English by descent. If it could not be proved that he was English – all unknown cases were assumed to be Norman – the law laid a murder fine on the hundred in which the crime took place. Similarly if an accused person who was in frankpledge went into hiding and failed to appear in court, the other members of his frankpledge group were fined for allowing him to break the law. Such communal punishments, intended to be a sharp spur to villagers and townspeople to bring their erring neighbours to justice, do not seem to have achieved much success. Probably because it was so difficult to arrest and punish criminals, the law even allowed plaintiffs to settle criminal matters out of court. Before the justices of eyre in Shropshire in 1203, for example,

Sibil, daughter of Engelard, accuses Ralph of Sandford that he, in the king's peace wickedly and contrary to the peace given her in the county court by the sheriff, came to her lord's house and broke open her chests and carried off her goods, and treated her so violently that he killed the child that was living in her womb.

Later she came and said that they had come to an understanding and she withdrew the charge, for they had agreed that Ralph shall satisfy her for the loss of the goods as seen and assessed by lawful men. And Ralph has agreed to do this.

It is apparent from the examples already quoted that royal justice was not reserved for the rich. Manorial courts possessed either severely restricted authority or no authority at all over criminal offences, and such local courts as the hundred and county courts, which were themselves in a true sense royal courts, could only deal with comparatively petty offences. Anything serious had to go before the king's justices, and the plea rolls paint a picture of these dignified gentlemen being constantly faced by woebegone plaintiffs accusing poverty-stricken defendants. In the records of two assizes, Lincolnshire, 1218–19, and Worcestershire, 1221, which Lady Stenton edited in volume 53 of the Selden Society publications, there are over eighty cases in which unsuccessful or absent litigants were said to be so poor that it would be useless to fine them. From their names and apparent social connexions this is often unexpected. At Lincoln they included Henry, brother of Roger the dean, Simon of Hough on the Hill who was a well-known juror, and Richard Sulee and Roger of Hawthorpe, the two sureties

for the prior of the Gilbertine house of Sempringham; at
Worcester, Richard the chaplain, son of Robert of Holt,
Gilbert of Feckenham and his wife Juliana, and the priest,
Walter of Leicester. That they were just as likely to be plaintiffs
as defendants is a telling comment upon the availability of the
king's justice. Warin, son of Guy le Buis, came before the
justices at Lincoln to claim a bovate of land which had previously been farmed by his father, but which was then held
by Nicholas le Buis. He maintained that since Guy had been a
freeman, the land should have been inherited by him, his heir.

The jurors say that the aforesaid Guy was a free man as regards his
body and that he died seized [possessed] of that land, but he, like the
other villeins in the same village, held it in villeinage and performed
all the customary obligations of a villein.

They therefore found in favour of Nicholas, but Warin could
pay no penalty for making a false claim because, son of a free
man though he was, the jury acknowledged he was 'very poor'.
The Worcester jury disallowed the claim of Rannulf of Clifton
to half a virgate of land, falsely said to have belonged to his
father, but again no penalty could be imposed because Rannulf
'is a poor man and has nothing'.

Other civil cases help us to assess the dominant interests and
scale of values which men had in thirteenth-century England.
They remind us continually that almost everyone had a direct
interest in farming, and that land completely outclassed all
other forms of wealth. Conflicting claims to hold or fence land
or to enjoy inherited freedoms and rights of way took up much
of the time of the courts, for such possessions and privileges
were highly prized and, therefore, frequently contested. No
changes could be made without vigorous protest from those
who considered themselves the injured parties. A typical case
at this same Lincoln assize of 1218–19 concerned three villagers
of Bicker, who accused the abbot of Owston in Leicestershire
of enclosing part of their common pasture. They failed to
convince the jury: 'the jurors say that he [the abbot] has not

disseized [taken away from] them of any common belonging to their tenement'. A similar but more complicated issue heard at Worcester in 1221 had to be referred to the bench at Westminster for final judgement. A score of villagers from Yardley complained that Thomas of Swanshurst, a neighbouring free man, had attempted to enclose part of the common land, contrary to a judgement given by King John at Nottingham. Therefore they had 'thrown down the hedges'. Thomas, with the backing of his lord, Ralf de Limesi, contended that

such is the law in Arden that where there is a great pasture, he who possesses the land may erect buildings, raise hedges, and dig ditches within the pasture, providing they be not in the commoners' entry or exit or to their hurt.

The plaintiffs countered this argument by claiming that Thomas's enclosure was blocking their way on to the pastures, but Thomas denied that it was infringing any common rights. He asserted that the villagers had acted 'contrary to the custom of that country'. Most serious disputes concerning common rights and landholding were settled by the itinerant justices with the help of a jury, the members of which were not directly concerned in the case but were local enough to know the traditions and customs of the area.

The records of manorial courts, which were concerned with administration as well as with breaches of the law, give us further abundant evidence about medieval agriculture, local government, and the life of the free tenants and the servile villeins and serfs. They are an essential source for all who seek knowledge of economic and social conditions in the medieval countryside. It was during the thirteenth century that lords of the manor began to ape the king and keep systematic records on parchment court rolls. They were interested in recording changes in landholding, rights and customs in the open fields and common meadows, and personal disputes between tenants, as well as such offences against manorial law and custom as trespass, stealing of wood or pasture, or neglect of labour services. Manorial courts varied considerably. They might meet once or twice a year, or as frequently as every two or three weeks. Their authority was determined by local tradition, royal grants of privilege, and the social status of the lord, but, for the sake of prestige and profit, most lords of the manor tended to push their legal authority as far as the superior courts allowed them to do. In the thirteenth century they recognized little difference between the court baron for free men, the court customary for the unfree, or the court leet authorized by a royal grant. All three, where they existed together, tended to merge into one all-purpose manorial court, and their records to be written on the same court roll.

The manor court's lack of legal dignity and rank does not make its records less welcome to the historian. The matters it dealt with were petty, but the court rolls demonstrate with infinite examples fundamental features of medieval life – that custom ruled the lord as well as the serf, that the sworn evidence of juries established facts, or that the bailiff in administering and disciplining the manor relied upon the help of reeve, hayward, pinder, and constable, court-appointed villeins or serfs, who, probably reluctantly, held office for a year at a time. Thousands of court rolls are scattered throughout libraries and record depositories. Many have recently found their way into county record offices and the hands of local historians, but there will have to be much more detailed study of them before we can claim that our knowledge of the lives of humble folk in the Middle Ages is both comprehensive and sound.

Such landholders as the king, the barons, and the monastic houses held many manors. For them the court roll served not only as a necessary record but also as a check on the work of their steward. The abbey of Bec, like other Norman abbeys, had acquired the lordship of a scatter of English manors. The abbot's steward toured the manors twice a year. In October 1247 he presided over the court at Tooting in Surrey.

The whole vill gives 2½ marks for the abbot's tallage.

William Jordan is in mercy because he ploughed the lord's land badly. Arthur is his pledge. Fine 6d.

John Shepherd is in mercy because he encroached across the boundary of his land. Walter the reeve is his pledge. Fine 6d.

Lucy Rede is in mercy because her cattle were found on the lord's pasture after ward had been made. Hamo of Hageldon is her pledge. The fine is forgiven.

Elias of Streatham is in mercy for default of service in the autumn. Fine 6d.

By early November the same steward was presiding over the same abbey's manor court at Deverill in Wiltshire.

William Miller appears [before the court to prove] he was not the pledge for William Scut of Hull, whose sheep were found in the lambs' pasture. Pledges for him are William Swineherd and Thomas Guner.

Arnold Smith is in mercy for not producing the said William Scut whose pledge he was.

The parson of the church is in mercy for his cow caught in the lord's meadow. His pledges are Thomas Guner and William Coke.

The township gives 3 marks for the abbot's tallage.

From Martin Shepherd 6d. for the wound he gave Pekin.

Once all the business had been done at Deverill, the steward moved south. In mid-December he was at Povington, Dorset, and by early February back near London at Ruislip, Middlesex. During the six months of winter it must have been an exacting circuit, for monastic lodgings could be most Spartan, and footpads and muddy potholes made medieval roads dangerous.

2. CHANCERY DOCUMENTS

Of all the documents filed in the chancery or secretariat, the charter, with its formal language and large appended seal, is the most impressive. We have already examined those charters which are the title deeds of boroughs, and everyone knows of the Great Charter which John sealed at Runnymede. But the crown issued hundreds of charters for dozens of purposes, including the granting of lands, titles, offices, and privileges to monasteries, churches, colleges, schools, and individual clerics and laymen. Both the king and the recipient wanted everyone to know the terms of the charter, and therefore the king addressed it to as wide a group of people as he considered necessary. He set no time limit to the rights it conveyed. Most charters which the Norman kings and Henry II issued to corporations were undated. Many have been lost, but we know of their existence either because the corporation – monastery, borough, church, or college – confirmed them with later charters, or because, from Henry III's reign onwards, the king issued an *inspeximus*, by which he acknowledged that his officers had examined and accepted a particular charter. A corporation sought a new charter for a number of reasons, varying from the practical need to renew a faded or damaged parchment to the political prudence of re-establishing its traditional and treasured rights and privileges with the new authority enthroned by civil war. It often wished to transform the vague terms of an early charter into a more detailed and precise statement. To raise money and to protect themselves against fraudulent claims, some kings, such as Richard I and Henry III, threatened not to recognize any charter granted by their predecessors unless the holders bought a confirmation. Such documents could be expensive. The chancellor, vice-chancellor, and protonotary added their fees to the purchase price, and even the cost of the parchment and of the wax for the seal appeared on the bill as separate items. But most corporations preferred to pay these costs than risk losing their cherished liberties.

Not all charters, of course, were issued by the crown. Just as the seigniorial boroughs sported charters from neighbouring landholders, so other corporate bodies and individuals enjoyed liberties granted by earls, barons, abbots, bishops, and lesser dignitaries in church and state. At the end of the twelfth century

Baldwin fitz Baldwin awarded Geoffrey, chaplain of Tothill, half a messuage in Westminster, on condition that he paid 18d. each year and employed a man to cart hay or corn for one day a year for the abbot of Westminster. In 1234 the prior of the Cluniac house of Lenton confirmed the right of Robert Ingram of Nottingham to pasture his cattle in a meadow belonging to the church of St Stephen, Sneynton. Robert could hope to pass on this right to his heir, but after Walter Hervey, mayor of London in 1270, had granted charters to groups of craftsmen allowing them to regulate trade, the next mayor refused to recognize such privileges. This was a risk all charter-holders had to take.

Many charters exist which are no more than ordinary civil contracts. The business could just as easily have been dealt with by a final concord; the types of agreement recorded in these private charters and in feet of fines are indistinguishable. But to most historians the matter of the document is more important than the form. From such a private charter as that granted in the early thirteenth century by Hugh, son of Adam of Ringston, they can establish that in the name of piety it was possible and laudable for a landholder to give a villein with his family 'to God and St Mary and to the abbot and abbey of Sulby in Northamptonshire', and from the following charter, transcribed from the deeds of the Shakerley family in *Early Cheshire Charters*, they can gather a number of details about Cheshire salt and about some of the people who lived in the county in the days of King John.

Peter, clerk of the earl of Chester, to all clerics and laymen, both those now living and those who are to follow, to whom this present writing shall come, greeting.

Know that I have given and granted and by this present charter of mine have confirmed to Thomas of Croxton for his homage and service half a salthouse of the fee of Roger Mainwaring, and another half salthouse of the fee of Ralph Brereton which Gilbert, chaplain of Middlewich, gave me, as well as all the land which Erneis the chaplain held between the estate of William Brun and the brook which runs close to the earl's bakehouse. These grants are to be possessed and held freely and quit of charge by the aforesaid Thomas and his heirs of me and my heirs, or of those whom my heirs or successors shall nominate, in exchange for rendering annually to me and my successors, for all service and claims belonging to me and my successors, fourteen shillings, seven to be paid on the nativity of John the Baptist [24 June] and seven at the feast of St Martin [11 November]. If, moreover, the aforesaid Thomas and his heirs will both charge the two aforesaid salthouses and the aforesaid land with a payment of seven shillings and eight pence to the Hospital of St John at Jerusalem and quit them from all other charges, I, Peter, and my successors will solemnly guarantee that Thomas and his heirs shall hold these two half salthouses with the aforesaid land against all men and women. These are the witnesses: Liulf the sheriff, Richard his son, Richard Lokeharm, Richard of Clive, Henry of Weaver, John of Occleston, Stephen son of Edric, Ingulph son of Matilda, Hugo the smith, Richard the clerk and many others.

The list of witnesses is often the most useful part of the charter to the historian. It helps him to date the documents, and is a primary source when he is building up a genealogy or seeking evidence for such things as the foundation of a parish church or the presence of an early schoolmaster.

Letters patent and letters close are the most voluminous categories of chancery documents. The king used them for sending orders to his officers, but equally frequently they are, like the charter, the crown's answer to a subject's petition. They lack the flamboyant address of the charter and do not carry so imposing a list of witnesses, but to the recipient they frequently conveyed privileges or instructions of considerable importance, and to the historian they offer just as rich a field as the charters for investigation. Out of hundreds of similar items, the following short list has been selected from the calendars of letters patent of Henry III and Edward I in order to show the types of business which the crown transacted by attaching the great seal to these documents.

August 1233. Mandate to the sheriff of Nottingham to permit no one to prevent the execution of the will made by Sarra, late wife of

Hubert, son of Ralph, concerning her goods and movables.

September 1234. Royal assent to the election of Reginald, prior of Grimsby, to be abbot of Grimsby, and a mandate to the bishop of Lincoln to do his part herein.

February 1238. Grant for life to Emma Biset, sometime damsel of the queen, of £10 a year at the exchequer for her maintenance.

September 1242. Licence for Randolf Tusk of Parma, James Charbonet, James of Siena, Hugh Symonet of Florence, Alemannus of Florence, Forez of Pistoja and Guy of Lucca, merchants of Rome and Italy, to come safely to England with goods and merchandise, and for the protection of them in so doing.

March 1263. Bond to Nicholas of Lyons, Walter Pedargent and others, merchants of Douai, in £221 18s. 0d. for cloths bought of them for the king's use by Richard de Ewell and Hugh de Turri, buyers of the wardrobe, in Winchester fair in the 46th year [of Henry III's reign, i.e. 1261–2] and in Bury St Edmund's fair in the 47th year: which money the king will pay to them at the next Boston fair.

March 1264. Licence for Richard Foliot and his heirs to enclose his manor of Grimston, Nottinghamshire, with a ditch and wall of stone and lime, and to fortify and crenellate it.

December 1275. Appointment during pleasure of Ralph of Sandwich to the custody of the castle of Devizes and the manor of Rowde, with the forests of Chippenham and Melksham, and mandate to John of Havering to deliver to him the castle with the armour, and the manor with the stock, corn, and other goods.

March 1277. Safe conduct, until midsummer, for the abbot of Cluny coming to England.

June 1280. Acquittance to Joseph of Cancy, sometime treasurer of the exchequer, of the exchequer, of the writings, silver, gold, jewels and other goods of the king, which have been at any time in his hands, and which he has surrendered.

September 1281. Pardon to Henry the Sauser, in the gaol of Winchester for the death of William the Prikere, on testimony before the king of William of Brayboef and William of St Clare, justices appointed to deliver that gaol, that he killed himself by misadventure.

September 1281. Commission of oyer and terminer to Geoffrey Aguillon and Alan of Walkingham touching the persons who carried away 60 marks and other goods of William of Wintringham, clerk, at Beverley, Yorkshire.

Much political as well as economic and social history is wrapped up in these royal letters. Journeys undertaken by the court, important meetings of the great council, and military campaigns are all heralded by a spate of letters, some open and some closed, making necessary arrangements. The king gave general orders, but relied upon the accumulated experience of his chancery clerks to see that the details were competently handled. At the end of 1276 Edward I determined to launch full-scale war on Llewelyn of Wales in the following summer. On 12 December his clerks sent letters to 14 earls, 2 archbishops, 19 bishops, 20 abbots, 4 abbesses, and about 170 other tenants-in-chief ordering them to be present with 'horses, arms, and all their service at Worcester in the octave of St John the Baptist next [last week of June], to set out on the king's expedition against Llewelyn, son of Griffith, prince of Wales, and his accomplices'. In addition the chancery instructed each sheriff to require all who held of the crown by knight service, or their substitutes if they were unable to bear arms, to be at Worcester at the same time. But this summoning of the feudal host was the beginning and not the end of the chancery's work. By 28 December the clerks had written to Edmund, earl of Lancaster, and twenty other major landholders conveying Edward's orders to prohibit 'corn, wine, honey, salt, iron, arms, or other things whatsoever, whence the rebels might have any maintenance' from passing through their lands into Wales, and in February 1277 they began to issue a long series of letters patent granting protection to individual gentlemen who were 'going to Wales on the king's service'. They sealed more than 200 of these letters in the first three weeks of July when the main army had assembled, and when, in order to feed the troops, they were sending Edward's instructions to the sheriffs of all counties from Gloucester to Lancaster to prohibit the holding of markets and to encourage owners of surplus stocks to sell to the king's officers. Edward wanted efficiency and the willing co-operation of all. Through his chancery he urged his sheriffs to speed war supplies through their shires, but, in order to minimize grumbling and apprehension, as early as 5 February he took the trouble to send letters to the commonalty of Shropshire and Hereford assuring them that

their courtesy and aid of horses and arms and other their power to Henry Lacy, earl of Lincoln, Roger de Mortuo Mari and others, who have gone on the king's service to the parts of Wales against Llewelyn son of Griffith, prince of Wales . . . shall not be taken to establish any new right on the part of the king nor be construed in any way to their prejudice.

Thus, from the chancery letters alone, we can appreciate both the assembling of the necessary food supplies, arms, ships, labourers, and soldiers, and Edward's preliminary actions, by which, in the early months of 1277, he quickly recovered the lands in mid-Wales which Llewelyn had recently occupied, and forced his enemy back on Snowdonia. The letters make it clear that by the time Edward had amassed his midsummer force at Worcester, he had already done much to smooth its path to victory. A moderate measure of historical imagination can easily convert these facts, together with the evidence of expenditure derived from other chancery and exchequer records, into a full narrative of the preparations for the Welsh war.

Feudalism based itself on the axiom that the king owned all the land in his kingdom. In order to have the benefit of a variety of services, however, he allowed certain favoured subjects, his tenants-in-chief, to hold estates during their lifetime. When a tenant-in-chief died his estates returned to the crown until his heir had established his right to succeeed and had paid the required relief, which was often the equivalent of one year's rent. An inquiry or inquisition *post mortem* held by the king's escheator determined who was the rightful heir to the deceased. The exchequer was the most interested section of the administration because it did not wish to lose any revenue that might be owing from wardships, reliefs, or any profits from the estate between the death of the holder and the succession of the heir, but it was the chancery which ordered the inquisition and which filed the escheator's report. These documents give us most detailed information about the extent and value of the lands held by the deceased, about subtenants of his who owed military service, about his heir, and about his widow and her dower. They show as separate items the worth and size of the demesne ploughlands, meadows, gardens, mills, fisheries, woodlands, the holdings of the free tenants, and the customary gifts and perquisites belonging to the manor. They should be most reliable documents because local jurors, the people most likely to know, gave the escheator all the facts on oath.

During the reign of Henry III inquisitions *post mortem* gradually assumed a rigid pattern, and the Record Office has published fourteen volumes of the *Calendars of Inquisitions Post Mortem* to cover the years from 1236 to 1377. The calendars do not print all the details – a local historian particularly might require the omitted names of the jurors or the subdivisions of the demesne – but they give an adequate description of the whole estate, and abundantly illustrate the complicated pattern of landholding which inheritance, marriage, sale, and gift had created within two centuries of the Conquest. Inquisitions *post mortem* of major tenants-in-chief could be most involved. Even in the summary form of the calendars they run into several pages. Equally, of course, the essential details of the estate of a minor tenant do not occupy more than a few lines of the calendar. An inquisition held in Nottinghamshire in September 1268 declared that Hugh de Stapleford, aged twenty-five years, was the son and heir of Richard Heriz, and that Richard held on his death

Nottinghamshire. Stapleford. 23 bovates land, $\frac{1}{2}$ watermill, and 4s. 6d. rent. Derbyshire. Mapperley. 3s. 0d. rent.
All held of the king in chief of the honour of Peverel by service of 1 knight's fee.

More typical of the general run of inquisitions is that which was held in north-west Devon early in September 1274 after the death of Henry de Tracy, a kinsman of William de Tracy, one of the four knights who murdered Becket. Tracy held land in different parts of Devon, and therefore the escheator arranged four inquiries, each of which was served by local jurors. Two of the juries stated that Henry's rightful heir was his grand-daughter Maud, the wife of Geoffrey de Canvile; the other two made no statement on this matter. The first jury gave details of the lands which Henry had held at Upex of the king, at Greenslinch of Sir Walter fitz Payn, and at Kilmington of Walter de Merton. The second jury dealt with Barnstaple: Henry had held

the borough, including a place called the castle, around which a wall is almost built, and there is a *mota* in which are a hall, chamber, kitchen, and other houses almost built, a market and fair, a priory founded on the lord's demesne with its custody when vacant, and the advowson of the church, held of the king in chief as head of the barony of Barnstaple by service of 2 knights or 4 esquires at his own cost for 40 days when the king shall have need.

The third jury stated that Henry had held the manor of Bovy Tracy as part of the barony of Barnstaple, and the fourth gave details of his holdings in Fremington, Tawstock, Nymet Tracy, Holsworthy, Toriton, Nymet St George, Lew, Hele, Ilfracombe and Winkleigh. The first three of these manors he held as part of the barony. For the remainder he paid rent or owed service to other gentlemen, Richard Tremalet, John de Umfraville, William de Cluynguy, none of whom were his social superiors. The borough of Ilfracombe he held of Henry de Campo Arnulphi for a rent of eight marks a year.

Among the more specialized of the chancery records the fine rolls and the liberate rolls are of most use to the historian. Not only do the fine rolls list the payments made to the crown for charters, writs, privileges, and pardons, but they also record the appointment of royal officers and quote the orders which the king sent to sheriffs, escheators, and exchequer officials about financial matters. As long ago as 1835 the Record

Commissioners published transcripts of the fine rolls of John's reign, the earliest of all, and extracts from those of Henry III's reign, and since 1911 the Public Record Office has produced twenty volumes of calendars covering the years 1272–1471. It has not yet given the same attention to the liberate rolls, for apart from the transcripts of a few from John's reign, the only printed versions are calendars for most years in Henry III's reign. Liberate rolls record writs which either ordered or warranted the spending of the king's money. They cover many varied topics from the heavy costs of a military expedition or a diplomatic present to a fellow monarch to trifling expenditure on a charitable gift, the expenses of a messenger, or a servant's wages. They are unexpectedly enlightening on the constant care and attention which the crown had to give to its castles and houses to keep them up to date and in good repair. Some of the modifications and additions are historically significant or architecturally interesting. In 1240, for example, Henry III ordered that the gate and houses of his castle at Hadleigh, Essex, (later to be completely rebuilt by Edward III), should be repaired without delay, and further that

a suitable porch be made before the king's hall at Havering-atte-Bower, and to cause the king's chapel there to be wainscoted and repaired, and to cause six glass windows to be made in the said chapel, and to cause a penthouse of the king's chamber to be enlarged the length of ten feet and to cause a private chamber and a wardrobe to be made there for the queen's use.

Twenty-five years later Henry III decided to overhaul Hereford castle out of fines and amercements due to him from that county. He ordered the sheriff

to fit the tower of Hereford castle with joists and roof it with lead; to make a bridge to the tower, repair the king's and queen's halls, chambers, and kitchens, the larder, the knights' chambers, the king's chapel, the stable and two turrets; to finish a chamber lately begun for the king's clerks; to make a bakehouse; to repair the walls descending from the tower to the city and the Wye; to repair the king's hall belonging to the almonry, the halls where the county courts are wont to be held, the exchequer chamber in the castle, the wall round the castle, and the towers in the inner bailey; and to make a building for housing engines, the gate beneath the tower, the swing-bridge there, and a prison within the castle, with all necessary repairs. . . .

These liberate rolls offer much information to the social historian. Like the rest of the judicial and administrative records they do not give him a narrative of events, but they reveal details which stimulate his imagination, bring people alive, and enable him to assess the chief interests and scale of values of the king and some of his leading subjects. What a man spends his money on is often a trustworthy guide to his personality.

3. ROYAL INQUISITIONS

Just as the royal officers of the twelfth and thirteenth centuries incidentally provided historians with detailed primary sources when they began to make chancery, exchequer, and judicial administration more systematic, so the kings from Henry II onwards, in their anxiety to take from their tenants a full tally of feudal services, caused records to be compiled, which reveal in considerable detail changes in tenure, the comparative values of estates both in different parts of England and in different generations, and a long register of tenants' names. Local juries provided most of the information for these records, and the sheriffs, as they did with their Easter and Michaelmas accounts, handed them into the exchequer. Today, these lists of landholders and feudal obligations are readily available in print in two books, *The Red Book of the Exchequer* and *The Book of Fees*. They are neither complete nor free from obscurities, but they are more explicit and detailed than the lists of tenants-in-chief in Domesday Book. Nineteenth-century historians used them extensively for genealogical studies. They picked out of them the stepping stones which enabled a favourite family to make its way across the thirteenth and twelfth centuries, so that, with courage derived from imaginative invention, it could leap across the difficult gap of the next three or four generations and land triumphantly in the middle of William's army on the slopes of Senlac Hill. Obviously such records must contain much valuable genealogical evidence, but they can also provide considerable raw material for economic and military historians.

In his settlement of England after 1066, William I gave land to his chief supporters in return for the services of an agreed number of armed horsemen for forty days each year. There was no fixed relationship between the number of acres and the number of soldiers, and, thanks to royal confiscations, grants to new tenants-in-chief, gifts of lands to churches and monasteries, and the ordinary feudal conventions of inheritance, the pattern of landholding in England rapidly became most complicated. Therefore, in 1166, Henry II determined to find out what services he was entitled to have. He asked his sheriffs how many knights each tenant-in-chief in their shire should provide; of these he required to know for how many the tenant himself was responsible, how many came from subtenancies created before the death of Henry I, and how many from subtenancies created more recently. The answers to these questions are to be found in the *Red Book of the Exchequer*. They constitute the first detailed record of feudal holdings since Domesday Book.

Different landholders arranged their replies in slightly different forms. Richer de Laigle, who held the honour of the Eagle in the rape of Pevensey in Sussex, made his report thus:

Richer de Laigle, to his very noble lord, Henry king of the English, greeting and faithful service.

Know that I have 35 knights' fees and a half, and I had so many on the day and in the year that King Henry your grandfather lived and died. Nor have I enfeoffed any since that day. These figures are correct:

> Richard son of William holds 15 knights' fees
> Ralph of Dene, 6 knights
> William Malet, 4 knights' fees

William son of Richard, 3 knights' fees
William Malfed, 3 knights
William of Echingham, 2 knights
Robert of Horsted, 2 knights
Andreas of Alfriston, half a knight.

The abbot of Glastonbury gave the king the names of the tenants who were holding his knights' fees in 1135 and those who held them 'at present', in 1166, but most landholders kept their reports as terse as possible.

Henry II used the figures of these reports for calculating scutage, the tax which tenants-in-chief paid when they did not do military duty. He and his successors assessed a tenant's liability on the number of knights he was required to provide.

In 1212 John held another major inquest of service. He instructed his sheriffs

to cause diligent inquiry to be made, in the best possible way, concerning all knights' fees and all kinds of tenements, within boroughs or without, which are held of us in chief in your shire by knights' service, or by any serjeanty, and of those who hold them and by what service. Likewise, you will inquire about all holdings which used to be held of us or our predecessors, the kings of England, which have been given away or alienated by marriage, service, alms, or any other means so that they are no longer held of us in chief, . . . [and ascertain] the names of those who hold them, by what service, of whom, by whom, and for what reasons they have been given away or alienated from the service, which used to be rendered to us or our ancestors . . .

This writ, dated at Westminster on 1 June, optimistically ordered the sheriffs to have their reports into the exchequer by 25 June. The sheriff of Oxfordshire managed to get his there almost on time, but it has signs of being hastily compiled. Certainly it was tabloid in form and almost certainly incomplete.

Earl William Marshal 6 knights
Earl of Chester 2½ knights
Earl of Salisbury 1 knight

Earl of Essex 2 knights . . .

. . . The abbot of Westminster holds the manor Islip by the will of the lord the king . . .

. . . The bishop of Winchester holds Witney and Adderbury, but we do not know for what service.

Thomas son of Richard holds 1 carucate of land, and for it serves as forester of Wychwood and pays into the exchequer £7 annually . . .

. . . In the town of Oxford. The lepers of St Bartholomew have annually £19 15s. 5d. for food by the gift of Henry I king of England, 65 shillings for clothing by the same gift. And the abbot of Oseney 9s. 5d. from a certain weir by the gift of the empress [Queen Matilda] and the confirmation of the king. And the prior of St Frideswides has by gift of the empress 48s. 6d. annually . . .

Oddly enough, the sheriff of far-away Cumberland made his return by 'the day after John the Baptist's day', as the writ required, but the other reports trickled into Westminster throughout the summer. They varied considerably in the detail they gave the king – and give the historian. The sheriff of Lancashire was one who took some trouble over his work. Here is part of his return for the small barony of Penwortham, which had belonged to the Bussel family probably from the Conquest to the first years of the thirteenth century. In 1202 Hugh Bussel was found guilty of perjury in a civil case which he had fought against his uncle, Geoffrey Bussel. When he failed to pay his fine of 400 marks, King John compelled him and Robert Bussel to sell the barony to the powerful Roger de Lacy, constable of Chester.

In the barony of Penwortham there are five knights' fees, counting those within the county and those outside. Thorp [Thorp-Morieux in Suffolk], a fee of one knight, was given in dower to Gutha, sister of Ranulf de Glanvill, and so was alienated from the barony, and the jurors do not know who holds that tenure now. Brocton [Nether Broughton, Leicestershire], a single knight's fee, was given to Geoffrey of Valoines by Albert Bussel, and they do not know who holds the tenure now.

Warine Bussel [died c. 1150] gave Ranulf son of Roger five carucates of land when he married his daughter. And the heir of this same Ranulf is the ward of Eustace of Moreton who [temporarily] manages the whole of that land. [The pipe rolls reveal that Eustace paid £100 for the wardship.]

The same Warine Bussel gave Gillemichel son of Edward on marriage with his daughter four carucates of land, of which his heirs [sic] hold three and is [sic] the ward of the archdeacon of Stafford and William of Harewood. And the heir of Theobald Walter, who is the ward of the lord the king, holds one carucate in Mithop [Kirkham parish] of that barony. . . .

Albert Bussel [died c. 1193] gave one carucate of land in Elston to the Hospital of Jerusalem. . . .

Warine Bussel gave three bovates of land in Penwortham and two bovates in Longton to the church of Penwortham in pure alms. Richard Bussel gave four bovates of land in Longton and one carucate of land in Farington to the same church in alms. Albert Bussel gave two bovates of land in Leyland to the same church in alms. The abbot of Evesham holds that church with all these lands.

Richard Bussel gave the abbey of Chester in alms one carucate of land in Rufford which the abbot of Chester holds.

Richard Bussel gave one bovate of land in Penwortham to Bolton Priory in alms.

Albert Bussel gave Gerald of Clayton four bovates of land for his homage that he might be his seneschal. . . .

Roger de Lacy gave Robert Bussel two carucates and two bovates of land in Longton and Leyland and the service of two carucates in Euxton for returning the service of the tenth part of a knight. . . .

Warine Bussel gave Norman three carucates of land in knight's fee in Kirkdale, where ten carucates constitute one knight's fee: and today Quenilda, daughter of Roger, holds that land by the same service . . .

This story of the Bussel estates is not at all exceptional. Land-holders frequently gave away parts of their estates in order to secure new services, complete a marriage settlement, or make a pious gift. The crown was indifferent to the details of such transactions, but it wished to safeguard the obligations attached to the estates. It took the view that if it did not allow the tenants-in-chief to escape paying their full quota of knight's service, or its cash equivalent, they in turn would keep similar pressure on the subtenants. Hence all these royal inquests are concerned primarily with tenants-in-chief.

Henry III too ordered several major inquiries. In 1235 he instructed his sheriffs to collect an aid – two marks for each knight's fee – which 'the earls and barons and all others of our whole kingdom of England, of their own free will and not according to custom, have granted to us' to pay the expenses of the marriage of his sister, Isabella, to Emperor Frederick II. In the following year he pressed for more details, requiring from his sheriffs information about those who held land by serjeanty (an agreed service other than military service) or by socage (rent), as well as by knight's fee. In 1242 he turned the collection of the special scutage to pay for his expedition to Gascony into a triple inquiry into feudal tenures. He sent successive writs to the sheriffs in May, October, and December demanding increasingly detailed returns about the location, value, and number of fees held by tenants-in-chief, and, as later in 1254, he tried to bring into the inquiry and subsequent scutage all who held land worth £20 or more, whatever their status.

The marked reluctance of many lesser landholders to undertake the military duties of knights was another factor which compelled Henry III and his son Edward I to take new steps to safeguard their rights. Both kings several times ordered the sheriff to fine those who held land worth more than £20 a year and who yet refused knighthood. They used this money to hire soldiers. Under Edward changes were taking place which, by the mid fourteenth century, were destined to transform the royal army from the traditional, cumbersome, feudal host into the smaller, efficient force used by Edward III in Normandy, but these changes did nothing to temper

Edward I's determination to keep his tenants up to scratch. In 1277 the earl marshal compiled a new register of obligations for tenants-in-chief, and in 1282 the sheriffs ordered all who possessed £20 worth of land to report at Northampton or York for military duty, and those who held £30 of land to provide a fully-equipped warhorse or its equivalent in cash. The financial pressure of war in Scotland and Gascony in his later years compelled Edward to continue these periodic shrieval inquiries and demands to the end of his reign.

By themselves these thirteenth-century lists and accounts are sufficient to demonstrate the complicated pattern of land-holding: used together with such other sources of information as inquisitions *post mortem* or lay subsidy rolls, which give lists of village inhabitants with assessments of their wealth, they can paint a clear and detailed picture of a family, a manor, or a county. The Great Inquisition of 1212 stated that the king had granted the wardship of the estates of the Somery family of Dudley, Worcestershire, to the earl of Salisbury during the minority of the heir.

The earl of Salisbury has in custody $10\frac{3}{4}$ knights' fees of the honour of Ralph de Somery with the heir of the said Ralph, by the precept of the lord the king.

By 1235, when Henry III was collecting the aid to finance his sister's marriage, Ralph's heir, Roger de Somery, had come of age, and the collectors' report, under the heading *Fees of Roger de Somery*, was

Envil 1; Morf $\frac{1}{2}$; Amblecote and Himley 1; Wombourne, Swindon, Oxley 1; Overton, Bradley 1; Penne Buffard 1; Bushbury and the other Penne 1; Essington 1; Barre and Alrewich 1; Perry 1; Little Barre $\frac{1}{2}$; Handsworth 1; Tresel and Seisdon 1.

Sum $11\frac{1}{5}$ fees. Sum of payments 22 marks 5 shillings, of which he paid 20 marks by the hands of Henry de Kerbrinton, and there remains to pay 32 shillings.

Later in the report a Margaret de Somery, possibly Ralph's widow, was charged for half a knight's fee of the barony of

Dudley, and almost at the end, the collectors showed that Roger was liable to further demands.

> Roger de Somery renders account of 50 fees of ancient enfeoffment, and of one fee in Mere and in Clent [Worcestershire]; nothing paid to the treasury. And in the balance there are £13 and half a mark of his fees in this county as is set forth in the roll by which the collectors have paid into the treasury. And he owes £56.

The documents connected with the scutage to pay for Henry III's expedition to Gascony in 1242 give details of how Roger sublet his land. He retained one knight's fee in Swinford, Clent, and Mere as demesne land, and had the following tenants:

The heirs of William de Envil, 1 fee, in Envil.
Robert de Bushbury, 1 fee, in Bushbury.
Robert de Waure, $\frac{1}{5}$ fee, in Amblecote.
Henry de Morf, $\frac{1}{2}$ fee, in Morf.
William Buffry, 1 fee, in Penne.
Philip de Lutley, $\frac{1}{4}$ fee, in Hagley.
Robert de Essington, $\frac{1}{3}$ fee, in Mosley.
Walter de Overton, 2 fees, in Overton, Wombourne, Swindon and Oxley.
Thomas de Stirchley, 1 fee, in Tresel and Seisdon.
Peter de Selle, $\frac{1}{3}$ and $\frac{1}{40}$ fee, in Himley.
William de Englefeld, $\frac{1}{3}$ fee, in Himley.
John de Parles, $\frac{1}{5}$ fee, in Handsworth.
William de Perry, 1 fee, in Perry.
Hugh de Bowles, $\frac{1}{2}$ fee, in Rushale.
Robert de Weston and Robert de Heniton, $\frac{2}{3}$ fee, in Essington.
Richard of Little Barre, 1 fee, in Little Barre.

The two lists of 1235 and 1242 do not coincide, but the differences between them could easily be explained by inevitable minor changes in the seven years' interval. Their stark statements whet the appetite for more detail, and happily much more light is thrown on the Somery estates by the inquisition *post mortem*, which was held on Roger's death in 1273. It began with a valuation of the manor of Clent:

there is a chief messuage with a garden worth yearly 2s. There are 2 virgates of land worth yearly 10s. 8d. . . . on each acre it is possible to sow one quarter of barley, two quarters of oats. Also the meadow there contains . . . half an acre, and it is worth yearly 4 shillings. Also the pasture in the moor of Halenmor and Hodenhull is worth yearly 3s. Also the rent of assize in the manor is worth £6 17s. 9½d. Also the pleas and perquisites of the court with heriots and reliefs, and the merchet of daughters are worth yearly 20 shillings . . . Total of this extent £8 17s. 5½d.

Also the advowson of the church of Clent belongs to the lord of the manor, and the said church is worth 10 marks yearly.

There followed similar extents of the manors of Dudley borough, Cradeley, Sedgley, and Swinford, compiled by the escheator with the help of a different group of jurymen. The rents from the burgesses of Dudley were valued at £5 15s. 5d.

Some burgesses owe pannage for their hogs yearly whether or not there be mast, and it is worth 5s. a year. Also the pleas and perquisites of the hundred are worth yearly 30s., because they are sure. Also the tolls of the markets of Dudley are worth 40s. yearly. Also there is a wood called Penniak, one mile in length . . . and half a mile in breadth, and the pannage in the said wood is worth yearly 20s. . . . The pasture of the wood cannot be valued because it is in common. The profits arising from the sale of dead wood and underwood in the said wood are worth 13s. 4d., and there is one enclosed park the pasture of which is worth 13s. 4d.

. . . in demesne in the manor of Cradeley there are 14 acres of impoverished land, 25½ feet to the perch, and they are worth 1 mark a year. There are also 18 villeins, each of whom holds half a virgate [4 acres], and they give and render 50s. 10¾d., and one windmill is worth 4d. . . .

. . . there is a castle newly begun at Dudley [actually in the manor of Sedgley, Staffordshire], which cannot be valued because it is unfinished; but the garden there, and the pasture of the close of the castle are worth 4s. yearly. [Henry III recognized Roger's services in the Barons' War by letters patent allowing him to enclose his house with a ditch and stone wall, and fortify and crenellate it.] Also the rent of the freeholders [in the manor of Sedgley] is worth £9 2s. 9½d. yearly. . . . Also the rent of Mogsi the forester is 2 lbs. of pepper and

2 lbs. of cumin; the rent of Roger de Brierley is 2 lbs. of pepper; the rent of Himley is 1 lb. of cumin, and they are worth yearly 2s. 11d., the price of pepper being 8d. a pound, and of cumin 1d. Also the rent of John de Chasepool is 4 barbed arrows unfeathered, worth 2d. yearly. Also the rent of John le Messeg is one pair of gloves 1d. Also the rent of the assorted tenements is worth £5 10s. 9d. a year . . .

. . . John de Ferhull, who ploughs the 'Monendays earth' between the Purification [2 February] and Easter whenever the plough can be used . . . and a day's ploughing is worth 2½d. He is required also to reap the lord's corn, and it is worth 1d. He has to mow the meadow which is ancient demesne, and it is worth 2d., and to make hay, which is worth ½d.; and to carry the hay from the meadow from Overton in Warwickshire to the castle of Dudley, and the carting is worth 3d. He is required to measure the lord's corn, when he has any to be measured, and the service is worth 8d. And he has to gather the nuts and every year give one measure of nuts at Lent or 3d. instead, and the service is worth 4d.; and carry wood from Dudley Park for Christmas and this is worth 3d. a year.

Also 23 customary tenants do all the services on the same tenure and they are worth 67s. 1d. . . .

. . . there are 2 water mills which are worth 53s. 4d. yearly. Also the mill of Penyval is worth a mark. Also there are 5 large shops [probably iron-smelting furnaces] each of which pays yearly 40s., and they are not fixed nor certain, because they are only at the will of the workman, but by estimation they are worth £6 a year. Also four coal pits of sea coal are worth £4 a year. . . .

This inquisition valued the whole Somery estate in Staffordshire and north Worcestershire at slightly more than £150 a year, and in addition Roger had held land in ten other counties. His heir was his eighteen-year-old son, a second Roger. He died in October 1291, less than twenty years later, and another inquisition *post mortem* had to be held. The details of this document provide some interesting comparisons with his father's inquisition. The value of the son's property in Staffordshire and north Worcestershire was assessed at just over £500, more than three times that of his father. The manors of Clent, Sedgley, and Swinford appeared in both inquisitions, but the son's inquisition began with Handsworth, Rowley, and Mere, three manors not included in his father's. By 1291 the castle at Sedgley was finished and had become the chief residence of the Somery family: 'it is held of the lord the king by the service of three knights . . . and together with the rabbit warren, vegetable garden, and grange . . . is worth 26s. 8d. yearly'. The coal mines were priced down in the second inquisition – they were said to be worth only the same as the castle – but iron mines were included and valued at £8 a year, and far more detail was given about subtenancies. Apparently William de Birmingham had become Roger's main tenant: he held several knights' fees himself, and sublet others to tenants of his own.

The inquisition of the younger Roger was the occasion of a scandal. One sub-escheator, William de Mere, was accused of cutting down trees on the Somery estate, selling them to charcoal burners, and keeping the money: the other sub-escheator, Adam de Elmbrugg, was similarly accused of misusing his authority and temporary control of the estates not only to cut down trees for charcoal, but also to poach a large number of deer. Both accused men were brought before William de Beresford, one of the king's justices, at Dudley in October 1292. Their crime is a dismal reminder of the ever present danger of administrative corruption, but to economic historians the court record is welcome evidence of a seller's market for charcoal in the bloomeries of thirteenth-century Staffordshire.

A historian rarely quotes a source document in full; he takes from it the facts and the phrases he requires. His choice of detail and the way he stresses this point and minimizes the importance of that statement stamps his writing with his personal interests, prejudices, and interpretation. Of course, much depends upon what he is trying to do. If he is writing a history of the Somery family he will probably use the lists of fees and the inquisitions quoted above as a basis. Then he will search the patent and close rolls, the feet of fines, and other administrative and judicial records for further information, and look round for helpful writs, wills, letters, lay subsidy rolls, cartularies, or any other documents which might add to his growing store of knowledge. But if, instead of recording the family's history, he is studying the pattern of feudal landholding, or estimating the effectiveness of royal inquests, or investigating the methods by which thirteenth-century kings recruited and financed their armies, or seeking evidence about medieval prices, agricultural methods, or industry, he will merely file the evidence he extracts from these Somery records, and continue to examine the exchequer lists and inquisitions of scores of other landed families. Only when he can set it alongside a large quantity of comparable evidence can anyone possibly decide in what ways the Somery story is exceptional or typical of family experience in the thirteenth century.

4. AN ECCLESIASTICAL MISCELLANY

The surviving ecclesiastical buildings of the Middle Ages are almost universally admired. Even those critics who find nothing aesthetically satisfying except the simplicity and perfect proportions of classical architecture cannot help throwing a word of appreciation to medieval masons and carpenters for their ingenuity and skill in erecting such noble buildings as Battle Abbey, Ely Cathedral, and St Mary's Church, Beverley. Timber was the usual building material. Therefore almost the only medieval buildings to survive, even in ruins, have been stone-built castles, churches, monasteries, and the oldest quadrangles and chapels at Oxford and Cambridge. The rest have perished, or more probably were pulled down in the sixteenth and seventeenth centuries to make way for 'modern' stone or brick buildings.

Cost was the simple reason for the men of the Middle Ages building so little in stone and brick. Only the king, the richest of the noblemen, or the church with its various branches growing richer every year could possibly afford the expense. Even they had often to build their castle or monastery piecemeal, living for many a long year partly in stone buildings and partly in temporary wooden structures waiting for more money and labour to become available. When necessity decreed, as it did with the erection of the North Wales castles, the king could compulsorily muster skilled and unskilled workmen to labour continuously until the project had been completed. But he could only do this by robbing other sites of masons and carpenters. There was no surplus of building experience and skill.

Stone and timber cost comparatively little: their transport to the building site could be much more expensive. But easily the chief charge the medieval builder had to meet was the paying of wages. D. Knoop and G. P. Jones, who have published so many enlightening studies of medieval builders and building methods, have worked out that of the total amount of money spent on building at the new Cistercian abbey of Vale Royal in central Cheshire during 1278, 1279, and 1280, tools and materials took 4·4 per cent, cartage 24·5 per cent, and wages 71·1 per cent. These figures are not typical because Vale Royal had much timber and stone given to it, but they indicate how false is the widespread belief that labour costs were comparatively low before the twentieth century. Facts about costs and methods of thirteenth-century building rarely come from straightforward documents such as account books or balance sheets. They have to be gleaned from less obvious sources. Letters patent, letters close, and the liberate rolls are likely papers to yield information about royal castle building: after patient search, deeds, petitions, court records, annals, and the occasional will or letter might tell us something about the progress and problems of building a particular church or abbey. The following three documents are not specifically concerned with building costs, but incidentally they speak of the expense and rate of building of Edward I's foundation at Vale Royal. The first is an extent or inventory of the abbey's possessions made in 1291, by order of the king, before the justiciar of Chester and Adam of Wettenhall. Nine jurors gave evidence about the abbey's receipts from the usual scattered estates, properties, and perquisites:

> . . . in Little Over one carucate, and it is worth 40s. a year; and in Twemlow one messuage and one carucate of land, with a small area of wood and pasture worth 30s. a year; and in Stanthurl one messuage and 15 acres of land, which are worth 10s. a year . . . etc.

The total came to £108 13s. 0d. Much more unusual were the payments made by the crown.

The abbot of Vale Royal shall receive yearly from the king towards the building of the aforesaid abbey 890 marks, of which he shall receive at the feast of All Saints [1 November] £100, and in the first week of Lent 200 marks and on Ascension Day 200 marks, and on the feast of St Peter ad Vincula [Lammas, 1 August] 160 marks. Moreover, the same abbot ought to receive 180 marks, namely 45 marks at each of these terms, and he shall receive his first payment on Ascension Day next to come. The king shall henceforward pay him the said sums at the said times in manner aforesaid upon a writ of payment, in the name of Master William de Luda; and of these the abbot received on the feast of All Saints £100 from the wardrobe, and £100 after Christmas; and so there was wanting at the time of All Saints 45 marks, and at the first week in Lent 95 marks, which he shall receive from the exchequer.

In the parliament of the lord king at Acton Burnell [in Shropshire in 1284] it was ordained that the abbot of Vale Royal should receive from the wardrobe for the works of his abbey every year between the feast of St Michael [29 September] and Christmas £100, and between Christmas and Easter 200 marks, between Easter and the feast of St John the Baptist [24 June] 200 marks; between that feast and Michaelmas 160 marks; and in addition to this, out of the issues of the county of Chester, by the hands of the justiciar there, 790 marks. And altogether he shall receive for the said works £1,000 yearly.

To the abbot of Vale Royal for the works of his church at the festival of All Saints at the end of the 11th year – £100.

To the same abbot for the same purpose for the 12th year, as well out of the exchequer by Mark de Luca [sic] as out of the wardrobe – £526, 1 mark.

To the same abbot in the 13th year by the same hands £300.

To the same abbot in the 14th year by the same hands £723, ½ mark.

To the same abbot in the 15th year by the hands of merchants and from the exchequer – £363, ½ mark.

To the same abbot in the 16th year from the exchequer and by merchants – £516, 1 mark.

To the same abbot in the 17th year from the exchequer and by merchants – £570.

To the same abbot in the 18th year from the exchequer only upon writs for payment by Master William de Luda – £260.

To the same abbot in the same year upon the last writ for payment – £100.

Total £3,480 [sic].

Further in the same document there is a reminder that 'according to the account of his treasurer', the king had paid £32,000 for 'the new work of Vale Royal'. This probably referred to Edward's initial grant to pay for the first work at the site in 1278 and the following years. Later, he obviously discharged his obligation – for this abbey was a royal thank-offering – with regular limited payments.

The second of the three documents is an undated petition, addressed probably to Edward II or just possibly to Edward III, asking the king to rescue Vale Royal financially.

To our Lord the King and his council. His chaplains, the abbot and convent of Vale Royal, show that, whereas they were founded by the most honourable King Edward, the king's forbear, and since the time of their foundation, from year to year according as they were able, they have built a part of their church and a part of their communal house, so that by reason of the great sums spent by the convent and the bad years there have been, they must forthwith perish unless they receive some timely assistance; they therefore pray our said Lord the King, that for the love of God, as a work of charity and for the souls of his ancestors, he will be pleased of his especial grace to grant them some assistance, so that they may maintain and continue their works; which cost £37,000 from the treasury of our lord the king, who founded the house. And whereas the aforesaid ancestor of our lord (whom God absolve from sin!) of his grace assigned to them £1,000,

£490 of which are in arrears, for, from the manor of Ashford in the Peak, which was assigned to them for the same sum, they have received only £80, may it therefore please the king to continue to assign that manor to them to provide for that sum, until they shall be paid, or else the vill of Northwich in the county of Chester, or else think fit to order the chamberlain of Chester to pay that sum to the said works out of his exchequer.

The third document is a postscript to a statement of income and expenses made at Vale Royal in 1336, nearly sixty years after the first stone had been laid. The statement, a kind of internal 'audit' within the Cistercian order, is addressed to the abbot of Morimont, a house in eastern France; the postscript, protesting the chronic poverty of the community, is a telling comment upon the speed of building even at an abbey which had a king as founder and patron.

But you should bear in mind, reverend father, that in our monastery we have a very large church begun by the king of England at our first foundation, but by no means finished. For at the first foundation he built it with stone walls, but the crypt remains to be built, with the roof and the glass and other ornaments of the church. Moreover, the cloister, chapter-house, dormitory, refectory and other offices of the monastery still remain to be built in a style corresponding with the church; for the accomplishment of which the rents of our house are insufficient. And this we have written to you, in order that you may know that, if there should remain anything over from our expenses, it should all be applied to the work indicated above.

Money for monastic and church building came from charitable and pious givers, for, from king to villein, men of the Middle Ages were ready to convey land, privileges, and services to the church in the belief or hope that their generosity would ultimately benefit their own souls and the souls of other members of their families. These gifts were allocated to particular monasteries, friaries, cathedrals, or parish churches, and before long it became administratively necessary for the bigger or more popular foundations to compile a register or cartulary of the estates and liberties they had acquired. Once the register had been made it needed keeping up to date, because land continued to be given to the eve of the dissolution. Many of these cartularies survive; several have been published chiefly by county record societies. At first glance they look dull and repetitive, but for several reasons they are valuable documents. Primarily they record the gift and the giver, and, if they mention the reason and intention for the gift, they contribute their mite to our understanding of medieval thinking. They preserve old spellings of the names of fields, villages, rivers, and hills; they identify areas of arable, pasture, and woodland, and often give us details of fisheries, mills, markets, tithes, and the advowson of churches. They are one of the chief sources for students of medieval farming, and in recent years have helped to show that different areas of England managed their open fields and enclosures in different ways. Themselves they demonstrate the chief sources of medieval wealth, for the demesne lands, rents, tolls, tithes, fishing rights, flocks, herds, and privileges which they list constituted the primary materials which medieval administration, ingenuity, brain, and brawn transformed into tall spires, graceful columns, fan vaulting, and hammer-beam roofs.

For the Sussex Record Society, L. F. Salzman has edited the cartulary of the Cluniac priory of St Pancras at Lewes, renowned in south-eastern England for its patronage of artists. Robert Auncell, the prior during the middle years of the fifteenth century, ordered the register to be made. Probably it superseded an earlier one; certainly it goes back to the beginning, for it quotes what purports to be the foundation charter granted to the priory by William de Warenne soon after the Conquest. There is reason to think that the text of this charter is not original, but the fifteenth-century clerk who embroidered the facts with the legends and traditions that had grown round them provided a most imposing preface to the record of the priory's possessions. In his second charter William de Warenne freed from feudal obligations all the lands he had previously given to the priory, granted further tithes, free pastures, and fishing rights, and then went on:

I give, grant and confirm to the said monks in the vill of Lewes preferential buying of logs for making their wood pile on three days of the week, namely Tuesday, Thursday and Saturday, from Whitsun to Lammas [1 August], and after the said feast common market with the men of Lewes if necessary. And of flesh and fish and all other things which they wish and require to buy for their own needs or those of their guests, not only in the vill of Lewes but also at Seaford and throughout my estates in all places where a market is held, I grant to the monks for ever that every day they may have without hindrance or impediment the pre-emption after sufficient purchases have been made for my own needs and those of my heirs. . . .

The next hundred documents in the cartulary record the benefactions of successive generations of the patron family, and they are followed by a long miscellaneous list of relatively small gifts from 'outsiders'. Increasingly from the thirteenth century onwards, the priory leased plots of land to subtenants, because it found drawing rents just as lucrative and less troublesome than farming its lands directly. The clerk recorded the leases in the cartulary as faithfully as he did the gifts. In 1258 the priory leased to Warin le Bat and his heir eighteen acres in Grinstead for 4s. 0d. a year and for undertaking to do all the services belonging to the land, and about the same time leased 'all the land of the Reddyke in the manor of Langrey' to Richard le Soper of Pevensey for 8s. 0d. a year and for

finding a man with a wagon and two horses and a cart for carting the lord's dung one day every year. And ploughing with half a plough [team] one day every year at the time of the Lent sowing and one day at the time of [blank] and harrowing with a man and a horse one day in each of the said seasons. And a hen at Christmas, and one pack journey in Lent with 3 bushels of beans from Langrey to Lewes Priory. And one job of carting in summer to fetch wood by means of a man with 2 oxen and a wagon with 2 horses and a cart. . . .

To the monks such services were just as important as the rent, and it is doubtful if the leased land would have yielded so much profit had the prior decided to keep it in the priory's demesne.

Owners of large estates are always in danger of becoming entangled in law suits. The monasteries were no exception. Since their possessions were so wide-flung – the Lewes lands were sited in at least eight counties – and since abbots and priors were apt to change more frequently than heads of families, they had to keep particularly alert watch on trespassers and on those who would assume rights which belonged to the monastery. In the thirties of the thirteenth century, for example, Lewes Priory had considerable trouble straightening out the tithes of the manor of Patcham. In 1230 an ecclesiastical court ruled that the small tithes of the demesne lands in Patcham belonged to the prior and not to the vicar. The prior subsequently granted the vicar, Osbert, all the tithes, with the exception of the tithe of pigs, on the understanding that he paid 2s. 0d. a year and that when he ceased to be vicar the tithes returned to Lewes. Nine years later a new vicar, Nicholas, was inducted, and assumed that since Osbert had collected the tithes they belonged to the vicar. It took another ecclesiastical court to resettle the matter in favour of the priory, and this time the prior leased only half the tithes of lambs, cheeses, and fleeces to the vicar, and charged him not 2s. 0d., but 16s. 8d. a year. Again the agreement stipulated that the tithes would revert to the priory when Nicholas died or resigned. On the whole medieval ecclesiastics had the reputation of being good landlords, but, like the church commissioners of today, they were neither amateurish nor casual in business matters.

Nearly three hundred miles of arduous and tedious travel separated the priory at Lewes from the isolated Premonstratensian abbey at Cockersand overlooking the mouth of the Lune. Yet Cockersand, like most of the houses passed on the way, had a cartulary very similar to the one at Lewes. It was compiled in 1267–8 by Robert of Lachford 'as much for the convenience of the younger brethren who are not used to legal documents as to avoid difficulties often experienced by those searching through the charters'. Robert wrote neatly and used abbreviations. Even so his cartulary took up 332 parchment pages three times the size of the pages of this book, and the Chetham Society needed seven volumes to print, translate, and edit it. It begins, as expected, with what the abbey considered were its most important documents – papal bulls granting privileges, and letters and charters from such noblemen as the earls of Chester and Lincoln and the lords of Wyresdale. But the bulk of the cartulary records small gifts, and these are the ones to interest the social and economic historian. This Cockersand document, properly searched and interpreted, is as eloquent as any other cartulary about farming conditions and the development of leasing, but because of Cockersand's geographical position, it has much to tell about early enclosures, and the assarting, or making arable, of forest, march, and waste lands. This type of information can often be supplemented by deeds, rent rolls, and manor court rolls, and since agricultural custom died hard, even a sixteenth- or seventeenth-century manor roll or estate map is not without relevance.

Farther north still, in north-west Cumberland and athwart one of the traditional Scottish invasion routes, stood the Cistercian abbey of Holm Cultram. Its cartulary has been edited by F. Grainger and W. G. Collingwood, and, as the extracts quoted below show, the abbey was deeply involved in all aspects of life in that border area. It cropped oats, bred cows and horses, pastured sheep, smelted iron, quarried stone, fished the rivers, profited from successful raids and campaigns across the border, suffered from invading Scots, and sent its monks and lay-brothers as traders to sell wool, destined for the Continent, in such markets as Boston, or as buyers and barterers across the sea to the Isle of Man and Northern Ireland. It owned property in Carlisle and Newcastle upon Tyne, and for a short time administered Skinburness as a borough, enjoying the profits from its Thursday market and its midsummer fair. But in 1305 the abbot reported to the king that the sea had swept away most of the borough, and petitioned that Holm Cultram should be allowed to transfer its rights to nearby Newton Arlosh. Edward I granted the request.

Very few of the recorded charters bear a date, and so the approximate date, as usual, has to be calculated from what is known of the principals and the witnesses. These calendared, or slightly shortened, extracts from the cartulary all concern gifts made to the abbey in the thirteenth century.

Lambert, son of Gillestephen of Waverton, grants to Holm Abbey land at the east gate of the vill of Waverton adjoining the land of the Hospital of Jerusalem, which Roger the provost held, except one half-acre held by the grantor's nephew, Robert.

Thomas, son of Thomas son of Cospatric, grants to Holm Abbey the fishery of Seton on the Derwent, and one free net in the Derwent, and one toft by the shore and easements needed by the fishers; also the liberty to divert the course of the water of the Derwent or any part, whenever and wherever such is required for the purpose of fishing.

Lambert of Multon grants to Holm Abbey 24 dozen loads of iron ore in Copeland to keep up a forge, to be taken yearly from a place where he and his men get iron ore. Also right of way for the monks and their men and goods when carrying and digging. But the monks are not to smelt this ore in his part of Copeland. They are to pay him half a mark of silver yearly.

Alice of Rumeli, daughter of William son of Duncan, in her widow-hood grants to Holmcultram a quarry in a field called Sandwith in Aspatria for building purposes, with right of way, 3 acres of her demesne in Aspatria in Northcroft between the crofts formerly of Henry and of Geoffrey, and common pasture for 10 oxen, 10 cows, 1 bull, 2 horses and 40 sheep.

Walter of Teindale grants to Holm Abbey all his land in Newcastle [upon Tyne] with the buildings between the land of the hospital of St Mary of Westgate and that which belonged to Ralph Long; paying farm to the king of three halfpence a year as a free burgage. [This charter was witnessed and dated, 12 March 1235, in the borough court of Newcastle.]

Robert Turp grants to Holm Abbey 14 acres of his demesne in Edenhall, of which 12 lie between Thurkilhou and land formerly held by Yvo of Seton, and between the Eden and the marsh; and 2 acres in Scalleflat on the north; also a vaccary on the way out of Edenhall in Thorbrandcroft, granted by his father to John of Crofton, and pasturage for 700 wethers and as many animals as belong to the said estate, with easements etc. according to the liberties and customs of the vill.

King John grants to Holmcultram the hermitage of St Hilda in his forest of Inglewood with the clearing which Roger Goki, late hermit, held there. They may cultivate it or keep it in pasture as they please. He agrees to them having a vaccary there for 40 cows, with pasture in the forest and with calves up to two years old, and as many horses and oxen as are needed for the cultivation of the land. [This charter dated and witnessed at 'Windeshore', 1 March 1215.]

King Edward confirms to Robert, abbot of Holmcultram, land worth 300 marks yearly, namely in Grevestone, the lands of the late Robert of Ros of Wark, a rebel; in Scotland, the lands of Richard of Glen, Patrick the Archer, Alexander of Folcardestoun, Gilbert Makiluagh, Robert of Moffet, Gilbert Makinoluagh, Chutbert Mackgilwinni and Gilcolm his son, Alexander Fraser and John of Luce, rebels, which they held on St Magdalen's day in the 20th year of his reign [22 July 1292]; the abbey rendering due services to the king and the lords . . . [Dated and witnessed at Carlisle, 25 September 1292.]

Olaf, king of the Islands, [Isle of Man], grants to Holmcultram free entrance and exit in his land with one ship and its boats for monks, lay-brothers and their men, goods and chattels, and leave to buy and sell for their own use whatever they need, without tolls.

Just as early in the twelfth century the first Cistercians had brought to England the ideal of austerity, so a hundred years later the first Franciscan and Dominican friars arrived to preach repentance and to practise absolute poverty. The Cistercians had disapproved of the wealth of the Benedictines and Cluniacs, but the friars were critical of all the cloistered orders, not only because they considered monastic ideals mistaken, but also because they believed worldly possessions and interests distracted a religious from the work of God. Yet, like the Cistercians before them, the friars soon found that they acquired gifts of land so quickly that, whether they liked it or not, they had in part to neglect their spiritual work in order to administer their estates. All clergy, and certainly all ecclesiastical communities, tended to play a double role. Bishops and parish priests spent a considerable portion of their time on such secular work as financial administration and the care of property. Friaries and monasteries might continue to be power houses for praise and prayer, but they also found themselves centres of small, scattered earthly 'kingdoms' that called for efficient, firm administration. When John de Celle, a devoted scholar, was elected abbot of St Albans, he wisely decided to leave the care of the buildings and the running of the estates to his prior and his cellarer, for saints or scholars, without any interest in secular matters and without ability to lead and manage men, could make disastrous abbots, priors, or bishops. The qualities required in all these offices were those possessed by Thomas Carlyle's hero, Abbot Samson of Bury St Edmunds. Had Samson been born in the twentieth century he would probably have had an outstanding career in business or as the vice-chancellor of a modern university. Jocelin, his Boswell, valued his talents for what they were. This is how he described the reforms which Samson initiated immediately after he had been appointed abbot in 1182.

After these things the abbot caused an inquiry to be made throughout each manor, concerning the annual quit rents from the freemen, and the names of the labourers and their tenements, and the services due from each; and he put all this into writing. Likewise he repaired those old halls and unroofed houses round which hovered kites and crows. He built new chapels, and likewise inner chambers and upper stories in many places where there never had been any dwelling-house at all, but only barns. He also enclosed many parks, which he replenished with beasts of chase, keeping a huntsman with dogs; and, upon the visit of any person of quality, sat with his monks in some walk of the wood, and sometimes saw the coursing of the dogs; but I never saw him take part in the sport.

He cleared much land, and brought it into tillage, in all things looking forward to the benefit likely to accrue to the abbey. . .

... Moreover, by his command, a general survey was made through-out the hundreds of the leets and suits, of hidages and foddercorn, of hen-rents, and of other dues and rents and issues, which, for the greater part, had ever been concealed by the farmers. He put it all in writing, so that within four years from the time of his election, there was not one who could defraud him of the rents of the abbey to the value of a single penny, whereas he himself had not received from his predecessors any writing touching the management of the abbey, except one small schedule, wherein were the names of the knights of St Edmund and the names of the manors, and what rent was due on each farm. This book he called his calendar, wherein also were entered the debts he had satisfied; and this same book he almost daily perused, as if in the same he were beholding the face of his honesty in a glass.

The first day that he held a chapter, he confirmed to us, under his new seal, sixty shillings from Southrey, which his predecessors had unjustly received from Edmund, surnamed the golden monk, for the liberty of holding the same vill to farm all the days of his life. He also proposed, as a general rule, that from thenceforth no one should pledge the ornaments of the church without the assent of the convent, as had been the custom heretofore, nor that any charter should be sealed with the convent seal, unless in chapter in the presence of the convent. He appointed Hugh as sub-sacrist, ordering that William the sacrist should not have anything to do with the sacristy, either in the manner of receipt or disbursement, unless by his consent. After this, but not on the same day, he transferred the former keepers of the offerings to other offices; lastly, he deposed the same William: wherefore those who liked William said, 'Behold the abbot! Lo, here is the wolf of whom it was dreamed! See how he rages!'

Jocelin, like Matthew Paris at St Albans, took a pride in his abbey's material welfare and reputation. He was gratified when King John decided to visit Bury so soon after his accession, but he was most scornful of John's stinginess:

... King John, immediately after his coronation, setting aside all other affairs, came down to St Edmund, drawn thither by his vow and by devotion. We, indeed, believed that he was come to make offering of some great matter; but all he offered was one silken cloth, which his servants had borrowed from our sacrist, and to this day have not paid for. He availed himself of the hospitality of St Edmund, which was attended with enormous expense, and upon his departure bestowed nothing at all, either of honour or profit, upon the saint, save thirteen pence sterling, which he offered at his mass on the day of his departure.

This double function of the medieval church is reflected in ecclesiastical archives. Liturgies, missals, martyrologies, antiphonaries, breviaries, psalters, and customaries lie alongside cartularies, extents, and other records of earthly treasure; copies of papal injunctions and manuscript books of theological exposition alongside such administrative documents as bishops' registers, or regulations issued by the Benedictine provincial chapters, the chapters-general of Cluny and Cîteaux or other monastic supervisory authorities. There are also extant a few collections of letters, some formal and some less formal, by which abbots, priors, bishops, and archdeacons conducted the business of their office. Of the administrative documents probably the bishops' registers are most used by historians. Most of the volumes published by the Canterbury and York Society are transcripts of registers, and a number of county societies have included local examples among their publications. Bishops' registers list and date both the institution of rectors and vicars and the episcopal confirmations of the elections of abbots and priors. They give the names of the patrons of benefices, and record any special conditions attached to the institution. Among the miscellaneous entries can be found details of dispensations, pensions, gifts of land, and the indulgences usually granted to those who contributed to the building of a new church, the repair of an existing one, or the erection of an additional part of a monastery or cathedral. Anyone wishing to write the history of an old parish church, or merely compile a list of its rectors or vicars, must consult the bishops' registers of the appropriate diocese. He can rely upon finding there the dates of the institution of the clergy and of major repairs to the fabric, and probably he will discover information about legal disputes, tithes, the endowment of chantries, relations between the vicar or rector and neighbouring houses of monks and friars, the provision of vestments and candles, and, nearly always, something quite unexpected. The register of Walter Gray, archbishop of York from 1215 to 1255, reveals, for example, that in May 1225 he allowed the vicar of Wilton to lease the vicarage for three years so that he could go crusading to the Holy Land, and that, although he turned the vicar of Rowley out of his living 'because he immediately succeeded his father therein', he gave him as compensation the corn tithes of two manors for life. Bishop Sutton of Lincoln showed similar charity when at the end of the century he had to deprive Robert of Wenham of the living of Frampton, because the archdeacon had discovered that Robert had been insane for the last five years. The parish historian can supplement the registers a little by finding out the thirteenth-century value of the benefice from the *Taxatio Ecclesiastica* of Pope Nicholas IV which was compiled in 1291, and was considered so important a document by the Record Commissioners that they chose it as the first to be printed, when in 1802 they decided to publish the major historical documents of England and Wales.

In the scriptoria of monastic houses and cathedrals clerical and lay scribes were just as busy in the thirteenth century as they had been in the twelfth, making copies of the Bible, service books, and of the writings of such fathers of the church as St Jerome and St Augustine, and of such favoured pagans as Aristotle and Euclid. Most of the scribes spent their days on expendable, working copies: a talented few produced the magnificent illuminated manuscripts, so much treasured then and ever since. Those monastic houses which took a pride in their libraries set their scribes copying manuscripts which they had borrowed from other collections, and detailed suitable monks to continue the annals, which previous generations had bequeathed to them. A number of thirteenth-century chroniclers succeeded in writing works which form the backbone of our knowledge of contemporary political events, and the century can boast the remarkable writings on theology and natural science of the bishop, Robert Grosseteste, and the friar, Roger Bacon. Like their predecessors, the chroniclers compiled their histories by uncritically merging extracts and summaries from previous chronicles, but what most of them had to say about contemporary events makes their work valuable to historians today. As we have already seen, St Albans set a high standard with Matthew Paris, who, among many other works augmented and rewrote the *Flores Historiarum* of his distinguished predecessor, Roger of Wendover, and continued the chronicle to 1253. In turn, after his death, Matthew's work was added to by other monks of St Albans. John Tayster and his two continuators of Bury St Edmunds and Bartholomew Cotton of Norwich wrote interesting accounts of events in the troubled middle years of the century and in Edward's reign, and several northern chroniclers, notably Walter of Guisborough and the author of the *Lanercost Chronicle*, had much to say about the Anglo-Scottish wars. Simon de Montfort and King Edward both inspired songs of praise, and one or two thirteenth-century chroniclers wrote in verse, the author of *Le Brut* and Langtoft of Bridlington in French verse, and Robert of Gloucester, who graphically described the battle of Evesham, in English verse. But it was not until the next century that English poets wrote those works which are the most helpful to historians of medieval England.

Bibliography of Thirteenth-Century Documents

Eyre and Spottiswoode, the publishers of *English Historical Documents*, intend to follow Vol. II, covering the years 1042–1189, with Vol. III to continue as far as 1327, and with Vol. IV to the Battle of Bosworth. Both volumes are in active preparation.

The Selden Society has published more than seventy volumes, almost all of which contain transcripts or extracts from medieval judicial records. Quotations from Vols. 1, 2, and 53 have been used in this chapter. See also *The Earliest Lincolnshire Assize Roll, 1202–9*, edited by D. M. Stenton, Vol. 22 of the publications of the Lincoln Record Society.

The Public Record Office has published calendars of charter rolls from 1226, patent rolls from 1216, close rolls from 1227, inquisitions *post mortem* from 1216, and fine rolls from 1272. All these series continue to varying dates well beyond the end of the thirteenth century. The published calendar of liberate rolls as yet only covers the years 1226–51. In addition, extracts from the charter rolls, 1199–1226, the patent rolls, 1202–32, the close rolls, 1204–27, and the fine rolls, 1216–72 have been printed by the Record Commissioners. A translation of Magna Carta, by J. C. Dickinson, was published by the Historical Association in 1955. *Early Cheshire Charters*, ed. G. Barraclough, was published by the Record Society of Lancashire and Cheshire in 1957.

The Red Book of the Exchequer, edited by H. Hall, was published in 1896, *The Book of Fees* in 1920–31. Both works are in three volumes. For local examples see *Lancashire Inquests Extents and Feudal Aids*, ed. by W. Farrer (Lancashire and Cheshire Record Society, Vol. 48), and Vol. 36 (1911) of the publications of the William Salt Archaeological Society.

The accounts or cartularies of Vale Royal, Lewes, Cockersand, and Holm Cultram will be found respectively in Vol. 68 of the Lancashire and Cheshire Record Society's, Vol. 38 of the Sussex Record Society's, Vols. 38–40, 43, 56–7, and 64 (New Series) of the Chetham Society's, and Vol. 7 (Record Series) of the Cumberland and Westmorland Antiquarian Society's publications.

Reference is made in the chapter to the following chronicles:

The Chronicle of Jocelin of Brakelond, ed. H. E. Butler, Nelson's Medieval Texts.

The Flores Historiarum by Roger de Wendover, ed. H. G. Hewlett, 3 vols. Rolls Series (1886–9).

Chronica Majora of Matthew Paris, ed. H. R. Luard, 7 vols., Rolls Series (1872–83).

Lanercost Chronicle, ed. J. Stevenson, Bannatyne Club (1839).

The Chronicle of Walter of Guisborough, ed. H. Rothwell, Vol. 89, Camden Third Series.

Historia Anglicana of Bartholomew Cotton, ed. H. R. Luard, Rolls Series (1859).

THE FOURTEENTH CENTURY

I. POEMS

No wise historian neglects the literature of the age he sets out to study. At the least it will tell him what matters interested the people of that time, what virtues they admired, and what evils they denounced; at the best it will describe for him their towns, countryside, means of travel, houses, furniture, dress, food and drink, education, and entertainment, and illustrate and discuss the problems that most vexed their minds. If only one in a thousand of our modern novels survives, future historians should not find it difficult to picture twentieth-century London, or appreciate current concern about the misuse of atomic energy, the colour bar, or the parking problem. The writings of Shaw, Wells, and Galsworthy are obvious sources for anyone trying to recapture the atmosphere of the early years of this century, just as the novels of Dickens and Jane Austen or the prose works of Milton and Bunyan must be read by those who seek to understand the outlook of the working and middle classes in the nineteenth century or explore Puritan thought two hundred years earlier.

Men of letters were comparatively rare in the Middle Ages, but fourteenth-century England was well blessed with creative writers whose work has survived. Both as a poet and as a social commentator, Chaucer shines much more brightly than the rest, but his brilliance should not blind us to the historical value of the writings of Gower and Lydgate, or of the anonymous mystery and miracle plays, or of the many lyrics written in the century, or of such narrative poems as *The Pearl* and *Sir Gawain and the Green Knight*, or, above all, of William Langland's *Piers Plowman*. In the fourteenth century both the small group of intimates in the solar and the miscellaneous crowd in the hall enjoyed listening to long wandering stories in verse.

The idle found them a relief from boredom, and the humble and hardworking relished the vicarious romance which they brought into their lives. Most of these poems developed magical themes and carried the listener into fairy land, but somewhere in the labyrinths of the narrative the historian can usually find a few helpful comments on the contemporary scene, or a description of imagined banquets and beautiful dresses, or a character sketch of the poet's ideal man or woman. Amidst its blood-curdling, fairy horrors, *Sir Gawain* preserves in its alliterative verse good descriptions of fourteenth-century hunting, armour, and clothing. Into *The Pearl*, a tearful story of a baby's death, the poet introduced a topical theological discussion on the rival merits of grace or deeds as means of salvation, and the author of *Sir Orfeo* set the classical story of Orpheus and Eurydice in an English setting complete with the ever-popular medieval panegyric praising the month of May –

> Befell so in the coming of May
>   When merry and hot is the day
> And away be winter showers
>   And every field is full of flowers
> And glorious blossom on every bough . . .*

The miracle plays which were regularly performed in most of the important towns made no pretence of recreating Biblical times. The chief characters might be Noah and his termagant wife or the Roman soldiers at the foot of the Cross, but the dresses and the props were all 'modern' and anachronisms abounded. When in *The Dancers of Colbek*, Robert Manning of Bourne in Lincolnshire retold a story of eleventh-century Saxony, he began by attacking the common misuse of church and churchyard by noisy revellers in fourteenth-century England.

> Carols [dances with songs], wrestlings, or summer games,
>   Whosoever haunteth any such shames

* In this extract, as in all extracts taken from English originals, the spelling has been modernized.

> In church, or in churchyard,
>   Of sacrilege he may be afeared;
> Or interludes, or singing,
>   Or tabor beat, or other piping –
> All such thing forbidden is
>   While the priest standeth at mass . . .

To sift all the historical value out of medieval literature the searcher must use a fine mesh so that small but valuable items do not escape him. It is not without constitutional significance that Sir Orfeo should have advised his subjects that, as soon as they received word of his death, they should

> Make you then a parliament
> And choose you a new king.

And it reveals a little of the awe medieval man felt in the presence of his few machines that the author of *Sir Gawain*, seeking to describe a wild, threatening, and unearthly noise, resorted to two mechanical similes –

> As one upon a grindstone had ground a scythe.
>   Hwat! it whirred and whette [made a grinding noise],
>   as water at a mill.

In a more straightforward way Langland gave us a list of fourteenth-century good causes, when, through his character Truth, he said that the right use of a merchant's profits was to repair hospitals, help people who were in trouble, repair bad roads and broken bridges, enable poor girls to marry or enter nunneries, feed the poor and the prisoners, send boys to school or apprentice them to a trade, and endow religious orders. Some good causes live through many centuries, but the presence and priority of those that have a shorter life contribute their mite towards our understanding of a particular age.

Fourteenth-century literature constantly illustrates the omnipresence of the church in medieval life, and the natural way in which medieval people thought in terms of Christian belief and practice. Authors frequently made comparisons with events in the Bible or with incidents in the lives of saints: they wove into their narratives, in Latin or in English, biblical texts and phrases from church services with obvious assurance that they would be readily recognized and understood. They were ever ready to criticize and satirize individual clerics or specific groups in the church, but they expressed no scepticism about the faith or the essential church. The only hint of wavering belief was in medical circles. In the twelfth century John of Salisbury had admonished physicians for giving too much credit to Nature and forgetting that Nature itself was one of God's creatures, and Chaucer observed that the knowledge possessed by his well-read doctor was based 'but little on the Bible'. Generally, however, men upheld Christian virtues without question. Whatever they practised themselves or saw practised by others, none denied that the wise were those who laid up for themselves treasures in heaven. Langland constantly returned to this theme.

'When all treasures are tried', quoth she, 'truth is the best . . .
    . . . Whoso is true of his tongue and telleth none other [tells nothing but the truth]
And doeth the works therewith and willeth no man ill,
    He is a god by the gospel aground and aloft [on earth and in heaven]
And alike to our Lord . . .

A thousand of men then thronged together
    Cried upward to Christ and to his clean [virgin] mother
To have Grace to go with them Truth to seek . . .

'Nay, by my soul's health', quoth Piers and [be] gan for to swear,
'I would not take a farthing for St Thomas's shrine!
Truth would love me the less a long time thereafter!
But if you willeth to wend well, this is the way thither . . .
. . . You must go through Meekness, both men and wives,
Till you come into Conscience, that Christ may know the truth
That you love our Lord God most loved of all things,
And then your neighbours next. . . .

Fourteenth-century folk were subjected to frequent denunciatory sermons about their sinful life, the nearness of death, and the inevitable, calamitous, final reckoning. Yet, whether preached by village parsons, wandering friars, or the dedicated Lollards, these sermons did not bring about a widespread religious and moral revival. Many of the preachers themselves were led from the narrow path of what they deemed to be righteousness by the powerful desire to eat, drink, and be merry, whenever it was possible to do so in so unaffluent a society. Langland painted a panoramic picture of his contemporaries at the beginning of *Piers Plowman*. He praised a minority who lived a worthwhile, hard-working life – the ploughmen, the pious religious, the honest merchants, and the minstrels who 'get gold with their glee'. But he had not the slightest tolerance for the majority, the sham, self-centred, and greedy – the beggars, the religious who did not observe their vows, and the lawyers who 'pleaded for pennies and pounds' and never once opened their lips 'for love of our Lord'. No one, he wrote, could get 'a mum from their mouth' unless he first showed them money.

The two authors who are the most rewarding for the historian of the fourteenth century lived in quite different environments. Chaucer, the son of a well-to-do London vintner, spent his youth at court and in the household of the duke of Clarence, and his maturity partly as a trusted servant of John of Gaunt and partly as a customs house official. He was always in touch with fashion and wealth, and all his life enjoyed such comforts as the fourteenth century had to offer. By contrast, Langland, slightly the older of the two men, lived humbly in Cornhill, one of the most crowded and boisterous quarters of medieval London. That these two should have looked upon their fellows from such opposite angles is fortunate for the historian. Not only does it give him the possibility of exploring a wider combined experience, but also it ensures that if he finds both authors holding the same opinion, he cannot dismiss it as prejudice springing from the one's wealth or the other's poverty. Both Chaucer and Langland, for example,

obviously disliked many friars, especially the limiters who did
the begging, and detested all pardoners. Had they been writing
today they would have been wise to protect themselves with
the usual formula that they intended no reference to any
person living or dead, for it is patent that when they were
writing such passages as the following they were writing out of
experience. Moreover, they expected that their pen-pictures
and opinions would be received with considerable appreciation
and approval.

> . . . But now can no man see none elves more
>   For now the great charity and prayers
> Of limiters and other holy friars
>   That search every land and every stream,
> As thick as motes in the sunbeam,
>   Blessing halls, chambers, kitchens, bowers,
> Cities, boroughs, castles, high towers,
>   Thorpes, barns, shippons, dairies,
> This maketh that there be no fairies . . .
>   . . . Women may go safely up and down
> In every bush, or under every tree;
>   There is no other incubus but he
> And he will not do them but dishonour . . .
>   'Wife of Bath's Tale'

I am Wrath, quoth he, I was sometime a friar,
   And the convent's gardener for to graft shoots;
On limiters and listers lies I grafted
   Till they bore leaves of low [flattering] speech lords to please
And since then they [have] blossomed abroad in bowers to hear
      shrifts [confessions].
   And now is fallen thereof a fruit, that folk would much rather
Show their shrifts [say their confessions] to them than shrive them to
      their parsons.

Piers Plowman

I [Chaucer's Pardoner] preach of nothing but for covetousness
   Therefore my theme is yet and ever was
The root of all evil is money.

Thus can I preach against that same vice
Which that I use, and that is avarice.

'The Pardoner's Prologue'

Here preached a Pardoner, as [if] he a priest were
    Brought forth a bull with bishop's seals,
And said that [he] himself might assoil them all
    Of falsehood, of fasting, of vows broken.
Lewd [ignorant] men believed him well, and liked his words,
    Came up kneeling to kiss his bulls;
He bonched them with his brief [thrust his parchment at them] and
        bleared their eyes,
    And raked in with his roll rings and brooches.
Thus they give their gold, gluttons to keep . . .

Piers Plowman

Chaucer and Langland are not the only witnesses to the greed of
fourteenth-century friars. Gower in the *Mirour de l'omme* is just
as hostile – 'the halfpenny he takes if there is no penny' – and
there are three or four mid-century edicts of the church itself
against the activities of unscrupulous pardoners.

Chaucer and Langland were at one in denouncing several
other fourteenth-century evils. Neither approved of the growing practice of parish priests 'leaping to London' to seek lucrative chantry appointments, and both spoke unfavourably about
the excessive drinking of their day. Their frequent references
to fraud and deceit supplement and confirm the evidence of
other writers and of judicial records that dishonest trading was a
common medieval scandal. Gower explained in *Mirour de l'omme*
how Fraud made money out of the 'ladies of the city', who on
their way to church or market 'to the tavern came tripping':

. . . he will assure them
That they shall have, if they will wait a bit,
    Vernage, Greek, and Malmsey.
To make them spend the more
    Many a wine he names to them . . .
. . . From a single tun he draws them
    Ten kinds of wine, if so he can keep them
Sitting in their chairs. . . .

Vintners and brewers were ever suspect; so were millers and bakers. Chaucer's reeve chose to tell his story about a fraudulent miller, and to depict Covetousness, Langland described a man who as an apprentice had been taught to lie, give false weight, and 'stretch ten or eleven yards into thirteen'. His wife, a weaver who had taken to brewing, regularly sold indifferent ale in short measure at high prices, and to increase his ill-gotten wealth, Covetousness made big profits by barter and money-lending. In the third book of *Piers Plowman*, Langland urged those who administered the law to punish cheating brewers, bakers, butchers, and cooks by putting them in the pillory or on the ducking-stool for, he claimed, 'they poison the people privily and oft' and grow rich at the expense of the bellies of the poor.

However much they agreed upon topics such as these, Chaucer and Langland, as one would expect, did not have identical views about wealth. In the fourteenth century the outward sign of personal wealth was immoderate dress. Richard II's court set the fashion with gaily-coloured, extrava-gantly-cut clothing, ridiculously long shoes 'resembling the claws of demons', and crazy, flamboyant hats. As Thomas Hoccleve wrote in *The Regiment of Princes*,

> But this me thinketh an abusion,
>   To see one walk in gowns of scarlet,
> Twelve yards wide, with pendant sleeves down
>   On the ground, and the rich fur therein set.
> Amounting to twenty pound or bet [ter];
>   And if he for it have paid, he no good
> Hath left him wherewith for to buy a hood.

Chaucer amused his readers by poking gentle fun at those who aspired to such fashions. Through his reeve he described the holiday clothes of Simkin the miller, and his wife –

> With his tipet [strip of cloth] bound about his head,
>   And she came after in a skirt of red;
> And Simkin had hose of the same [colour]

and he asked us to picture the wife of Bath with her head covered with heavily-embroidered kerchiefs, her legs encased in scarlet, well-gartered stockings, and her feet sporting soft new shoes. He introduced Absolon, the parish clerk in 'The Miller's Tale', as a highly-fashionable young man:

Curled was his hair, and as the gold it shone,
   And strouted [spread out] as a fan large and broad;
Full straight and even lay his jolly shode [handsome parting].
   His rode [complexion] was red, his eyes grey as goose;
With [St] Paul's window carven on his shoes,
   In hose red he went elegantly.
Clad he was full small [slender] and properly [comely]
   All in a kirtle of a light wachet [blue cloth]
Full fair and thick were the points set.
   And thereupon he had a gay surplice
As white as is the blossom upon the rys [branch].

Langland, however, could not bring himself to speak lightly of such vanities. He did not mix with well-dressed people, and automatically associated riches with sin and the exploitation of the poor. Therefore, when he introduced into his story Lady Lucre, the daughter of Falsehood and the wife of Fraud, he described her as heavily bejewelled and richly and extravagantly dressed:

Her robe was full rich, of red scarlet ingrained,
   With ribbons of red gold, and of rich stones;
Her array me ravished, such richness saw I never . . .

It seemed to him, writing in Cornhill, that this was appropriate costume for so despicable a character.

All fourteenth-century writers, including the scientists, had a healthy respect for astrologers. They sincerely believed that the movements of the heavenly bodies forewarned the initiated of revolution, sudden death, and other disasters, determined the inborn desires and abilities of all mortals, and governed the success or failure of physicians and surgeons. No doctor could hope to practise successfully unless, like Chaucer's doctor, he was 'grounded in astronomy'. Even John Arderne, the most

renowned of English surgeons in the fourteenth century, concluded his practical and sensible advice to his fellow practitioners
by declaring that above all else they must not operate at a time
when the 'astronomers' considered the omens unfavourable.
The medieval eye looked for signs and portents in all kinds of
things. Ranulf Higden of Chester, a fourteenth-century monk,
explained in his *Polychronicon* that the Dee, which, he said,
divided England from Wales, periodically changed its course:

> . . . but whether the water draw more toward England or toward
> Wales, to what side that it be, that year men of that side shall
> have the worse end and be overset, and the men of the other side
> shall have the better end and be at here above [be over them]. When
> the water changeth so its course, it bodeth such happenings.

The interpretation of dreams intrigued medieval people. Not
by chance did Langland and Chaucer both choose dream forms
for their allegorical poems, for in their day men and women
were used to examining dreams to find their inner meanings.
Majority opinion accepted them as one of God's ways of showing mankind the pattern of future happenings. The garrulous,
philosophical Chanticleer in 'The Nun's Priest's Tale' held this
view, and supported it with many a classical and biblical
example.

> By God, men may in old books read
>   Of many a man . . .
> . . . [who] has well founded by experience
>   That dreams be significations
> As well of joy as tribulations
>   That folk endure in this life present.
> There needeth make of this no argument;
>   The very proof showeth it in deed. . . .
> . . . And furthermore, I pray you looketh well
> In the Old Testament, of Daniel,
>   If he held dreams any vanity.
> Read also of Joseph, and there shall you see
>   Where dreams be sometime (I say not all)
> Warning of things that should after fall.

Chanticleer had been moved to such rhetoric by his favourite wife, the fair and practical Pertelote, who, like a small but growing number of fourteenth-century people, rejected the idea that dreams were portents, and explained them away as by-products of disorders in the stomach.

Nothing, God knows, but vanity in sweven [dreams] is.
　　Swevenses engendered of repletions
And oft of fume, and of complexions
　　When humours be too abundant in a wight.

Her remedy for bad dreams was to use 'digestives' and laxatives to readjust the balance of the four humours in the body. The nature of the dream told her which humour needed reducing.

Certes [in truth] this dream, which you have met tonight,
　　Cometh of the great superfluity
Of your red cholera ...
... A day or two you shall have digestives
Of worms, ere you take your laxatives ...

Pertelote quoted Cato as her authority for this advice, but what she prescribed for her feathered husband the most scientific of fourteenth-century physicians would have prescribed for their human patients – with suitable changes of ingredients. To justify such treatment they could have quoted many medical writers and reliable doctors including Galen the Greek, Avicenna the Arab, and the almost-contemporary Englishman, Dr John of Gaddesden.

Chaucer's doctor, that 'very perfect practitioner', made much of his wealth during pestilences. In the middle three years of this century the Black Death swept through England from south to north, and, together with subsequent sporadic outbreaks, almost halved the population. The revolutionary economic consequences of this disaster bewildered the generations which struggled to control them. Langland had no wish to see a new England: however critical he might be of the court and royal administration, he obviously agreed with the government's attempt to use statutes and force to keep things as they had been. He looked sceptically at the growing number of merchants – 'it seemeth to our sight that such men thriveth' – and, a little like Cobbett in a later age, he pined for the return of a simpler economy when the young men who were not born to riches chose either to learn a craft or 'to till and travail' with a plough 'as true life asketh'. He mistrusted the increasing use of money for paying wages and rents, and thought it more ethical as well as sounder economics that men should be rewarded in kind and pay with services. To earnest and honest Langland money was the corrupter – it 'over-mastereth law and much truth letteth'. It encouraged ambition and greed, and was as much the primary cause of bad governors and unworthy judges as of dishonest traders and of priests who deserted their parishioners and went to

> . . . London to dwell,
> And singeth there for simony, for silver is sweet.

Langland longed for a time when money should no more be

> . . . master, as she is now,
> But love and lowness [humility] and loyalty together,
> These shall be masters on earth.

For him a money economy was the antithesis of a Christian society.

Though neither Langland nor Chaucer straightforwardly described political events, their writings could hardly help but reflect something of them. Langland's fable of the rats and mice plotting to bell the cat caricatured the failure of the Commons to curb the hostility of John of Gaunt; and the Nun's Priest compared the clatter and enthusiasm of the farmer's household chasing the fox with Jack Straw's jubilant attack on the Flemish merchants in London in 1381:

> So hideous was the noise, a benedicite!
>   Certes, he Jack Straw, and his meynee [household]
> Ne made never shouts half so shrill,
>   When that they would any Fleming kill
> As thilke [the same] day was made upon the fox.

Perhaps the most interesting political lines in contemporary literature are those which comment on the attitude of Englishmen to foreigners in the fourteenth century. Jews had long been fair game for Christians to attack, and the Prioress began her anti-Jewish story with words which left no doubt of her personal opinion:

> There was in Asia, in a great city,
>> Amongst Christian folk, a Jewerie [a ghetto],
> Sustained by a lord of that country
>> For foul usury and lucre of villainy,
> Hateful to Christ and to his company ...

In *Confessio Amantis*, Gower wrote a similar derogatory passage which began:

> I am a Jew, and by my law
>> I shall to no man be fellow
> To keep him truth in word nor deed ...

and John Mandeville recorded some widespread fantastic beliefs which men held of Jewish plans 'for to destroy the Christian people'. But during the fourteenth century there appeared increasing signs of hostility against other Christians. The merchants and populace in London resented the way continental merchants sailed from Dover or from the Thames with rich profits made in England, for it seemed to them that these Lombard bankers, Hanse merchants, or Flemish traders could only have grown rich at the expense of Englishmen. As in 1381, anger and jealousy occasionally boiled over into rioting and murder, and the Lollards were not the only people who resented the steady flow of money from England to Rome. In two ironic passages Langland commented that a king, as guardian of the realm, was bound to distribute handsome gifts – especially to foreigners; and to prevent gold and silver from 'filling the pockets of Papal robbers' and from crossing the Channel, he advised the king to have his officers search all those leaving Dover, except merchants and their men, messengers with merchants' letters, priests, penitent pilgrims, and those seeking livings from Rome – all, of course, the culprits who were widely believed to be constantly taking treasure out of England. This vague feeling of national exclusiveness, nourished no doubt by the long war which began in 1340 between the English and French crowns, led Langland to deplore the appointment of foreigners to English benefices, and to disapprove of pilgrimages to foreign shrines. St James, he declared, should be sought in English churches and not at fashionable Compostella: let no one go to Galicia except to stay there. Even when put into the mouths of fictional characters such sentiments betray the presence of those fibrous roots, which, in the next two centuries were destined to feed the ever-growing tree of nationalism. They contributed considerably to the destruction of medieval Europe, and to the creation of modern nation states.

2. SIGNIFICANT ADMINISTRATIVE CHANGES

In 1348, to commemorate his triumph at Crécy and to honour St George, Edward III founded the Order of the Garter. Together with the other twenty-five members of the brotherhood, he dedicated his life to the 'advancement of piety, nobility, and chivalry', and proclaimed truth, honour, freedom, and courtesy as the ideals to be pursued by this exclusive fellowship. When he founded his Order, Edward was deliberately imitating the legendary King Arthur. He intended his knights of the Garter to be the companions of a new Round Table, an inspiration and an example to the remainder of Europe's chivalry. To add colour to the picture he encouraged jousting, which rapidly became the most popular sport of the aristocracy. At royal command the constable and marshal arranged the tournaments, and household officials provided food and drink in plenty for interminable banquets. The competitors decked themselves and their horses as richly and gaily as they could afford. They observed elaborate formalities, for the spectators, especially the ladies, were as essential to jousting as the knights and chargers. Chivalry had become a cult, and heraldry, its squire, was fast developing into a complicated science, which needed heralds to interpret and control it. Crests and coats of arms became the universal decoration. No longer did knights confine them to utility use on helmets, shields, surcoats, and seals, but began to display them on banners and pennants, towers and gatehouses, illuminated manuscripts and decorative tiles, and, most permanently, in churches and on tombs.

This colourful and romantic surface of the fourteenth century should not mislead the student of the Middle Ages. The fourteenth was not the most feudal of centuries, but the one which witnessed significant changes, which we can now see marked the end of the true feudal age and began paving the way for the strong monarchies, nation states, and national wars of the sixteenth century. Much fourteenth-century 'medievalism' had become artificial and self-conscious. Already men were finding it a little curious. It was acquiring an antiquarian interest and losing its usefulness. It was ceasing to belong to the real world of practical living.

Perhaps the most obvious change which took place in the fourteenth century was in methods of recruiting. We saw in the last chapter that Edward I still called on his tenants-in-chief to fulfil the feudal obligations imposed on their estates: he expected them to provide him with an agreed number of armed men pledged to serve for forty days a year. But in his Welsh and Scottish campaigns Edward found the feudal host unsatisfactory. He required longer service from his troops and a better system of command, and therefore he raised an increasing number of 'regulars' by means of indentures. His successors, especially Edward III in the French wars, used the new method far more than he had done. Indentures were businesslike agreements made between the crown and suitable and willing commanders. They ensured that the king would be served by adequately equipped, professional soldiers, ready to campaign, winter as well as summer, for as long as he continued to pay them. They stipulated the number and categories of troops as well as the agreed rates of wages. When Edward III sailed for Normandy in July 1346, he sealed indentures, for example, with the earl of Northampton for 302 soldiers – himself, 2 bannerets or subordinate commanders, 46 knights, 112 esquires, and 141 mounted archers – with Lord Talbot for 157, including 82 archers, and with Sir Walter de la Pole for 5 – himself, 2 squires, and 2 archers. The king agreed on a fixed rate of wages for each rank. He paid Northampton, as an earl, 6s. 8d. a day, Talbot, as a baron, 4s. 0d., and Sir Walter, as a knight, 2s. 0d. Mounted archers and hobelars, who were the lightly-armed horsemen often used for foraging, received 6d. a day, unmounted archers 3d., and Welsh foot-soldiers 2d. Considering the value of money in the fourteenth century, this was a far better paid army than the one which fought on the same Somme territory in 1914–18, or than the British section of the allied force which landed on the same Contentin peninsula almost exactly 600 years later.

In turn the commanders who served the king made similar agreements with the men who were to form their retinue. At every level in the social hierarchy wages were becoming the accepted bond between master and man: the Black Prince and John of Gaunt received their daily wages from the crown just as naturally as the humblest archer or foot-soldier took his wages from his captain. At first employer and employed struck verbal bargains, but most of the troops who fought for Edward III overseas seem to have had the security of a formal indenture. A clerk wrote the agreement twice on the same piece of parchment. He then cut zig-zag between the two copies, handing one copy to the master and the other to the man. Because the irregular edges of genuine indentures would always fit when placed together, both parties enjoyed a simple precaution against forgery. And these zig-zag cuts gave the documents their name, for they reminded the fanciful of upper and lower teeth.

The general purpose of all indentures was the same – to bind the soldier in service to his master, and, on the other hand, to ensure the soldier a reasonable reward. But naturally indentures differed considerably in detail. In August 1372 John of Gaunt sealed the following agreement with Sir Walter Urswick, a knight who had already served him well for many years as a chief forester in Lancashire.

This indenture, made between our lord John, king of Castile and Leon etc., of the one part, and Sir Walter Urswick of the other part, witnesses that the said Sir Walter is retained and will serve our said lord for life in peace and in war. And our said lord has given and granted the said Sir Walter, for the good and satisfactory service that he has long rendered and will render in the future, £100 sterling [a year] for life from the revenues of the manors of Gryngley and Wheteley from the hands of the lord's receiver, who will pay at Michaelmas and Easter in equal portions. And if the said £100 be unpaid in part or in whole a month after the aforesaid feasts, our lord wills and gives leave to the said Sir Walter to distrain on the said manors or either of them, and to keep as he wishes what he distrains until he receives full payment with any arrears there may be. Given at Langdon Abbey in the county of Kent on the 28th day of August in the 46th year [of Edward III's reign].

Sir Walter could count himself fortunate or particularly deserving, for most indentures were far less generous. The agreement made between Gaunt and Sir Roger Trumpington on the next day, 29 August 1372, is much more usual:

... our lord has granted the said Sir Roger for life, for himself and a squire, forty marks a year in English coinage in time of war and twenty marks in the same coinage in time of peace, to be taken from the revenues of the manors of Glatton and Holm in the county of Huntingdon, and to be paid by the lord's receiver at Michaelmas and Easter in equal portions. Both in peace and war the said Sir Roger will be required to serve our said lord, and to go with him to war wherever he wishes, with a squire suitably and well equipped. And each year he will take his fees of war, as stated above, for himself and his squire, together with such wages as are paid to others of his rank. And the said Sir Roger shall begin his year of war on the day he sets out from home to join our said lord in accordance with instructions which will be sent to him, and thus he shall be entitled to wages for himself and his squire for reasonable travelling time going and returning. And the said Sir Roger shall provide such adequate equipment for himself, his men and horses as can be reasonably expected. As for war-horses taken and lost in our lord's service, and as for prisoners or other prizes taken or won by the said Sir Roger or his esquire or one of his servants, our lord will recompense him as he will recompense others of his rank. Given at Sandwich . . .

Some indentures made provision for the soldier to bring other troops with him, if the employer specifically asked him to do so. Thus the indenture sealed at Pontefract in July 1381 between Gaunt and William Tunstall stipulated that in time of war William should receive

by the hands of the duke's treasurer of war, such wages and consideration for himself and the men-at-arms and archers, which he shall bring at the duke's command, as the duke himself receives from the king of England for men-at-arms and archers of similar condition; or, if the duke is campaigning on his own, as much as he gives to other esquires, men-at-arms, and archers . . .

In 1347 Edward III sealed a similar, but more specific indenture with Henry Husee.

This indenture, made between our lord Edward king of England and of France and lord of Ireland of the one part and Henry Husee of the other part, witnesses that the said Henry has undertaken the defence of the Isle of Wight until next Michaelmas with forty men-at-arms and sixty archers at the king's expense. He will begin to be responsible for these same men and for the island immediately after Easter, and he will be paid wages for the said men at a rate agreed between himself and the treasurer of our lord the king.

In witness of this, our said lord the king holds the part of this indenture concerning the said Henry, and the said Henry holds the other part of the same indenture concerning our said lord the king. And they have attached their seals.

Given at Westminster the 22 day of March, the year of the reign of our said lord the king, namely, of England the twenty-first and of France the eighth.

Occasionally the soldier, for personal reasons, insisted upon limiting his service. Roger Perewick declined to be bound to serve across the sea, and the indenture made between Gaunt and Sir John Swinton, a vassal of the king of Scotland, contained this extra clause:

... the said duke wills and grants that he [Sir John] will not be held to serve him against his allegiance. And if the said Sir John be not in the duke's service for any time because of his allegiance, the said John wills that for the same period the duke shall be quit of paying the aforesaid fees and wages whether it is in time of peace or war.

The success of indentured troops rapidly put an end to the feudal levy altogether. Richard II's attempt to revive it for a Scottish expedition in 1385 was discouraging, and no other king tried to raise it after that. But when the country was in danger of invasion or insurrection, the king could call out the shire levies. The Statute of Winchester in 1285 had clearly defined each man's obligation.

Every man shall have in his house equipment for keeping the peace, according to the ancient assize; that is to say, every man between 15 and 60 years of age shall be assessed and obliged to have arms according to the quantity of his lands and goods; that is, he who holds land worth £15 a year, and goods worth 40 marks, shall have a coat of mail, an iron helmet, a sword, a knife, and a horse; from land worth £10 and 20 marks of goods, a coat of mail, an iron helmet, a sword, and a knife; from land worth £5, a doublet, an iron helmet, a sword, and a knife; and from 40 up to 100 shillings' worth of land, a sword, a bow and arrows, and a knife; and they that have less than 40 shillings' worth of land shall be sworn to keep halberds, knives, and other smaller weapons; and they that possess goods worth less than 20 marks shall equip themselves with swords, knives, and other smaller weapons; and all others out of the forest shall have bows and arrows, and within the forest bows and bolts.

The view of arms shall be made twice each year. And in every hundred and franchise two constables shall be appointed to make the view, and the constables shall bring before the justices, when they come into their area, the defaulters whom they have discovered ...

The king began mobilization by issuing commissions of array. As commissioners he usually chose local barons, knights of the shire, or his household officers. From their specified area, the commissioners selected such men as they required for the job in hand.

Details of commissions of array are listed in the calendars of patent rolls. The following are typical entries.

12 November 1371. Commission of array in the county of Kent to the keepers of the peace and the sheriff of that county: and order to secure the observance of the statute of labourers.

Similar commissions sent to the keepers of the peace and sheriffs in all counties of England [except Durham].

10 July 1381. Commission to John Mowbray, earl of Nottingham, Robert, lord of Willoughby, William, lord of Bardolf, John, lord of Beaumont, John, lord de la Warre, John, lord of Welle, Philip, lord of Darcy, Philip le Despenser [and twenty other named gentlemen] to assemble and array the king's lieges in the county of Lincoln to resist the insurgents.

The insurgents were, of course, the men and women who were followers of Wat Tyler, Jack Straw, and John Wrawe in the Peasants' Revolt. June had been a bad month for the government, and by the time Richard II issued this commission, his officers had far more confidence. Within the next fortnight, the king sent similar commissions to the bishop of Norwich, the earl of Suffolk, Thomas Morley, and Hugh Hastings in Norfolk and Suffolk, and to John Montagu, Thomas West, and nine other gentlemen in Hampshire and Wiltshire. Occasionally arrays did not work out according to plan, or the king found it necessary to issue subsequent instructions. In 1385 Richard II was hard pressed. While he was trying to mobilize the feudal levy against Scotland, the threat of French and Flemish raids forced him to call out the shire levies along the south-east coast. The men of Orford in Suffolk resented being ordered to other parts of the county, leaving their own homes exposed to possible attack. To them service in the shire levy meant very local service indeed. The king upheld their objection and sent the following instructions. The letter is calendared in the close rolls.

1 June 1385. To the arrayers of men at arms, hobelars and archers in Suffolk.

Order, upon petition of the men at Orford, themselves or one of them to repair thither in person and oversee the arraying of the petitioners, causing them to be arrayed and kept in array according to the king's commission, compelling them to guard the town against attacks of the enemy if any shall invade those parts, and telling them to be intendent to Isabel countess of Suffolk lady of a castle there in regard to ward of the castle if peril happen, and order to release any distress made upon the said men to appear before the arrayers without the town; as on their behalf it is shown the king that the said town and castle are upon the sea shore, that the king's enemies of France and Flanders lately appeared with a great fleet off that coast at a place near called Orford Ness, and are purposing to invade and destroy the town and castle and lay waste the neighbouring parts if they be not manfully resisted, and that the arrayers are distraining the petitioners to appear without the town in distant parts of the county, although at every array the men of the town used to be arrayed within the same, praying the king to make provision for the defence of the town and castle, and to order the petitioners to be there arrayed, as used to be done.

The king took no responsibility for arming or clothing the levies, but if he required shire troops to serve abroad, he paid them wages as if they were indentured men. Sailors were recruited in similar fashion. When the Black Prince was preparing to sail for his Poitiers campaign in May 1355, the exchequer entrusted William of Wenlock with £380 to pay the wages of the mariners serving 'the prince and other people going to Gascony'. His instructions were to pay them for twenty-eight days. If he paid every sailor serving in the forty-four ships of the expedition, their wages would average out at about $3\frac{1}{2}$d. a day.

Indentured soldiers won surprising victories in Scotland and across the Channel. At Halidon Hill as well as Crécy and Poitiers the English longbowmen and men-at-arms shattered formidable opposition. But campaigns, however victorious, demanded endless money, and Edward III was fortunate that a silent revolution in national administration kept him adequately supplied. The back-room boys in these wars were men like William Edington, John Thoresby, and William Wykeham, mostly clerics who spent many years in royal administration. They improved the machinery of government, and without provoking the jealous opposition of the magnates, succeeded in keeping the landholders and the merchants actively behind the war effort.

Edward I had centred his war administration in the wardrobe, an efficient, personal organization which he kept separate from exchequer and chancery. He used the privy seal, the sign of the wardrobe's authority, for recruiting and paying troops, but when Edward II tried to follow his father's lead, his barons insisted upon bringing the wardrobe under their control. To counter this, Edward II created a new household organization called the chamber, but neither he nor Edward III ever made the chamber very efficient. After 1340 the war in France was far too big an undertaking to be financed out of the king's pocket or administered by the chamber. It required the mobilizing of all possible resources, and the creation of an efficient, systematic, administrative machine. The chancery, with its two subsidiary departments, the office of rolls and the office of hanaper, took charge of executive government. The exchequer steadily gained full control of finance. It transferred funds to the wardrobe, which acted as the war treasury abroad, but it required from it accounts of how the money was spent. In the late 40s it began to audit and administer the chamber's accounts, and in 1356, in order to promote harmony, Edward gave it control of the last of the estates from which the chamber had drawn its independent income. It also held directly responsible to it both the great wardrobe, which supplied clothing and equipment to the king's forces, and the privy wardrobe, which maintained and repaired the royal stocks of arms and armour in the Tower. Each department had its specialized function, and the hierarchy of command enabled the administration to work steadily and efficiently without constant royal supervision. Edward's absence in Normandy did not impede the work of the chancery and the exchequer at Westminster. Nevertheless, the whole purpose of the administration was to serve the king by carrying out his commands. Writs under the privy seal informed the chancellor or the treasurer what the king willed, and the king relied upon his chief administrators to see that his will was put into effect. Parallel changes were taking place in judicial administration. Routine and precedent, which had begun to stake their claim in the thirteenth century, grew stronger throughout the fourteenth. Gradually they completely ousted from the bench judgement given by the king in person. Nevertheless, the courts were not divorced from the crown; they still dispensed royal justice and upheld the royal prerogative.

Naturally, this new administrative and judicial machinery called for more clerking. It could not work without registers, writs, financial accounts, letters patent, and letters close in plenty. The historian can only welcome the increase in the number of departmental papers, because, at the cost of a little duplication, it affords him means of checking facts, and of course reduces the chances of total loss. Many of these papers for the fourteenth century are easily available in print, at least in calendar form. The Public Record Office has published calendars of the patent, close, fine, and charter rolls for the whole of the century, inquisitions *post mortem* and miscellaneous inquisitions as far as 1377, and various chancery rolls and chancery warrants (instructions sent by the king to the chancellor) up to the year 1346. Exchequer papers are not so easily examined, but as long ago as 1837 the Record Commissioners published *Issues of the Exchequer*, which consists of translated extracts from the accounts of different departments from the mid thirteenth to the mid fifteenth century, and the Public Record Office has since published *Inquisitions and Assessments Relating to Feudal Aids, 1284–1431* in six volumes which cover the counties in alphabetical order. In addition *Archaeologia*, the journal of the

Society of Antiquaries of London, printed details of the 1377 poll-tax in Volume 7 (1785), of a few wardrobe accounts of Edward II, Edward III, and Richard II in Volumes 26 and 31 (1836 and 1846), and of the repayment of some royal loans in Volume 28 (1840). The historian has to explore as many such records as he can lay hands on, and out of them take those facts which seem to him to throw light upon the problem he is investigating. Almost certainly he will be left with a few gaps and inconsistencies. The gaps, if not too big, he can try and fill by careful inference; the inconsistencies he must attempt to resolve by deciding which one of the differing records has come from the department most likely to have been best informed. In the end he will probably be surprised at the volume of information he has acquired.

In 1897, for example, George Wrottesley gathered together, in Volume 18 of the publications of the William Salt Archaeological Society, all the primary sources he could find on the Crécy campaign. From writs and letters patent listed in the French Roll, Norman Roll, and the Memoranda Roll of the Queen's Remembrancer (the exchequer official responsible for collecting documents preparatory to the audit), he took information about recruiting and about the privileges and pardons acquired by soldiers serving in the campaign. The accounts of Walter Wetwang, keeper of the wardrobe from April 1344 to November 1347, gave him information about the number of troops on the payroll, the names of the commanders, and the rates of pay for each rank; and the letters written to England by Michael de Northburgh, one of the clerks in the king's household, enabled him to put an alternative story of the campaign against that of the French chronicler, Froissart. It is particularly interesting, and not a little perplexing, to compare the numbers of troops in the various documents. Quite apart from indentured troops, the king summoned the levies from all but the most northern counties, and ordered London and the larger towns to send sizeable contingents to Portsmouth, the embarkation point. The commissioners could only have chosen a small percentage of eligible men from each county, because according to Wetwang's accounts – a most reliable document for such information – the total number of men in the king's pay, including workmen as well as soldiers, was no more than 32,303. Of these about 5,340 were men-at-arms and over 16,000 archers on foot, but these figures included Henry of Lancaster's forces fighting in Gascony, and North-ampton's troops in Brittany. When Edward III moved towards Calais after the battle of Crécy, he reinforced his army in order to besiege the town more effectively. Froissart assessed the size of Edward's army at Crécy as about 3,000 men-at-arms and 5,200 archers. When every allowance has been made for wastage and for men employed on other duties, it seems likely that he underestimated the numbers engaged.

This fourteenth-century progress towards systematic na-tional administration is mirrored in the changes which the great magnates and certain bishops and abbots were making in their households. The laws of inheritance, especially the one con-cerning the disposal of lands of heiresses, tended to concentrate many extensive and scattered estates into a few hands. In the last half of Edward III's reign the duke of Lancaster could boast himself as rich in land as Edward, prince of Wales; and half-a-dozen other landowners such as Richard Fitzalan, earl of Arundel, or Thomas Beauchamp, earl of Warwick, ranked only slightly inferior. Each of them saw the advantage of centralizing their estates. They could not consolidate them into an unbroken block of territory, but they could bring them under a common administration. They took the royal administration as their guide. From his wardrobe in the city of London and his treasury in Westminster, the Black Prince administered his lands in Cheshire, Cornwall, and Wales. His local officers accounted to his treasurer in Westminster for the revenues they collected, in the same way as the sheriffs accounted to the royal exchequer. His keeper of the wardrobe, sometimes called chancellor, issued his writs, and his central judicial officers travelled to his estates to reinforce the authority of his regional justiciars, and to report back to his central administration. In 1351 Sir John de Wengefeld and Sir Richard de Stafford, both London-based officers of the prince, paid a formal visit to the earldom of Chester. Among other things, they investigated cases of trespass in the Forest of Wirral. A month or two later the forester received the following orders from London.

Edward, son of the illustrious King of England, Prince of Wales, Duke of Cornwall and Earl of Chester, to William de Stanley, forester of the Forest of Wirral, Greeting,

Without fail you and yours must be present at the next County Court of Chester at our exchequer [i.e. the exchequer of the earldom] at the same place, and bring with you all the debts, listed below, which are due to us in your bailiwick, concerning amercements, assarts, purprestures [encroachments], corn grown in the Forest and dogs not lawed and other trespasses committed to the injury of the Forest, in the enquiry concerning the Forest of Wirral held before Thomas de Ferrars, justiciar of Chester, and John de Wengefeld and Richard de Stafford of the Council of the Lord the Earl, on Wednesday the morrow of the Conversion of St Paul in the twenty-fifth year of the reign of the Lord Edward the King, our Father [26 January 1351], namely:

Agnes who was the wife of John de Mollington for enclos-
    ing one grove against the assize of the Forest   12d.
Hamon de Massey for the same   12d.
Richard son of Simon de Becheton for the same   12d.
Hamon de Massey of Puddington for the destruction of
    one grove   12d.
Roger Gyle for breaking up one acre of land in Ledsham
    in a tristera [a hunting station] which is not permissible 12d.
The same Roger for cropping the same acre for 2 years   4s.
    [etc.]

Altogether the writ listed 126 offences, and the fines totalled £22 1s. 4d. William de Stanley paid them into the earl's exchequer at Chester, and Thomas de Ferrars, 'our justiciar of Chester', countersigned the writ on 20 May as evidence that it had been obeyed. On 18 July the London chancery sent out a second writ concerning more serious offences than those previously entrusted to Stanley:

> To Sir Thomas de Ferrars, justice of Chester, or his lieutenant, and Master John de Brunham, the prince's clerk and chamberlain there. Enclosed is a schedule indented containing the names of those persons who were lately indicted before the justice, Sir John de Wengefeld, and Sir Richard de Stafford of trespasses committed in the Forest of Wirral, together with the sums which the prince orders that they pay for their fines and the sums wherein he orders that they be bound for good behaviour towards him and his ministers and towards those who indicted them.

The said schedule:

Bonds for good behaviour	Names	Fines
	John Dounville the father	100 marks
200 marks	John Dounville the son Matthew his brother William de Bradburn, his son-in-law	10 marks
	John de Leighton	20 s.
	Henry de Neston	20 s.
£40	Robert de Berneston	20 marks
	Warin Trussel	40 s.
40 marks	John Doune	10 marks
	[etc.]	

The writ quoted a further twenty-six names, and the fines varied from £5 to half a mark.

Similar evidence of the centralizing of seigniorial administration in the fourteenth century can be found in *John of Gaunt's Register*, a collection of administrative documents published by the Royal Historial Society. Gaunt's inheritance was unusually complicated. To his own estates he added, in 1362, the duchy of Lancaster, which his first wife, Blanche, had inherited from her father, Henry. After 1371, the year in which he married his second wife, Constance of Castile, he laid claim to the crown of Castile and Léon, and in 1377 he received from his father, Edward III, palatine powers in Lancashire. Gaunt was particularly proud of the independence which he enjoyed in the county palatine. He continued to use the chancery court which his father-in-law had established at Preston, and in addition set up a palatine exchequer court at Lancaster. He also employed in the county a chief justice of the forests, a chief steward, and an escheator, and he dated writs issued under his great seal, which he used exclusively for business concerning the palatinate, according to his 'regnal' year, which began on 28 February 1377 when his father had first conferred the honour upon him. But whatever independence it enjoyed, the county palatine only constituted part of the duke's total possessions, and therefore its officers were subordinate to the duke's central officers, who, until its destruction by rioters in 1381, were based in London at the palace of the Savoy. Gaunt's two chief ministers at headquarters were his chancellor, who kept his privy seal and usually travelled with the household, and his receiver general, who supervised the work of local receivers and allocated money for household expenses and the various administrative departments. Both ministers, of course, had adequate staffs of clerks. The chancery informed the local officers of the duke's will. In 1372, for example, it dispatched a series of letters to his officers in different areas of England and Wales demanding the collection of an aid from all his tenants. This is the letter sent to the south-eastern counties:

John, son of the king of France and of England, etc., to all our seneschals, bailiffs, provosts, and all our other officers whatsoever within our estates in Kent, Surrey and Sussex, who will see or hear read our letters, greeting.

Know that, because of the great necessity we have at present, we have charged our dear and well-beloved John Colepepper and John Edward to go to all our land and estates in the said counties, and assemble all our tenants, both free and bond, on one occasion or on several, according as shall seem better to them, and request all the freemen of the towns and boroughs, and order all the bondmen that they make us an aide, each individually so that each one can be of service to us in this matter, giving the aforesaid John and John full power and authority to do all the things stated below, and to punish all and each of the bondmen through their bodies and goods sparing none who might refuse or oppose the aforesaid order. And if any free-man farms bonded land and refuses to pay the aforesaid aid let all the bonded land in his possession be seized and held until he has submitted to our aforesaid officers. We order and command our aforesaid officers and each one of them that, if there be any obstacle in carrying out the aforesaid instructions, they and each one of them shall let us know without delay what they know of the matter. Accordingly we order you and each one of you, requiring that you help the aforesaid John and John and each of them in the aforesaid business, advising them conscientiously in the light of all the facts, and of what they will enable you to do on our behalf.

In witness of which we have issued these our letters patent. Given at our manor of the Savoy on the 28th day of February in the year of the reign of our said lord the king of England the 46th and of France the 33rd.

The clerks at Gaunt's treasury in London kept a close watch on the accounts of the stewards, receivers, feodaries, and other officials who worked in different areas of the provinces, and the receiver general sent out auditors on regular tours of inspection. The following is a routine instruction sent from the treasury to officers in Hertford.

John, etc., to our dear and well beloved Thomas of Hardwick, auditor of accounts of our ministers and officers within the county of Hertford and elsewhere, and John Hallstead, our receiver in that county, greeting.

Because our dear and well beloved Richard Icklingford has made us full payment of a sum of £34 15s. 9½d., which he owed us on the last account he rendered to you in the said county, and which we have acknowledged by a receipt given to him under our privy seal, we order this same Richard to be discharged of this sum of £34 15s. 9½d., and be quit of this debt for ever. And these our letters will be for you a warrant for doing so.

Given under our privy seal at the Savoy on the 21st day of February in the reign of the year of our said lord the king of England [Richard II] the 3rd. [1380].

After Gaunt had died and his son had been crowned King

Henry IV, the centralizing of the Lancastrian estates was drawn even tighter. Hitherto, duchy and county palatine had been considered one and the same territory, but Henry enlarged the duchy vastly by including in it all the lands which his father had held not as duke of Lancaster, but by such lesser titles as earl of Lincoln or earl of Leicester. He established in London the court of duchy chamber, and manned it with the chancellor and chief officers of this enlarged duchy. He intended it to serve both as the supreme administrative and judicial body for all his patrimonial lands, and as an appeal court for dissatisfied suitors at the palatine chancery court at Preston. The duchy of Lancaster formed a state within a state, and because, since 1399, the duke has always been the reigning monarch, its separate administration, emasculated somewhat by Gladstone's reforming zeal, has survived to our own day.

In the later part of the Middle Ages, the duchy, however remarkable its size and efficiency, was not unique. Not only other magnates, but also bishops and the abbots of the major houses built up administrations which were increasingly formal and hierarchical, and did not need their actual presence in order to work effectively. As we have seen in the last chapter, the change from the simpler, personal administration began in the thirteenth century, but it became more widespread and more firmly established in the fourteenth. It was a practical necessity that political bishops, such as Adam Orleton of Hereford in the first half of the century and Henry Despenser of Norwich in the second, should have adequate deputies in their dioceses, and that those bishops who were fully employed by the king in secular administrative work should have a competent diocesan administration, based on a developing canon law and manned by such major officers as the registrar, the official, the suffragan bishop, and the vicar general at the centre and by the archdeacons and the rural deans in the parishes. Walter Reynolds was bishop of Worcester from 1308 to 1313, but he could not personally conduct the affairs of the diocese because he was the king's treasurer for the first half of that period and his chancellor for the rest. Thomas Arundel served Richard II as chancellor for most of the years he was bishop of Ely and archbishop of York, and Thomas Brantingham was treasurer for about a third of the long time, 1370–94, he was nominally in charge of the diocese of Exeter. The kings of the fourteenth century usually appointed secular priests to administrative offices, but abbots and priors could no more easily free themselves from temporal responsibilities. The Black Death accelerated the process by which monastic houses were leasing their lands to tenant farmers for cash rents, and though this relieved monastic officials from close supervision of sowing and harvesting, it brought with it new forms of inspection and the need to keep more accounts. Each diocesan or monastic official had well-defined duties and authority. Nearly always his duties entailed keeping a roll or a register, or presenting accounts, and, therefore, the historian of the fourteenth century can make profitable use of such of these departmental records as have survived. Many of them have been printed; they include such varied documents as the fabric rolls of York Minster, the halmote court rolls of Durham Priory, the records of the episcopal visitations made to the religious houses in the diocese of Lincoln, the registers or letter-books of the Cathedral priory of Canterbury, and many bishops' registers published by the Canterbury and York Society and a number of county record societies.

Another significant change in fourteenth-century England – and incidentally a by-product of the evolution of a more systematized national administration – was the growth of parliamentary power. This was the century in which the earls and barons established their right to be summoned to parliament and be considered the natural advisers of the king, and in which knights and burgesses made good their claim to be consulted about taxation and to present petitions to the crown. Parliament still had a long struggle ahead before it could claim that 'the king in parliament assembled' was the highest authority in the land, but, by the end of the fourteenth century, it would have been most difficult for a king to ignore its voice.

To attempt to determine the origin of parliament is to become enmeshed in the issues of a complicated problem, which constitutional historians have argued about for generations. Yet no one doubts that by the end of Edward I's reign a definite parliamentary pattern had begun to take shape. The peers of the realm, as they were learning to call themselves by the 1340s, were discussing with the king's ministers, and sometimes with the representatives of the lesser landed gentry and the merchants, petitions to be presented to the king. They offered the king advice which they expected him to take, and increasingly maintained that the king and lords sitting together in parliament constituted the most authoritative court in England. They even claimed in Edward III's and Richard II's reigns that the king's ministers could be held responsible to this court. Representatives of the commons were chiefly concerned with authorizing taxation and presenting grievances.

At first the activities of these early parliaments were recorded in various chancery and exchequer files, but, certainly from 1341 onwards, a separate parliamentary roll, kept by the clerk of parliament, recorded the petitions presented to the crown. Although discussing and presenting to the king petitions which could not be satisfactorily presented to other courts was easily the most frequent of parliamentary tasks, no records of argument or debate have come down to us. There is no medieval equivalent of Hansard: the rolls list the petitions, and the statute rolls, which date from the last years of the thirteenth century, give details of the enactments which the king decreed on the advice of his peers and at the request of his subjects. Statutes had the force of law, but medieval kings did not hesitate to ignore them when it suited their convenience.

Parliamentary petitions were of two sorts. In the early parliaments, the majority were private petitions asking for a favour, or relief, or judgement on behalf of a single person or small group of people. The petition on behalf of John Maltravers, which was unsuccessfully presented at Westminster in 1339 and is quoted below, is an example of this kind of petition. Occasional petitions, such as the second one quoted below which was presented in 1327, had relatively wide support, and claimed to be in the name of the people of England. Such petitions were the earliest parliamentary bills.

To our lord the king, his liegeman John Maltravers shows that as he was wrongly, and without law and reason, banished out of the kingdom of England in the parliament at Westminster – which judgement was and is in error according to many previous rulings, for in your first parliament it was ordained that no man should be lawfully judged without the right of reply, yet this said judgement was made in the absence of all the greatest peers of the realm and without their approval and their will, and without calling the said John to reply; further neither our lord the king nor the said peers of the realm gave any consideration to nor had, by appeal or indictment, any information concerning the matter which was alleged in John's absence – for which reasons the said John prays the said our lord the king that the aforesaid judgement be reviewed and examined, and because those faults and other irregularities contained therein, contrary to the laws of your kingdom, be reversed and annulled.

And may it please our lord the king of his good grace to grant that the said John may come safely into the kingdom of England, as one who, at all peril, will be ready to make answer to all, according to the law of the land, for whatever charge man will lawfully prefer against him. And because he is not ashamed to meet any man, he prays our lord the king that he may have his protection so that he may come safely to reply to all in the manner aforesaid.

To our lord the king, the community of the realm prays that as, by examination of prelates, earls, and barons and of the community of the realm in full parliament, it was formerly found that Hugh Despenser the father and Hugh the son were traitors and enemies of the king, and of the kingdom and of the crown, and because of this, by common consent of the king and his baronage, the said Hugh and Hugh were exiled from the kingdom of England never to return unless by common consent of all, given in full parliament by those lawfully summoned, which decision and exile was affirmed by common consent by statute in the same parliament. And after this parliament certain prelates, urged on by certain clerks who were adherents of the traitors, petitioned the king that the said enemies might be recalled to the kingdom: they alleged the exile of the aforesaid traitors to be wrong, so that the king recalled them to the kingdom against the conditions of the exiling. These enemies then made war on the peers of the realm to take revenge for their false quarrel, against law and reason and the great charter, so that they caused the death of the good earl of Lancaster and the good earl of Hereford; and many others, both great and small, died and were imprisoned and exiled and suffered confiscation of their goods and lands. Because of these things the community of the realm prays, in the name of the good prelates, earls and barons as in the name of those worthy messengers sent to our holy father the pope to acquaint him with the great wrongs that have befallen the kingdom and to beseech that henceforward he will be pleased to reserve the bishoprics and other offices of England, and allow the churches to have free elections according to former royal grants and according to the confirmation of the holy fathers the popes his predecessors:

That it may please our lord and king and his council and all the prelates and all other people by common assent, to the honour of holy church and for the betterment of the state of the kingdom, to plead by means of their letters and the aforesaid messengers for the canonization of the noble earl of Lancaster and Robert archbishop of Canterbury of holy memory.

Next, that it may please our lord the king that he may maintain the estate of holy church in all matters according to the great charter of liberties providing that the points which need to be made clear are made clear in this parliament. And that the record and proceedings of the false judgements made by the bad advice of Hugh the father and Hugh the son, Edmund earl of Arundel, Robert Baldock and others of their persuasion against the earl of Lancaster and all others of his cause, of which some are dead, and others exiled and disinherited, and others put to great expense to save their lives and their lands and others to remove fines from their lands, be repealed and quashed, and that heirs of those who are dead be given back their inheritance . . . and that the exiled, imprisoned, and disinherited be restored, reinstated in their lands and possessions. . . .

Next, that the people show our lord the king that Edward his father, as soon as he became king, by the evil counsel and co-operation of Hugh, father and son, Edmund earl of Arundel, Robert Baldock one time chancellor, and other evil counsellors, without cause and accusation, took into his own hands the temporalities of the bishops and all the goods and chattels found therein. And since the temporalities were in his possession for a long time and since he took all the profits during the same period, great damage, waste and destruction occurred to possessions, parks and woods. Because of these aforesaid matters the said people pray that due restitution may be made to the said bishops and to others of holy church in such circumstances.

Another thirty-two items follow. They all have the same purpose – to ensure that the young and newly-crowned Edward III would reverse many of his father's decisions, and would compensate the members of the faction which had been unsuccessful, and therefore had suffered, in his father's reign. The political ups and downs of the fourteenth and fifteenth centuries caused several succeeding parliaments to play a similar role. The parliament which met in January 1377, for example, repealed most of the achievements of the Good Parliament which had met the previous year, the parliament of 1397–8 reversed the decisions of the Merciless Parliament of 1388, and naturally, a century later, Yorkist parliaments undid much that had been done by the Lancastrians.

3. STATUES AND PICTURES

The Victorian schoolma'am taught history as a list of dates and a sequence of kings and queens. At best she regarded the subject as bald narrative interspersed with trite, inflexible judgements, and properly restricted to good and bad monarchs, to outstanding battles, and, here and there, to law-making and the suppression of revolts. She was not to blame for such cramped and limited thinking. Many of the historians of her day seemed to study in blinkers. Macaulay and Freeman saw little in history beyond past politics; Carlyle searched the centuries for a hero to exalt or a moral to expound; and the scientific historians towards the end of the reign set out to discover laws in the evolution of human affairs, or limited their study to establishing or confirming historical facts. Nowadays, thanks partly to the groundwork established by these same past historians, history is a far wider and fuller subject. Its aim is to re-create and interpret the past as truthfully as possible. This requires more than a string of facts. It calls for an understanding of how men reasoned, what scales of value they had, what standards of living they enjoyed or endured, how they dressed, what tools they used, and what foods they ate. 'The historian's duty', said Philip Guedalla, 'is not merely to catalogue dry bones in a museum, but to make them live.' To do this, the historian must see his characters as clearly as the novelist sees his. Yet, unlike the novelist, he cannot invent. He must re-create from established facts, not conjure up men and women from a fertile imagination.

In this part of his work the 'modern' historian has great advantages over his 'medieval' colleague, for he can usually find photographs or realistic portraits of the men and women he is writing about. Names such as Lloyd George, Alfred Tennyson, George III, Oliver Cromwell, and Mary Stuart immediately bring a facial image into the mind's eye. But what mental image is provoked by such names as Anselm, Matilda, Simon de Montfort, Langland, or Richard of York? The National Portrait Gallery displays a few pictures of medieval kings. One or two fifteenth-century portraits, like those of Edward IV and Richard III, were painted near enough the Renaissance possibly to be faithful portraits, and therefore useful stimuli to the historical imagination. Yet we do not know who painted any of them, and it is quite likely that at least one or two were painted from memory or imagination. Before the fifteenth century we are pushed back to tomb monuments – by the very nature of things sculptured post-humously – to stylized portraits on the great seals, or to the featureless faces which stare at one from a twelfth-century penny or a fourteenth-century groat. Medieval people other than kings have left us no real likenesses of themselves, although there are odd drawings of doubtful date, such as those of Chaucer and Humphrey, duke of Gloucester, in the National

Portrait Gallery. Warwick the Kingmaker, late though he lived in the fifteenth century and important though he was in his generation, is portrayed only in a formalized drawing in the Rows Roll. This displays his heraldic shield in detail, and gives a good picture of full plate armour, but it conveys no impression at all of the features or the stature of the man. In the same way, the medieval artist gives no topographical information about particular villages or towns. His pictures have no perspective, because he was primarily interested in pattern and ornament. He did not attempt naturalistic painting: that was one of the features of the many-sided Renaissance which brought medievalism to its end.

Yet, despite its obvious disadvantages, the work of medieval artists is not without value to the historian. The painter, sculptor, and embroiderer usually took their subjects from the Bible or from legend, but, fortunately for us, they did not attempt to clothe their characters in eastern clothing, or place them against a Palestinian background. It is true that Gothic art, which gradually replaced Romanesque during the second half of the thirteenth century, brought touches of natural behaviour and human emotions into pictures and sculpture, but Gothic artists still dressed their Herods in the clothing of medieval kings, their Roman soldiers in mail or plate armour, and their Virgins in the heavy kerchiefs fashionable in the fourteenth century. They drew their battle and hunting scenes from life around them, and seated their Old Testament characters at medieval banquets in Gothic halls. They filled in their backgrounds with drawings of contemporary buildings, and depicted the countryside of the Holy Land as if it were no different from that of Kent or Essex.

Churches have preserved medieval art. We can study the evolution of medieval architectural styles and techniques in most of our cathedrals, in monastic ruins, and in scores of medieval parish churches scattered throughout the land. Because the cathedrals and churches have been daily used by every generation since they were built, medieval work has often been elbowed aside, overlaid, or removed altogether. Yet tombs, brasses, figures, wood carvings, wall-paintings and windows can all be found in sufficient numbers to enlighten the social historian. Each one of these features of the medieval church has been the subject of technical studies, which have increased our knowledge of medieval skills and views on art, but we are concerned here only with the way these remains help us to envisage the people of the Middle Ages and the kind of life they led.

To begin in Salisbury Cathedral in front of the stone effigy of the thirteenth-century earl of Salisbury, and thence to move in turn to the brass of Sir John Daubernon in Stoke D'Abernon Church, Surrey, to the brass of Sir Hugh Hastings, in Elsing Church, Norfolk, to the tomb of the Black Prince in Canterbury Cathedral, and lastly to the bronze casting on the tomb of Sir Richard Beauchamp in its chantry chapel at Warwick is to see displayed the main stages in the development of armour from the thirteenth to the fifteenth century. William of Salisbury died in 1226. In accordance with convention his effigy shows him armed for war. Chain mail covered him from top to toe, but over his armour a sleeveless, knee-length surcoat, held in at the waist by a leather sword-belt, hung from his shoulders. Instead of a helmet he wore a dome-shaped mail coif, and he carried a long sword and a triangular shield almost three feet in height. Daubernon lived half a century later. He still wore chain mail, a coif, and a surcoat, but at his knees plate armour reinforced the mail. He carried the long sword, but his shield was much smaller than Salisbury's, and his right arm crooked a lance decorated with a pennon, the insignia of the knight banneret. Hastings died in the middle years of the fourteenth century on the eve of the Black Death. His brass shows that over his mail he carried plate not only at his knees but also on the outside of his arms and right round his trunk. On his head he wore a bascinet, a cloche-shaped helmet, which was fitted with a hinged visor which closed on to a heavy plate beaver. Instead of a surcoat, he wore a tight bodice, or jupon, with a short skirt, and carried a small triangular shield and a sword of lighter weight than Daubernon's. Sir Hugh's generation endured the worst armour of all, for the only way it knew of improving chain mail was to add extra weight to it. The French wars, however, stimulated more experiment, and the effigy of the Black Prince displays the success achieved. By the end of Edward III's reign, articulated plate had become the main protection of the man-at-arms. According to the evidence of his effigy the prince wore a conical helmet which had side pieces to cover his ears; to these side pieces was connected the mail aventail which rested on his shoulders and protected his throat and neck. He carried no shield, and his long thin sword hung in a baldric at his hip. A tight-fitting jupon decorated with his coat of arms covered his body armour, beneath which, it may be confidently assumed, he would wear a mail shirt. By the time William Austen, the London coppersmith, was casting Beauchamp's effigy in the middle of the fifteenth century, plate armour had developed even further. The mounted knight had discarded both jupon and shield as unnecessary; he gleamed in plate from head to foot. Shoulders, elbows, and hands carried extra armour, the helmet protected the whole of the face, and a plate gorget replaced the mail aventail round the throat. The armourer could do little more to safeguard the man-at-arms. He had made him wellnigh invulnerable – so long as he could stick on his horse.

Effigies and brasses are not confined to knights in armour. They also illustrate ladies' fashions in clothes, hair styles, and head-dresses. They depict the richness of ecclesiastical robes, and, in the wool churches of the Cotswolds and East Anglia and in some of the churches in London and the home counties, they parade the magnificence of the dresses of the late medieval merchants and their wives. Medieval fashions changed slowly compared with twentieth-century fashions, but each generation contributed some ideas of its own. A 1370 brass at Chrisall in Essex shows Joan de la Pole dressed in a simple, full-length gown with extremely long sleeves. Her hair, a mass of small ringlets, probably reinforced with false hair, was braided with linen. This modest way of covering the head contrasts sharply with the mitre head-dresses of the mid fifteenth century, and with the striking butterfly hats of Edward IV's reign, one of which is magnificently illustrated in the brass of the wife of Sir Ralph Sentleger at Ulcombe, Kent. Monuments depicting 'popish' clerics were favourite targets for the Puritan reformers of the sixteenth and seventeenth centuries, but fortunately the image breakers left us sufficient to illustrate changes and details of dress. Sculptured priests, abbots, and bishops vary from humble representations, such as that of the fourteenth-century Richard de Vernon in St Mary's Church, Stockport, to splendid statues, such as that of William of Wykeham at Winchester or that of Bishop Drokensford at Wells. Of almost equal value to the social historian are the figures of anonymous robed ecclesiastics, which appear in comparative plenty either on alabaster panels round tombs, chantry chapels, or reredoses, or set in wall niches both outside and inside churches.

Wall paintings are obviously more vulnerable than brasses and statues. They too outraged the Puritan conscience, but their particular enemies through the years have been damp and man's natural wish to re-decorate. Fortunately whitewash preserves as well as obscures, and during the last hundred years it has been possible for some of these pictures to be restored to view. During the first half of the fourteenth century extensive schemes of wall painting were carried out in many churches. Their single-minded purpose was instruction: as one contemporary put it, 'I say boldly that there are many thousands of people that could not imagine in their heart how Christ was done on the rood, but as they learn it by sight of images and painters.' In the chancel of Chalgrove church near Oxford we can still see how the lessons were planned: some twenty-eight separate pictures depicting scenes in the lives of Christ and the Virgin are arranged in three tiers. They are all lively drawings, and it is easy to imagine how the parish priest or the visiting friar could use them to kindle the interest and rouse the feelings of the congregation. A baby impaled on a long spear, and a mother thrust aside by a soldier who seizes her struggling child bring home the horror of the massacre of the innocents. The sight of Mary sorrowfully fondling Christ's lifeless arm and of a disciple taking the nails out of His feet demonstrates the pathos in the story of the descent from the cross, and the picture of the risen Christ leading the naked souls from the mouth of hell would leave the congregation in no doubt about the meaning of atonement.

To see such pictures is to understand how simply and entirely medieval people accepted Christian teaching, and how the gospel stories, elaborated by some legendary traditions, early became an indelible factor in every person's life. For us in the twentieth century, the pictures have the added advantage that they portray fourteenth-century people as well as first-century events. At Idsworth, Hampshire, for example restorers have revealed a St Peter wearing the conical tiara, alb, chasuble, and pallium of a medieval pope, a Herodias clothed like a fourteenth-century queen in a fur-lined mantle and a long veil covering her head and falling on her shoulders, and a Salome, in one picture sitting demurely at the high table with her princess's coronet and veil covering her braided hair, and in the next dancing an acrobatic sword-dance before a crowned and bearded Herod clad in a red robe and yellow mantle, and, in the aristocratic fashion of the fourteenth century, wearing his hair curled in long rolls over his ears. Alongside these pictures, which in strip-cartoon fashion tell the story of John the Baptist, the artist painted an English hunting scene with stylized oak trees, a pack of hounds, and huntsmen carrying bows and arrows and hunting horns. At Chalgrove, in the picture of apostles and women adoring the Virgin, one of the apostles is tonsured, and the six women look as if they came from well-to-do houses in the parish. One woman is shown wearing a wimple and veil, and two others have their hair in nets, linen bands round their heads, and other bands, barbettes, underneath their chins. At the presentation in the temple, the Virgin's lady-in-waiting is stylishly dressed with barbette and circular hat, and a fourteenth-century fop or jester, in parti-coloured tunic and long pointed shoes, runs before Christ on His way to Calvary. In just the same way, among the wall paintings that once decorated St Stephen's Chapel, Westminster, one of the kings in the scene of the adoration of the magi stepped right out of the court of Edward III. He wore an olive-green mantle which was lined with white, trimmed with grey fur, and sur-mounted with a broad ermine cape. His tunic was patterned in crimson and gilt, and the scarlet of his pantaloons matched the decoration on his black shoes. His three attendants were hardly less colourful. All wore fashionable and highly-decor-ated shoes. Two carried heavy swords, and the most elaborately dressed of them sported a crimson mantle lined with white. His right leg and foot were clothed in a black stocking and a white shoe, his left in a light-blue stocking and a black shoe. Behind the attendants came the groom with his crimson cap, and his green tunic boldly and vertically striped in yellow. Such natural paintings are more evocative of the fourteenth century than the stiff, stylized pictures of Edward III and his family, which the artist also included in his decorations of St Stephen's Chapel.

The materials used by the embroiderer and the glazier did not give either of them the wall painter's freedom of expres-sion, but the illuminators found just as much scope for realistic observation and personal comment. Several well-known psal-ters, mostly written in East Anglia, have come down to us, from the first half of the fourteenth century. They were prob-ably illuminated by lay illuminators, who decorated the capital letters and filled the borders of the pages with leaf patterns, birds, animals, grotesques, and everyday scenes from life in town and countryside. Among the hundreds of religious pictures illustrating *Queen Mary's Psalter* are several that are irrelevantly secular – a group of gossiping pilgrims, a butcher killing and curing a pig, and a musician playing for dancers. The *Ormesby* and the *Luttrell Psalters* have pictures of men ploughing, harrowing, bird-scaring, and reaping, stacking, and carting corn, and the psalter of Robert de Lisle shows a man, camouflaged with leaves, trying to catch birds with a limed twig. The religious purpose of the psalter did not deter the illuminator from indulging his taste for satire. It was fashionable to poke fun by portraying animals, particularly monkeys, taking over human activities. The *Gorleston Psalter*, for example, shows ten rabbits, two of them robed as priests, conducting a funeral, and the *Luttrell Psalter* has monkeys busy with harvesting. This was a form of humour which the carver often used for misericords. Chester Cathedral has a fourteenth-century carved seat showing a fox, dressed in a friar's habit, presenting a gift to a nun, and Blackburn has one representing a fox preaching to a congregation of hens and geese. The bite in this humour came from the animals mimicking the humans exactly, so that, if we can ignore the pointed noses, beaks, and tails, we can accept these paintings and carvings as pictures of medieval life.

One of the most eloquent illuminated books from the fourteenth century is *The Holkham Bible Picture Book*, which was probably painted in London during the reign of Edward II. It contains eighty pages of pictures explained by a few notes in French. It tells three stories: the events of *Genesis* from the Creation to the Flood; the redemption of mankind by Christ and the Virgin; and the end of the world, when Christ will return in majesty, the blessed be received in paradise, and the damned be thrown ignominiously into hell. The choice and interpretation of the themes and even the apocryphal stories have historical significance, but once again the chief value of the pictures to historians is found in the incidental details. They show us the people of the fourteenth century at their ordinary daily work. Folios 13 and 14 depict shepherds in the fields and a farmer sowing seed. The sheep are small and thin like the Gadarene swine ten folios away, and the shepherd's dog looks more like a whippet than a modern sheep-dog. The sower carries his seed in a wicker basket strapped high on his

chest, and the horse which pulls the harrow is harnessed by
attaching ropes to each side of its collar. Folio 16 illustrates a
bread oven which had to be heated by burning faggots inside
it until it was hot enough to bake the dough, and the versos of
folios 20, 21, and 25, which tell the stories of the marriage at
Cana, Salome dancing before Herod, and Martha and Mary
entertaining Christ, give us details of a medieval banquet. The
meat and fish are served in dishes, but the bread is set down
upon the cloth. There are knives on the table, but no one has
a fork or a plate. The masons who are building on folio 27
have their long coats tied above their knees. One is working
from a ladder, another from an unfinished part of the building,
and their labourers, by means of a two-wheel pulley, are
hoisting faced stones from the ground in a round wicker
basket. Four pages farther in the crucifixion scenes we can
study carpenters at work. One is drilling wood with a two-
handed auger, and alongside, the blacksmith's wife is hammer-
ing nails on a small anvil at a forge, which is blown by two
pairs of bellows harnessed together on a pole. According to
medieval tradition the smith who was required to make the
nails for Christ's crucifixion pleaded a bad hand as an excuse for
avoiding the distasteful job, and here the artist shows him
pushed aside by his less scrupulous wife. The last folio depicts
fighting again. On the upper part of the picture the knights
are fully engaged. They are all dressed in mail reinforced with
knee cap, greaves round their shins, and star-shaped pieces of
plate protecting their shoulders. Over their armour they are
wearing the long, loose surcoats fashionable in the first half
of the fourteenth century, and their heads are protected with
visored bascinets. The lower picture shows us the common
folk at war. None have body armour, though some have
helmets. They are variously equipped with battle-axes, swords,
and bows and arrows, and some of them carry small, round
shields. The upper picture we could have deduced from effigies
and brasses of the period, but the lower picture puts in visual
form facts which with some difficulty we could only have

picked up piece by piece from scattered account books and odd lines in the chronicles or poems of that period.

Bibliography of Fourteenth-Century Documents

Edited texts of the fourteenth-century poets are to be found in almost all public libraries. Modern translations of *The Canterbury Tales* by N. Coghill, *Piers the Ploughman* by J. F. Goodridge, and *Sir Gawain and the Green Knight* by B. Stone are available in The Penguin Classics, and K. Sisam, *Fourteenth Century Verse and Prose* (1921), B. Ford, *The Age of Chaucer* (1954), and R. T. Davies, *Medieval English Lyrics* (1963) are good anthologies.

John of Gaunt's Register, ed. S. Armitage-Smith, is published in Vols. 20 and 21 of Camden Third Series; *Fabric Rolls of York Minster*, ed. J. Raine, and *Halmote Court Rolls of Durham*, ed. W. H. Longstaffe and J. Booth, in Vols. 35 and 82 of the Surtees Society Publications; and *Literae Cantuarienses*, ed. J. B. Shephard in three volumes of the Rolls Series (1887–9). A. Hamilton Thompson edited *Visitations of Religious Houses of Lincoln Diocese*, 3 Vols. (1914–29), but these are fifteenth-century documents. The documents concerning the Forest of Wirral are to be found in full in Vol. 101, *Transactions of the Historic Society of Lancashire and Cheshire*. The standard collection of parliamentary rolls is *Rotuli Parliamentorum* (1272–1503), 6 Vols. (1767). A number of fourteenth-century rolls are printed in *Rotuli parliamentorum anglie hactenus inediti*, Vol. 51, Camden Third Series.

The following are well illustrated works on fourteenth-century art:
English Art, 1307–1461, Joan Evans (1949).
Painting in Britain: The Middle Ages, M. Rickert (1954).
Sculpture in Britain: The Middle Ages, L. Stone (1955).
Architecture in Britain: The Middle Ages, G. Webb (1956).
(The last three books are in the Pelican History of Art.)
English Wall Painting of the Fourteenth Century, E. W. Tristram (1955).
Gothic England, J. Harvey (1947).
The Holkham Bible Picture Book, ed. W. D. Hassall (1954).

THE FIFTEENTH CENTURY

I. LETTERS

Letters, as we have seen already, are one of the most common of historical sources. Every generation has written letters, but the historian finds that the extant letters of different ages were written for different purposes and, consequently, have different values and variable utility in his researches. The letters which Paul, Peter, and John wrote to the early Christian churches are expositions of faith and belief. The many letters which medieval popes wrote to kings and archbishops and which medieval archbishops and abbots wrote to ecclesiastical or secular dignitaries are almost always official and momentous. Their recipients filed them carefully away, and so preserved them for historians. The letters of Horace Walpole, Charles Lamb, and other distinguished men of letters still delight and amuse us, but they were not dashed off in haste to catch the post as most letters seem to be today. Indeed they were carefully composed, corrected, and caressed so that when they were published – for the writers hoped that that would be their ultimate end – they would enhance their author's literary reputation.

A comparatively large collection of letters, many written in English, have survived from fifteenth-century England. The crown still sent out its traditional Latin letters patent and letters close, but in diminishing numbers. Edward IV and Henry VII in particular preferred less stereotyped letters, usually written in English and issued under the signet, the seal of the secretary. Several hundreds of official and semi-official letters, which members of the royal family and officers of church and state signed or sealed in the fifteenth century, have long been available in such standard collections as Rymer's *Foedera* and the anthologies edited by Henry Ellis and

Champollion-Figeac. Many of them are formal diplomatic papers such as letters of credence or safe conduct. A fair number, such as reports from ambassadors or Edward IV's letter to the men of Bruges after his restoration to the throne, constitute supplementary sources for political historians, and a few, like the one quoted here, successfully bring contemporary feeling and atmosphere across the years. After their defeat at Towton on Palm Sunday 1461, the defeated Lancastrian leaders retreated northwards. From her Scottish refuge Queen Margaret sent Lords Hungerford and Whittingham to seek help from Charles VII of France, but when the ambassadors arrived at Eu they found that Charles had died and had been succeeded by his apparently-hostile but unpredictable son, Louis XI. Hungerford and Whittingham did not know how the new king would receive them, nor how best they could inform their queen of the changed situation. This was the fourth letter which they sent hopefully on its long journey to Scotland. It uses artifice, but it conveys to the reader a keen appreciation of the dilemma in which the two Englishmen found themselves.

To the Queen of England in Scotland

Madam, please it your good God, we have since our coming hither, written to your Highness thrice. The last we sent by Bruges, to be sent to you by the first vessel that went into Scotland; the other two letters we sent from Dieppe, the one by the carvel in which we came, and the other in another vessel. But, madam, all was one thing in substance, of putting you in knowledge of the King your uncle's death, whom God assoil, and how we stand at rest, and do yet; but on Tuesday next we trust and understand, we shall up to the King, your cousin german. His commissaries, at the first of our tarrying, took all our letters and writings, and bore them up to the King, leaving my Lord of Somerset in keeping at the castle of Arques, and my fellow Whittingham and me, for we had safe conduct, in the town of Dieppe, where we are yet. But on Tuesday next we understand, that it pleaseth the said King's Highness that we shall come to his presence, and [there] are charged to bring us up, Monsieur de Cressell, now bailiff of Caen, and Monsieur de la Mot.

Madam, fear you not, but be of good comfort, and beware that ye adventure not your person, nor my Lord the Prince, by the sea, till ye have other word from us, unless that your person cannot be sure there as ye are, and that extreme necessity drive you thence; and for God's sake the King's Highness be advised the same. For as we be informed, the Earl of March is into Wales by land and has sent his navy thither by sea; and, Madam, thinketh verily, we shall not sooner be delivered but that we will come straight to you, without death take us by the way, the which we trust he will not till we see the King and you peaceably again in your Realm; the which we beseech God soon to see, and to send you that your Highness desireth.

Written at Dieppe the XXXth day of August.
Your true Subjects and Liegemen.
Hungerford.
Whittingham.

Such official and semi-official correspondence helps to give reality to the intricate and confusing story of international diplomacy, but most historians value even more highly the four large, fifteenth-century collections of family letters – Cely, Stonor, Plumpton, and Paston – which, by good fortune, have escaped destruction. Without them we should know considerably less than we do about social conditions and trade during the later stages of the Hundred Years War and the period of strife which followed. All four of these families enjoyed the comforts and the prestige which wealth bestows. They belonged to the landed and commercial middle class, which during the fifteenth century was steadily increasing its wealth and influence. They were not aristocrats themselves, but occasionally they corresponded or dealt with members of the most distinguished families in England. That all of them should be frequently fighting legal battles is yet another pointer to the ease and frequency with which the middle class resorted to the law: that all of them, despite their different localities, should write so much about social disorder and the dangers of travel, is indicative of conditions in the age in which they lived, and of the middle-class desire to continue money making undisturbed by political squabbles and dynastic wars. The letters show us how some of the wealth was gathered together, and allow us to share the pains and pleasures associated with the gathering of it.

The members of the Cely family made their money in wool. They bought clipped wool and wool fells in the Cotswolds, had their purchases carried by packhorse to London, and sold them for spinning and weaving either in London or Calais. They had many Flemish customers, and consequently shared the general opinion of the City that the maintenance of healthy trading between England and the Burgundian states in the Netherlands should be the permanent aim of English foreign policy irrespective of whether Lancastrian or Yorkist was sitting on the throne. Like all their contemporaries the Celys invested their profits in land. They bought estates in Essex, took a gentlemanly interest in hawks and hounds, and kept the customary sharp look-out for profitable marriages. With such a background we find, as we expect, that the family papers tell us about commercial matters at the staple in Calais, about trading in Flanders, and about the difficulties of travel in the fifteenth century. They show how the crown took its share of the traders' profits in customs and subsidies, and how it occasionally relied on the merchants to advance the pay of the garrison troops. Some of the letter writers also make incidental comments upon rather less obvious matters such as fraud among the merchants, the comparative decline of the Cinque Ports, and the profits to be made in horse-dealing. But it is little use going to these papers for political opinions. The Celys were no partisans. Apparently they took no interest in the struggle between Lancastrians and Yorkists unless immediate events were threatening the safety or prosperity of their business.

The following is a typical Cely letter. When Richard Cely wrote it from London on 13 May 1482 he was merely sending his brother George in Calais the latest business and family news. But however routine and ordinary it was to them, it furnishes us with interesting sidelights upon the mechanics of the wool trade, matrimonial skirmishes, the drinking habits of gentlewomen, and Edward IV's attempts to prevent the drain of silver from England.

Right entirely well-beloved brother, I recommend me heartily unto you informing you at the making [writing] of this, our mother, brother, my godfather, and the household are in good health, thanked be the good Lord.

Sir, the same day that I departed into Cotswold I received a letter from you writ at Calais the 13 day of April wherein I find the inventory of such goods that were our father's and money on that side of the sea. Sir, I spake not with the bishop's officers since that I received your letter; when I spake last with them they said that all things [concerning their father's will] should abide your coming. I understand by your letter that you will make over above £500.

I have been in Cotswold these 3 weeks and packed with William Midwinter 22 sarplers [i.e. 22 tons of wool in sacks] and a poke [a half-filled sack] whereof be 4 middle. William Bretten says it is the fairest wool that he saw this year, and I packed 4 sarplers at Camden of the same bargain [contract] where are 2 good 2 middle. There will be in all with blots [blemishes] 27 or 28 sarplers whole. Sir, I cannot have William Midwinter's fells under £3 3s. 4d. the 100, and I shall go to that price. I pray you send me a letter shortly. Sir, I have bought in Cotswold upon the point of 7,000 reasonably good fells and I pay £3. I can get none under. . . .

The same day that I come to Northleach on a Sunday before mattins from Burford [?] William Midwinter welcomed me and in our communication he asked me if I were in any way of marriage. I told him nay, and he informed me that there was a young gentlewoman whose father's name is Lemryke and her mother is dead and she shall inherit from her mother £40 a year as they say in that country [district], and her father is the greatest ruler as richest man in that country . . . When I had packed at Camden and William Midwinter departed [to London] I came to Northleach again to make an end of packing, and on Sunday next after, the same man that William Midwinter brake [approached] first came [to] me and told me that he had broken to his master according as Midwinter desired him . . . and if I would tarry [till] May Day I should have a sight of the young gentlewoman and I said I would tarry with a good will . . . to mattins the same day come the young gentlewoman and her mother-in-law [step-mother?], and I and William Bretten were saying mattins when they come into church, and when mattins were done they went to a kinswoman of the young gentlewoman and I sent to them a pottle [half a gallon] of white romnay and they took it thankfully for they had come a mile afoot that morning and when mass was done I come and welcomed them and kissed them and they thanked me for the wine and prayed me to come to dinner with them, and I excused me and they made me promise to drink with them after dinner and I sent them to dinner a gallon [of] wine and they sent me a heron 'sew roste' [stewed and roasted?], and after dinner I come and drank with them and took William Bretten with me and we had right good communication [talk] and the person pleased me well as by the first communication she is young little and very wellfavoured and witty and the country speaks much good by her. Sir, all this matter abideth the coming of her father to London that we may understand what sum he will depart with [give as a marriage portion] and how he likes me. He will be here within 3 weeks. I pray send me a letter how you think by this matter ... Sir, they have begun to ship at London and all our wool and fells is yet in Cotswold save 4 sarplers; therefore we can do nothing at this time. Sir, I think money will be good at this mart for the King has sent to the mercers and let them know that he will have 3 'wissels' [exchanges for money], one at Bruges, another at Calais, the third at London, and as I am informed, what merchant of the staple that 'fellys' his 'whe'? [fills his way? i.e. finishes his selling?] he may buy what wares that he will again, and they that buy nowhere shall bring in their money into the King's 'wissel' at Bruges or Calais and be paid at London at a month to the day, and the money shall be stablished at 8s. The mercers be not content therewith. I pray you remember our boys. No more. Writ at London the 13 day of May per Richard Cely.

The heron which the two ladies sent to Richard for his dinner was a delicacy highly prized by medieval men and women, who, by modern standards, all seem to have been gargantuan flesh-eaters. A cookery book of the mid fifteenth century gives the following recipe for roasting heron.

Take a heron; let him blood as a crane [i.e. in the mouth], and serve [treat] him in all points as a crane, in scalding, drawing, and cutting the bone of the neck away. And let the skin be on, etc.; roast him and sauce him as the crane [i.e. with powder of ginger, vinegar, and mustard]; break away the bone from the knee to the foot, and let the skin be on.

I can find no recipe for 'heron sew roste', but very probably the preparation was similar to that given in the same book for stewed partridge, except that in the first part of the preparation the bird was roasted and not boiled.

Take a moderately strong broth of beef or of mutton when it is boiled enough, and strain it through a strainer, and put it in an earthenware pot. And take a good quantity of wine, as it were half a pint. And take partridge, cloves, maces [spices] and whole pepper, and cast into the pot, and let boil well together. And when the partridge been [in] enough, take the pot from the fire, and then take fair bread cut in thin browes [slices] and couch them in a fair charger, and lay the partridge on top. And take powder of ginger, salt, and hard yolks of eggs minced, and cast into the broth, and pour the broth upon the partridge into the charger, and serve it forth, but let it be coloured with saffron.

Several letters in the Cely collection, which H. E. Malden edited in 1900, illustrate the constant danger of piracy in the Channel. On 13 May 1480 William Cely wrote from Calais to George Cely in Bruges:

... on the 12 day of May there was 2 Frenchmen chased an English ship afore Calais, and Federston and John Dave and Thomas Owerton lay in Calais Roads but themselves were on land, and as soon as they saw them they got boats and went aboard and so did master marshal and Sir Thomas Everingham and Master Messefolde with divers soldiers of Calais and rescued the English ship and took the Frenchmen ... it is said here that after this day, the 12 day of May, there shall no man keep no lodging of guests, strangers, nor Englishmen without the gates of Calais ... and any man that hath housing without the gates is warned to remove his house as shortly as he can into the town. ...

The French were not the people always at fault. On 24 February 1484 William Cely reported from Calais that 'there be certain banished Englishmen that be on the sea hath taken 5 or 6 sail of Spaniards laden with wine coming in to Flanders'. These pirates were probably English refugees from the unsuccessful Buckingham revolt of the previous October. If they were, they were following the precedent set by the fugitive Warwick and Clarence, whose piratical activities in the mouth of the Seine in 1470 acutely embarrassed Louis XI. It suited the French king's scheming to support their cause, but he thought they would ruin his plans by provoking the dukes of Burgundy and Brittany to declare war before he was ready. In desperation he ordered two of his officers to get the English ships away from the Seine at all costs:

... see that all their ships sail away, for I shall not give them audience so long as they have their ships there: and if they wish to leave their ships for their men at Honfleur do not allow them to do it, for I will never be at ease until I know for certain that all their ships have gone. ...

Trade by land was just as precarious as trade by sea. The roads were never safe, but war increased their dangers especially when marauders snatched every advantage that it gave them. On 19 November 1487 William Cely described his recent adventures in Flanders, and passed on to Richard and George suggestions for avoiding future trouble:

... please it your masterships to understand that I am come to Calais in safety, thanked be almighty God, for I was never in so great jeopardy coming out of Flanders in my life for men were lying by the way waiting for English men, and also I and my company was arrested 2 days at Dunkirk, but for Sir James Tyrrell's sake [the English ambassador] we were let go, and so, sir, the world goeth marvellously in Flanders now, for it is open war between Ghent and the King of the Romans [Maximilian, afterwards Emperor Maximilian I] ... but Sir John de Lopis showed me at my departing that I should write unto your masterships to understand whether there shall be any jeopardy to bring wares out of the east parts into England now from henceforth or not as he supposeth that that act of the contrary shall be put in suspense for divers causes. Wherefore, sir, he adviseth you to bestow your money in gross wares now betimes at this Borre mart in such wares as your masterships thinketh will be best at London whether it be in madder, wax, or fustians, but I trow madder the best, and, so be that you will, Gomers de Sore shall buy it for your masterships and ship it in Spanish ships in his own name ...

The Stonors' family home was on the Oxfordshire–Buckinghamshire boundary, and during the fifteenth century they acquired estates in Kent, Devon, and Cornwall. In 1475 William Stonor, landed gentleman and sheep grazier, married Elizabeth Ryche, daughter of a London alderman and widow of a wealthy London mercer. Eagerly William accepted a business partnership with the experienced City merchant, Thomas Betson, but at the same time tried to maintain his family's traditional interests in Oxfordshire. In 1478 he represented that county in the Commons, and his growing wealth and influence brought him a knighthood in the same year. Within five years of their marriage, Elizabeth's death allowed Sir William to seek another wife. He chose Agnes Wydeslade, an heiress to estates in Devon, and for the next two years his attention was distracted from the London wool mart to legal battles and estate management in the south-west. So far Sir William had not become entangled in politics, but in 1481, when Agnes died and he made his socially most brilliant marriage with Anne Neville, niece of the Kingmaker, he could avoid taking sides no longer. The years immediately ahead were the most dangerous in the century for the politically-committed nobility. Stonor, probably guided by his close associate, Thomas Grey, marquis of Dorset, supported Richard of Gloucester when he seized the throne, but four months later made the mistake of joining the Buckingham revolt against him. Richard III seized the Stonor estates for the crown, and Sir William did not recover control of them until after the accession of Henry VII.

From the archives of such a family we might confidently have anticipated political letters more dramatic and well-informed than those to be found among the Stonor papers. Yet, to make amends, the mixed interests and varied acquaintances of the different members of the Stonor family have given us a collection of documents which touch on almost every aspect of well-to-do life in the fifteenth century. There are the expected letters which discuss legal actions, marriage settlements, and the sale of wool, but there are others which let us see the comparative dearness and the range of quality of shoes and clothes, and appreciate the expenses involved in feeding the Stonor household, buying wine, and lighting the chapel.

Mr William Stonor, knight. Inprimis [first] to my master himself 15 [word missing] price the pair 7d., summa [total], 8s. 9d. Item, to the same a pair of long boots to the knee, price 16d. Item, to the same a pair of boots repairing, 12d. Item, to my lady 2 pair shoes, and 2 pair of clogs, price of all, 20d. Item, to my lady's gentlewoman a pair of shoes, 4d. Item, to my lady's children, 18 pair, price of all the pairs, 3s. Item, to master Fenn's son 4 pair, price, 12d. ... Item, to Mr Gatton [a ward of Sir William] 18 pair, price, 3s. 9d. Item, to your child of your chamber 8 pair, 2s. 8d. Item, to the same a pair of boots, price, 20d. Item, to the same a pair of boots, price 8d. Item, to Blake-hall, your child, 19 pair, price the pair, 5d., summa of all, 7s. 11d. Item, to Chowne of the stable 25 pair, price the pair 4d., summa of all, 8s. 4d. Item, to William Hypworth a pair of boots by your com-mandment, price, 2s. 8d. Item, to Chowne a pair of boots, price, 16d. Item, to the child of the buttery 8 pair, price the pair, 4d. ...

Item, 5 yards of tawny ... for you [Mary Barantyne], and for my master's at 6s. —— 30s.
Item, 3 yards of Russet for my master's, at 6s. —— 18s.
Item, a yard and quarter peau de lion [a trimming] for you at 3s. 3d. —— 4s.
Item, 2 yards and quarter of brown medley for your household ... at 3s. —— 6s. 9d.
Item, 2 yards and quarter of puce delivered to Sir William Staveley at 5s. 4d. —— 12s.
Item, a yard of cham medley [camlet = a wool and silk mixture] for a child of yours at —— 3s.
... Item, 3 yards and quarter of Russet for your Mastership [Sir Wm. Stonor] and for your son ... —— 24s. 4½d.
Item, 3 yards of purple-red that William Harbar had ... at 6s. 8d. —— 20s.

The expenses for Christmas [1478]. First about the Thursday afore Christmas 18 geese, 6s. 9d. Item, the same day a dozen capons, 4s. 3d. Item, the same day 6 dozen larks, 12d. Item, 2 dozen setters [large birds], and great birds 12d. Item, 6 plovers, 6d. Item, 6 woodcocks 15d. Item, paid to Coventry on the morrow for 4 geese and 2 capons, 2s. Item, paid the same day to John Young's wife and to Blake of Watlington for eggs, 2s. 4d. Item, paid the Wednesday following for 2 dozen chickens, 2s. Item, for 4 capons, 16d. Item, paid the Thursday following for half a pig, 22d. Item, on the 12th day for pork, 12d. . . . Item, the Friday after the 12th day for 200 oyster and a gurnard, 2s.

[London, May 1482] . . . Sir, as for wine I have sent you by John Somer [a bargee], to be delivered to John Baker at Henley, 2 hogsheads of claret wine, a hogshead of red wine, a hogshead of white wine. And as for spices I spake to Master Rush; he looks for a galley coming now in, as he says, and then he will buy by the gross, and then you shall have with him as much as you will: but he will lay down no money for none. And as for candle, we can have none such as you sent for, as Tailbois can tell your mastership. And as for fish, I can none buy without money. And rysshes [? risschewes = balls or cakes made of fish or fruit] and soap I have sent you by John Somers's barge, the which will be at Henley upon Sunday or Monday at the furthest. . . .

Your own servant,

H. Unton.

To my worshipful Master, Sir William Stonor, knight for the body.

[London, 31 July 1478. A postscript.] First delivered unto my master Stonor: 1 hogshead white wine and 1 hogshead red wine the 11th day of December 1476 by Thomas Meryke my servant, and the same wine was delivered unto Goddard Oxbridge, your servant, price: £3 6s. 8d.

Item, sold by my wife unto my lady Stonor 1 pipe of red wine: for the which my lady must make the price as it pleaseth her for I gave my wife no other price but after 8 marks the ton. [£2 6s. 8d. was apparently the price charged for this pipe of wine.]

Item, I delivered unto my master himself, the which went to Stonor, 1 hogshead red wine, by the same token my master marked another hogshead wine into Friday Street. Price of both: £3 6s. 8d.

Item, for a butt of Romney to Stonor now of late, price £3 6s. 8d.

Item, paid for the costs [carriage] of the 2 hogshead wine that my brother, Thomas Betson, sent to Stonor, summa 16d.

These ensuing be the parcels [items] which my lady Stonor oweth unto Margaret Whitby of London, widow, that is to say:

First, delivered to her use the 8th day of February in the 16th year of the reign of King Edward IV [1477], 2 torches of wax weighing 2 lb. quarter and half [a quarter: i.e. $2\frac{3}{8}$lb.], price the lb. 8d. Summa 19d. Item, the 15th day of March for a roll of a quarter [lb.], 2d. Item, for a taper against Easter in the 17th year, weighing 5lb., for the making 5d., and 3 quarters and half waste 7d. Summa, 13d. Item, against Midsummer in the same year 7 tapers with the flourishing [decoration], weighing 14lb. 3 quarters and half, the making and waste, 3s. 3d. Item, for a garland of wax 1d. Item, the 29th day of August for a measure of wax, 1d. Item, for 3 branches of wax for the mind [remembrance] of Master Fenn, and 4 half lb. tapers with the flourishing, weighing together 20lb. and a quarter, the making, 3s. 4d. Item, wasted of the same branches 7lb. and a quarter, price 2s. $1\frac{1}{2}$d. Item, the 18th day of September in small candle, $\frac{1}{2}$d. Item, upon All Hallows Eve [31 October] for a taper of a lb. before St Anne, price, 6d. Item, against the feast of Candlemas [2 February] a taper of a quarter, and 2 tapers, every taper 1d., and a $\frac{1}{2}$d. candle price, 4d. Item, at the same feast for a roll, white and green, weighing a lb., price 18d. ...

Out of the dutiful letter of a confidential servant or the blandishments of a tradesman one can conjure a colourful mental picture. In the middle of a letter which he wrote from London to Sir William in July 1478, Thomas Hensham informed him,

I send downe by John Tailbois, your servant: Item, your demi gown of camlet; item your demi gown of black puce lined with green velvet, trussed in a sheet ...

And in 1479 Thomas Bradbury, a London mercer, sent Dame Elizabeth rolls of cloth to the value of £11 10s. 0d. They included 38 yards of green sarcenet at 5s. a yard, and Bradbury tried to sugar the pill of this unexpected high price by writing,

Madame, the sarcenet is very fine. I think most profitable and most worshipful for you, and shall last you your life and your child's after you, whereas harlatry [indifferent material] of 40d. or 44d. a yard would not endure two seasons with you. Therefore for a little more cost, methinketh most wisdom to take of the best. In certain I have bought the most part of the sarcenet, for I had not enough to perform it. I win never a penny in that ...

Not unnaturally three or four of the Stonor papers deal with funerals. The details of the funeral of Thomas Stonor, which cost the formidable sum of £74 2s. 5d., remind us that the nineteenth-century practice of 'dying richly' had a long parentage.

The Plumpton family letters take us north into the Knaresborough district of Yorkshire. They introduce us to a different circle of relatives and friends – men and women who looked upon the families of Percy, Darcy, Clifford, and Constable as their natural leaders, and upon Fountains Abbey and Bolton and Nostell and Newburgh Priories as the religious houses of influence and wealth. The long journey from London to Yorkshire tended to deflate the importance of political news from the court. Occasionally a Lancastrian, Yorkist, or Tudor king summoned the Plumptons to do this or attend there, and the threat of a Scottish invasion or the actuality of such a revolt as that attempted at Thirsk in 1489 periodically brought the family and neighbourhood face to face with the major political issues of the day. For the most part, however, the Plumpton letters are concerned with local events, and with the normal business of making life as comfortable and diverting as possible. As in the other family collections, there are Plumpton letters which quote prices for buying stock, selling surplus farming produce, or making clothes, and others which record family births, marriages, and deaths. One letter describes the difficulty of farming in a wet season:

... I have no oxen to get your corn with, nor none I cannot get carried, for every man is so busy with their own: for weather is so latesome in this country, that men can neither well get corn nor hay ... [Bristow's] cornland is overfloating with water ...

Another letter remarks on the severity of the winter of 1489-90:

... have me excused in that I send no wild fowl to you afore this time, for in all Lancashire could none be had for none money. The snow and frost was so great, none was in the country, but fled away to sea.

Several letters make comments upon sport, from the crown granting privileges of limited hunting in the forest, to Ralph Ryther requesting that his cousin, Sir Robert Plumpton, should give him '2 couple of conies to stocking of a little ground that I make at Ryther'. And inevitably there are reminders of the black aspects of medieval life, such as the helplessness of man before the ever-threatening evil of the plague and the increasing social scourge of vagabondage.

To my right worshipful master, Sir Robert Plumpton, knight.

After due recommendations to your good mastership and heartily desire of your welfare, for which of duty I am ever bound to pray for, and since I heard say that a servant of yours was deceased of the sickness, which hath been to your disease, I am right sorry therefor. Wherefore I would advise your mastership, my lady, and all your household, from henceforth to make promise and keep it, to fast the eve of St Oswald, king and martyr, yearly; and that promise truly intended to be performed, I trust verily ye shall be no more vexed with that sickness. And thus the Most Mighty preserve you and yours, this feast of Exaltation of the holy ghost [? of the Cross, i.e. 14 September 1499].

Your servant Robert Leventhorpe

To our master and lord, Sir William Plumpton, knight.

Beseecheth your good mastership all your tenants and servants of your lordship of Idle, William Rycroft elder, William Rycroft younger, John Rycroft, Henry Bycroft, and John Chaloner excepted. And that it please your good mastership to hear and consider the great rumour, slander, and full noise of your tenants of your said lordship . . . and for as much as the said William Rycroft elder, William Rycroft younger, John Rycroft, Henry Bycroft, and John Chaloner are dwelling within your said lordship, they all not having any cow or calves, or any other goods whereby they might live, nor any other occupation, and fair they are beseen and well they fare, and at all sports and games they are in our country for the most part, and silver to spend and to gaming which they have more ready than any other within your said lordship; and to the welfare of our sovereign lord the King and you, nothing they will pay without your said tenants [af] fray with them . . . And as for geese, grise [young pigs], hens, and capons, your said tenants may none keep, but they are bribed and stolen away by night to great hurt to your tenants. And for as much as these persons afore rehearsed are not labouring in due time, as all other of your tenants are, but as vagabonds live, your said tenants suppose more strangely by them. Wherefore at reverence of God and in way of charity, your said tenants beseecheth you to call all them before you, and to set such remedy in these premises as may be to your worship, and great profit to your tenants, and in showing of much unthriftiness, which without you is likely to grow hereafter, and your said tenants shall pray Almighty God for your welfare and estate.

Of the four collections of fifteenth-century family letters, the best known, and deservedly so, are the Paston letters from East Anglia. We owe their preservation chiefly to careful John Paston, who kept the letters of his father and mother, William and Agnes, and, when he died in 1466, passed them, together with his own and his wife's, Margaret's, letters, to his children. Some of the letters were received by the Pastons; some were copies of letters they had sent to relatives, friends, or business correspondents. Historians and historical novelists have been busy mining this correspondence ever since 1787 when John Fenn edited and published the first selection, but in the thousand or so letters there is still plenty of ore left for present-day miners, whether they are anxious to find political, economic, or social treasure. The Paston Letters are intimate and numerous enough to enable us to understand the mind and appreciate the outlook of the different members of the family, from the courageous, prudent, and practical Margaret to John II, her pleasure-loving, literary, impecunious son. They contain graphic descriptions of the local chaos which reflected the strife between the Lancastrian and Yorkist factions. In East Anglia, as elsewhere in England, local landed families took advantage of the distracted attention of the central government to settle old scores with their neighbours, or to attempt to seize coveted properties. It behoved families to look after themselves, for they had little hope of adequate redress in the courts if their estates and houses were taken or destroyed. It was far more useful to have a powerful patron or influential friend than a just cause.

Right worshipful husband, I recommend me to you, and pray you to get some crossbows, and windses to bend them with, and quarell [bolts to shoot]: for your house here be so low that there may no man shoot out with no long bow, though we had never so much need. I suppose ye could have such things of Sir John Fastolf if ye would send to him. And also I would ye could get 2 or 3 short pole-axes to keep doors with, and also many [padded, leather] jackets if ye may.

Partrich [a servant of Lord Moleyns] and his fellowship are sore afeared that ye would enter back upon them, and they have made great ordnance within the house, as it is told me. They have made bars to bar the doors crosswise, and they have made wyketes [loop-holes] on every quarter of the house to shoot out at, both with bows and with hand guns; and those holes that be made for hand guns, they be scarce knee high from the floor; and of such holes be made five. There can no man shoot out at them with no hand bows . . .

[Written by Margaret Paston *c.* 1448.]

Domestic matters ranging from the management of the Paston estates to household purchases; local gossip; news of such East Anglian magnates as the dukes of Suffolk and Norfolk, Sir John Howard, and Sir William Brandon; some comment upon national affairs, and even the occasional glimpse of historic events such as Margaret of York's marriage to Charles of Burgundy, or the tense situation at Calais in 1475 when Burgundy, pig-headedly insisted upon maintaining the siege of Neuss instead of keeping his Calais appointment with Edward IV – ' . . . the French king, men say, is come right to the water off Somme with 4,000 spears . . .' – all these diverse things are to be found in the Paston Letters. A few casual comments upon teaching and the best way of bringing up children illustrate the hard lot of boys and girls in the Middle Ages. Just as Langland's character Reason thought parents should 'spoil their children only with rods', so Margaret Paston instructed her son's new schoolmaster to 'truly belash him till he will amend' as had done a former Cambridge master, 'the best that ever he had'. The twenty-year-old Elizabeth suffered frequent hidings because she did not wish to marry the elderly Stephen Scrope, her mother's choice for her. Elizabeth Clere described the girl's predicament:

... for she was never in so great sorrow as she is nowadays; for she may not speak with no man, whosoever come, nor not may see nor speak with my man, nor with servants of her mothers, but that she beareth her a hand otherwise than she meaneth [accuses her of things she never meant to do]. And she hath since Easter the most part been beaten once in the week or twice, and sometimes twice in one day, and her head broken in two or three places. . . .

Wherefore, cousin [John Paston 1], think on this matter, for sorrow oftentime causeth women to beset [bestow] them [in marriage] otherwise than they should do; and if she were in that case I know well ye would be sorry. Cousin, I pray you burn this letter . . . for if my cousin, your mother, knew that I had sent you this letter she should never love me. . . .

Two letters from young William Paston at Eton and two from undergraduate Walter at Oxford give us brief glimpses of institutional education at the end of the fifteenth century. Despite the camouflage of outworn letter-writing conventions, all parents and elder brothers will recognize the perennial schoolboy in the following letter, which was probably written in 1478.

To his worshipful brother John Paston be this delivered in haste.

Right reverent and worshipful brother, I recommend me unto you, desiring to hear of your welfare and prosperity, letting you know that I have received of Alwedyr [a servant?] a letter, and a noble in gold therein. Furthermore, my tutor, Master Thomas, heartily recommended him to you, and he prayeth you to send him some money for my commons; for he saith ye be 20s. in his debt, for a month was to pay for when he had money last.

Also I beseech you to send me a hose cloth one for the holidays of some colour, and another for the working days – how coarse so ever it be it maketh no matter; and a stomacher, and 2 shirts, and a pair of slippers. And if it like you that I may come with Alwedyr by water and sport me with you at London a day or 2 this term time, then ye may let all this be till the time that I come. And then I will tell you when I shall be ready to come from Eton, by the grace of God, whom have you in his keeping.

Written the Saturday next after All Hallows Day, with the hand of your brother,

William Paston.

2. FOREIGN SOURCES

The word *foreign* in this sub-title begs a question. Today, *foreign* implies a world of passports, well-defined nation states, and sensitive feelings of exclusiveness. Medieval Europe was slow to acquire this habit of mind. It saw the need for letters of credence and safe conduct, and placed a high value on personal loyalty to one's lord, but such feelings of exclusiveness as its inhabitants possessed concerned social class and occupation rather than place of birth. That William of Jumièges and William of Poitiers are not regarded as foreign chroniclers is only partly explained by the fact that they were Norman subjects of William the Conqueror. No contemporary considered that Anselm was a foreign archbishop of Canterbury, although he had been born in Piedmont and had spent most of his life in the Norman monastery of Bec, nor, in its struggle against Henry III, did the baronage of thirteenth-century England see anything sinister or improper in accepting the leadership of Simon de Montfort, a nobleman born in France of French parents. But in fourteenth-century opinion and outlook it is possible to detect a change. Both the growing commercial rivalry overseas between London merchants and their competitors and the enthusiasm which victory roused among indentured troops in France helped to fan latent patriotism into a flickering flame. The Hundred Years War may have begun as a struggle for the French throne between Edward III, backed by his tenants, and Philip of Valois, backed by his, but Henry V was nationalist enough to suppress the alien priories and prevent their rents from crossing the Channel, and Joan of Arc's cry to drive back the Goddams into their own country did not fall on deaf ears. By the mid fifteenth century the long struggle had developed far more into a war between England and France than it had remained a personal quarrel between the kings of the two countries. Certainly in the sixties and seventies, when Louis XI on the one side and the dukes of Burgundy and Brittany on the other were trying to turn the civil war between Yorkists and Lancastrians to their own use, national feeling in north-west Europe ran stronger than it had ever done before. From this point, natural development easily carried it to the strident jingoism of Elizabethan England.

In the work of fourteenth- and fifteenth-century writers who lived outside England, therefore, English historians hope to find a new significance. They look for two things in particular – eyewitness, or at least fairly authentic, descriptions of events on the Continent in which the subjects of the king of England are involved, and partisan comment which, regarding Englishmen as rivals in business or enemies in war, is distinct from that which they would find in English sources. Broadly speaking, both fourteenth- and fifteenth-century foreign chroniclers and letter-writers furnish the first type of information, but only some of the fifteenth-century writers – and these usually from the second half of the century – have a distinctly *foreign* point of view.

Jean Froissart is the outstanding fourteenth-century foreign chronicler for English historians. He lived first in the county of Hainaut and then, after serving Philippa, Edward III's queen, as secretary for a time, at the French court, but he did not hesitate to describe events which took place in far-away places. He called his writings *The Chronicles of England, France, Spain, Portugal, Scotland, Brittany, Flanders, and other places adjoining*, and considering the difficulties of collecting news in the fourteenth century and the uncritical, credulous nature of most of his informants, he went some way to justify his pretentious title. For happenings in France or in the Netherlands historians must give Froissart's descriptions and comments considerable attention, but they find the chief value of the *Chronicle* in its three-dimensional picture of fourteenth-century life and manners, and in its natural, incidental explanation of fourteenth-century thinking. Such qualities hardly depend upon place of birth or upon residence at a particular court. Had Froissart been born in East Anglia or Franche Comté and served Edward III or Philip the Bold of Burgundy, he could have written a chronicle with similar characteristics. He was brought up in a burgess household, but the point of view he expresses is that of the fourteenth-century nobility. It is certainly not a Flemish or a French, as opposed to an English, point of view. His is the persuasive and romantic voice of the self-conscious age of chivalry. Little wonder that Henry VIII, who loved nothing better than jousting and pageantry, required Lord Berners to translate the *Chronicle* into English. It is from this sixteenth-century translation, edited by G. C. Macaulay, that the following extracts are taken.

Froissart's opening strikes the note for the whole of the *Chronicle*:

To the intent that the honourable and noble adventures of feats of arms, done and achieved by the wars of France and England, should notably be enregistered and put in perpetual memory, whereby the prewe [brave] and hardy may have ensample to encourage them in their well-doing, I, sir John Froissart, will treat and record an history of great louage [commendation] and praise. But, or [ere] I begin, I require the Saviour of all the world, who of nothing created all things, that he will give me such grace and understanding, that I may continue and persevere in such wise, that whoso this process readeth or heareth may take pastance [pastime], pleasure and ensample . . . Truth it is that I, who have enterprised to set in order this book, have for pleasure, which have ever inclined me thereto, frequented the company of divers noble and great lords, as well in France as England, Scotland and other countries, and had acquaintance with them. So I have always to my power justly inquired and demanded of the wars and adventures that have fallen, and especially sith the great battle of

Poitiers, whereat the noble king John of France was taken prisoner, as before that time I was but of a young age [he was 18 in 1356, the date of the battle] or understanding . . . All noble hearts to encourage and to shew them ensample and matter of honour, I, sir John Froissart, begin to speak after the true report and relation of my master John le Bel, sometime canon of Saint-Lambert's of Liège, affirming thus, how that many noble persons have oft-times spoke of the wars of France and of England, and peradventure knew not justly the truth thereof, nor the true occasions of the first movings of such wars, nor how the war at length continued: but now I trust ye shall hear reported the true foundation of the cause, and to the intent that I will not forget, minish [diminish] or abridge the history in anything for default of language, but rather I will multiply and increase it as near as I can, following the truth from point to point, in speaking and shewing all the adventures sith the nativity of the noble king Edward the III, who reigned king of England and achieved many perilous adventures, and divers great battles addressed, and other feats of arms of great prowess sith the year of our Lord God MCCCXXVI, that this noble king was crowned in England: for generally such as were with him in his battles and happy fortunate adventures, or with his people in his absence, ought right well to be taken and reputed for valiant and worthy of renown. . . . Also in France in that time there were found many good knights, strong and well expert in feats of arms; for the realm of France was not so discomfited but that always there were people sufficient to fight withal, and the king Philip of Valois was a right hardy and a valiant knight, and also king John his son, Charles [should be John] the king of Bohemia, the earl of Alençon, the earl of Foix, sir Saintre, sir Arnold d'Audrehem, sir Bouciquaut, sir Guichard d'Angle, the lords of Beaujeu, the father and the son, and divers other, the which I cannot their names, of whom hereafter right well shall be made mention in time and place convenient to say the truth and to maintain the same. All such as in cruel battles have been seen abiding to the discomfiture, sufficiently doing their devoir, may well be reputed for valiant and hardy, whatsoever was their adventure.

Here, boldly stated and without a trace of apology, is the medieval doctrine that gentle knights were born to fight, and that war ennobled all who engaged in it without fear and cowardice.

There is no partisanship: praise is given to all who fought valiantly, and prayers are offered impartially for those who fell in battle. Less than a century later Thomas Basin, another French chronicler, wrote, 'In the opinion of many, the English are not human beings and men, but senseless and ferocious beasts, which go about devouring people.' This has the authentic ring of war propaganda of modern times, and is ages away from Froissart in spirit if not in time. In the following passage Froissart describes how the Black Prince sacked Limoges in September 1370. The first part is valuable comment upon the way sieges could be made aggressive in these pre-gunpowder days, and the second shows how little Froissart and his fellows were concerned that townspeople should be murdered and property destroyed in order that honour could be maintained and that knights could fight with valour.

About the space of a month or more was the prince of Wales before the city of Limoges, and there was neither assault nor scrimmish, but daily they mined. And they within knew well how they were mined, and made a countermine there against to have destroyed the English miners; but they failed of their mine. And when the prince's miners saw how the countermine against them failed, they said to the prince: 'Sir, whensoever it shall please you we shall cause a part of the wall to fall into the dikes, whereby ye shall enter into the city at your ease without any danger.' Which words pleased greatly the prince, and said: 'I will that tomorrow betimes ye shew forth and execute your work.' Then the miners set fire into their mine, and so the next morning, as the prince had ordained, there fell down a great part of the wall and filled the dikes, whereof the Englishmen were glad and were ready armed in the field to enter into the town. The foot-men might well enter at their ease, and so they did and ran to the gate and beat down the fortifying and barriers, for there was no defence against them: it was done so suddenly that they of the town were not ware thereof.

Then the prince, the duke of Lancaster, the earl of Cambridge, the earl of Pembroke, sir Guichard d'Angle and all the other with their companies entered into the city, and all other foot-men, ready apparelled to do evil, and to pill and rob the city, and to slay men, women and children, for so it was commanded them to do. It was great pity to see the men, women and children that kneeled down on their knees before the prince for mercy; but he was so inflamed with ire, that he took no heed to them, so that none was heard, but all put to death, as they were met withal, and such as were nothing culpable. There was no pity taken of the poor people, who wrought never no manner of treason, yet they bought it dearer than the great personages, such as had done the evil and trespass. There was not so hard a heart within the city of Limoges, an if he had any remembrance of God, but that wept piteously for the great mischief that they saw before their eyen: for more than three thousand men, women and children were slain and beheaded that day. God have mercy on their souls, for I trow they were martyrs. . . .

Now let us speak of the knights that were within the city, as sir John of Villemur, sir Hugh de la Roche, Roger Beaufort, son to the earl of Beaufort, captains of the city. When they saw the tribulation and pestilence that ran over them and their company, they said one to another: 'We are all dead, without we defend ourselves: therefore let us sell our lives dearly, as good knights ought to do.' Then sir John of Villemur said to Roger Beaufort: 'Roger, it behoveth that ye be made a knight.' Then Roger answered and said: 'Sir, I am not as yet worthy to be a knight: I thank you, sir, of your good-will.' So there was no more said: they had not the leisure to speak long together. Howbeit, they assembled them together in a place against an old wall and there displayed their banners. So they were to the number of eighty persons. Thither came the duke of Lancaster, the earl of Cambridge and their companies and so lighted afoot, so that the Frenchmen could not long endure against the Englishmen, for anon they were slain and taken. Howbeit, the duke of Lancaster himself fought long hand to hand against sir John Villemur, who was a strong knight and a hardy, and the earl of Cambridge fought against sir Hugh de la Roche, and the earl of Pembroke against Roger Beaufort, who was as then but a squire. These three Frenchmen did many feats of arms: their men were occupied otherwise. The prince in his chariot came by them and beheld them gladly and appeased himself in beholding of them. So long they fought together that the three Frenchmen, by one accord rendering their swords, said: 'Sirs, we be yours, ye have conquered us: do with us according to right of arms.' 'Sir,' quoth the duke of Lancaster, 'we look for nothing else: therefore we receive you as our prisoners.' And thus the foresaid three Frenchmen were taken, as it was informed me.

Thus the city of Limoges was pilled, robbed and clean brent and brought to destruction. Then the Englishmen departed with their conquest and prisoners and drew to Cognac, where my lady the princess was. Then the prince gave leave to all his men of war to depart and did no more that season; for he felt himself not well at ease, for always his sickness increased, whereof his brethren and people were sore dismayed.

There is pity for the massacred townsfolk, but no horror at the outrage and no protest against the perpetrators. There is not even a suggestion that the noble and gentle knight, Edward, had disgraced his calling. He had been in a bad temper: that was sufficient explanation. It mattered far more that the three leading defenders had fought bravely before acknowledging defeat. Their conduct redeemed the occasion, and won the admiration of all men.

Froissart died in 1410, a little before Henry V renewed the war with France. If we move forward exactly half a century, through the victorious days of Agincourt and the Treaty of Troyes and the dark days of Joan of Arc and the reconquest of Normandy, we find ourselves in a very different political world. In 1460 the English nobility was divided into two warring groups, one supporting the Lancastrian king, Henry VI, and the other supporting Richard of York. During the last hours of that year Richard was killed in battle at Wakefield, but three months later in London his son was crowned Edward IV. From then until the death of Richard III at Bosworth in 1485, the see-saw struggle between the two parties dominated political events in England. Across the Channel a parallel but more purposive struggle was developing. Louis XI, who succeeded his father, Charles VII, in 1461, was determined to centralize the government of France so that his control would be absolute from the Channel to the Mediterranean and from the Atlantic to the eastern frontier. The biggest obstacle in his way was the entrenched resistance of the great feudatories, and, therefore, the political story of Louis's reign concerns failures and successes in his constant endeavour to destroy the independence of the French nobles, particularly Burgundy and Brittany. Both sides looked for allies in England. The very possibility of an understanding between Burgundy and the Yorkists could prompt Louis to offer help to the Lancastrians, and any sign that Burgundy and Brittany were becoming more friendly towards exiled Lancastrians impelled Edward and Louis to begin seeking a rapprochement. The historian may well find that the explanation of a sudden change in Yorkist diplomacy has to be sought in current negotiations between Louis XI and Charles the Bold, or in the latest happenings in Brittany or Navarre.

Fortunately, in studying this complicated political 'foursome', historians have the help of several contemporary commentators. As we shall see below, fifteenth-century England did not lack chroniclers, but in Burgundy and France there were as many, if not more, chroniclers and letter writers, whose work throws light upon English affairs. A number of these writings are anonymous, but the majority of the evidence is made more valuable because sufficient is known of each author to enable historians to gauge the extent of his partiality. They must make considerable allowances, for example, for the hatred Thomas Basin, bishop of Lisieux, had for Louis XI and his 'modern' ideas. Basin, a Norman who studied at Paris and Louvain and travelled widely, was something of a contradiction, for though as a scholar he was abreast of the radical humanist movement, as a politician he was a traditionalist who wished to conserve the decentralization of feudalism. He and Louis, both before and after 1461 when Louis became king, quarrelled several times on political issues. Eventually, Basin exiled himself to Rome, and spent his last years writing his *History of the Reigns of Charles VII and Louis XI* in as near Ciceronian Latin as he could achieve. His narrative is particularly accurate and reliable, but his portrait of Louis is venomous. Burgundy maintained at court a small group of official chronic-

lers, the chief of whom was verbose, old-fashioned Georges
Chastellain. He knew and liked Charles VII; he served both
Philip the Good and Charles the Bold, yet he never seemed to
have an inkling of the significance of the struggle for power
that was going on around him. He would have been more in
tune with his times had he lived in the days of Froissart. Two
other chroniclers at the Burgundian court were Jean de
Wavrin, who wrote a narrative chiefly concerned with English
affairs, and Olivier de la Marche, who delighted in jousts and
tourneys, had an eye for descriptive detail, and was a shrewd
judge of men. Jean Molinet, a fourth Burgundian chronicler,
unlike the others lived most of his life not at court but among
ordinary folk at Valenciennes. The glories of warfare did not
dazzle and fascinate him: on the contrary he condemned war as
the great destroyer of men and goods.

All these chroniclers, French or Burgundian, however, must
yield pride of place to Philippe de Commines, the supreme and
most sophisticated chronicler of his generation. He can be
rightly regarded as being both French and Burgundian, for
when in 1489 he sat down to write his memoirs, he could look
back on a long, eventful, diplomatic career, first in the service of
Charles the Bold, and then, after 1472, in that of Louis XI. No
one could have been closer to the centre of political affairs in
north-western Europe, for he had enjoyed the confidence of
both his employers, had met most of the outstanding men of his
day, and had witnessed many important occasions. Moreover,
his eyes penetrated below the surface of events: he recognized
Louis as forward-looking, and he knew that the age which
Charles the Bold symbolized was doomed if not already dead.
He wrote with moderation and yet with a sense of the dramatic,
but historians have to keep in mind that in his memoirs he was
'recollecting emotion in tranquillity'. Letters and dispatches
are always likely to be surer guides to contemporary opinions
and immediate reactions than are memoirs written at the end of
a long life. Fortunately, a large number of letters and diplomatic papers have survived from these fifteenth-century years.

Rymer's *Foedera* has preserved official instructions and the texts of treaties and truces in plenty. Dispatches which Milanese and Venetian ambassadors sent back to Italy from north-western capitals have been calendared and printed, and some 2,000 private and official letters of Louis XI himself, probably the most useful source of all, have been available in print since the beginning of this century.

These varied documents, which usually supplement and occasionally contradict one another, have three main uses for the English historian. First, they allow him to catch a glimpse of Englishmen or of outstanding allies or enemies of England from unusual angles. Commines, for example, described Edward IV:

> King Edward was not a person of any great management or fore-sight, but he was invincibly courageous, and the most handsome prince my eyes ever beheld.

Of the Kingmaker, he wrote,

> This earl of Warwick, because of the outstanding service he had given him and the care he had taken of his education, might well have been called King Edward's father. Indeed, he was a very great man; for, as well as his patrimony, he held several large estates which the king had given him, some of them crown lands and some that had been appropriated. He was made governor of Calais, and had other important offices, so that, according to what I have heard, he received annually in pensions and that kind of reward 80,000 crowns, besides his inheritance.

Olivier de la Marche described Francis II of Brittany as 'a poor and needy prince, but for the rest, handsome, virtuous, and of impressive appearance', and he said of Pierre de Brezé, the grand seneschal of Normandy who led a daring raid on the Kent coast in 1459, that he was 'a gentle and honourable knight, the most pleasant and gracious speaker I have ever met, wise, and a splendid organizer'.

The historian's second use for foreign documents is to find out from them what rumours and reports were current overseas, and what views the capitals of Europe were forming of English affairs. For several months after the battle of Towton in 1461, it was widely believed in north-western Europe that the Yorkists had captured the Lancastrian queen, Margaret of Anjou. Chastellain improved on this false rumour when he wrote:

. . . for Warwick has had it publicly proclaimed in London, and in the presence of the mother [Margaret], that she was a woman ashamed of herself, that the child that she had made believe to be the son of King Henry was a child of fornication, conceived in sin with a base-born man, a dancer, because of which he was not worthy to succeed to the crown nor to royal rank. . . .

Yet at the same time and from Bruges, where Chastellain was probably writing, the Milanese ambassador wrote to the duke of Milan prophesying that

before long grievances and recrimination will break out between King Edward and Warwick, King Henry and the queen will be victorious, and he who seemed to have the world at his feet will provide a remarkable example of what prudent men, in excuse for human errors, have called Fortune.

The third and most important advantage of foreign documents is that they interlock with English sources, and allow the historian of the fifteenth century to study all sides of the diplomatic and military campaigning in much the same way as modern historians, since 1945, have been able to piece together rounded accounts of the fall of France in 1940 or of D-day in 1944. The sequence of events which led to Edward IV and Louis XI signing the Treaty of Picquigny in August 1475 illustrates this interdependence of English and foreign sources very well. Lack of space forbids a full development of the complicated story, but the following account should be detailed enough to show how a handful of foreign documents give us a clearer delineation of the events, and help us to appreciate the motives and reactions of the principal characters.

In July 1474, King Edward promised Charles, duke of Burgundy, that he would invade France with 10,000 armed men

not later than 1 July 1475. On his part, Burgundy undertook
to contribute a similar number of troops to the joint force,
which the two allies hoped would be strong enough to conquer
France. The full details of this nicely balanced agreement and
treaty are set out in six long Latin documents printed in Rymer's
Foedera. The last document displays the magnificent confidence
which Edward and Charles professed to have in the success of
their scheme, for by it Charles 'promised and consented' that
he would allow Edward and his heirs to be crowned king of
France at Reims according to tradition, notwithstanding that
the second document of the treaty had included the county of
Champagne among those French lands which Edward agreed
to 'give, yield, and convey to our aforesaid brother'. During
the next months Edward busily prepared for the invasion. The
patent rolls give us details of 'the wheat, wine, ale, beeves,
muttons, sea-fish and fresh-water fish and other victuals for the
king's army soon to be sent to France for the recovery of that
realm'; of instructions to gentlemen in different parts of the
country, 'to make payments of money to fletchers for the
manufacture of "shefe arowes", to workmen for the manufacture of bows and "bowestaves", to smiths for the manufacture
of arrowheads, and to workmen called stringers for the manufacture of strings for bows'; of commissions to other gentlemen
'to take carpenters called wheelers and cartwrights and other
carpenters, joiners, stonecutters, smiths, plumbers, shipwrights,
coopers, sawers, fletchers, chariotmen, horse-harness men and
other workmen within the realm of England and the town and
marches of Calais and elsewhere under the king's obedience for
the works of the king's ordnance', and of the commandeering
of 'all ships and vessels of 16 tons and over and masters and
mariners for them'.

Despite such serious war preparations, however, Christofforo
di Bollato, a Milanese at Louis's court, informed the duke of
Milan that Edward and Louis were still in apparently friendly
communication. In August, he said, Louis had sent Edward a
gift of horses, and in return had received two greyhounds and

the suggestion that a marriage might be arranged between the dauphin and an English princess.

Meanwhile, Charles the Bold was not mobilizing his forces against France, but, in Edward's view, was wasting precious time and resources on a spectacular but ineffective siege of Neuss on the Rhine. About Christmas 1474, Morton and Montgomery, representatives of Edward IV, visited the duke's camp on their return from an unsuccessful mission to persuade the Emperor and the king of Hungary to join the Anglo-Burgundian alliance. A week or two later, they reached Calais and seem to have impressed the garrison and the merchants with their description of the siege. On 17 January 1475 Sir John Paston wrote from Calais:

. . . For it is so that as tomorrow I purpose to ride into Flanders to purvey me of horse and harness, and perchance I shall see the siege at Neuss ere I come again, if I have time . . . God send me good speed; in chief for that matter above written. . . . For as for tidings here, there be but few, save that the siege lasteth still by the Duke of Burgundy before Neuss, and the Emperor hath besieged also, not far from these, a castle, and another town in likewise, wherein the Duke's men be. . . . The King's ambassadors, Sir Thomas Montgomery and the Master of the Rolls [Dr John Morton] be coming homewards from Neuss; and as for me, I think that I should be sick but if [unless] I see it.

Louis did not allow the threat of invasion to fluster him into precipitate action; he decided to wait and see. Bollato wrote to Milan on 3 February that he had spoken to Louis

urging him in the name of your Excellency to attack the duke [Burgundy] before he can receive any help from the English or others. As he is engaged upon that enterprise at Neuss, a victory may result, especially as practically all Germany is provoked and hostile to him.

But Louis refused to do anything so positive. Time, he hoped, might bring a better solution: since 'the duke is constantly exposed to the perils of war, some day a bolt or a mortar will come and carry off his head'. This answer helped to persuade the duke of Milan that he would serve his own interests better if he signed an alliance with Burgundy instead of France. On 24 April his ambassador wrote back to him from Neuss:

In public he [Burgundy] will thank your lordship for the league with his Excellency, thanking you for the coming of Signor Ludovico. In private he will ask for men-at-arms, and to prevent the trade and passage of the Swiss [Burgundy's enemy] by Bormio, Como, Bellinzona, and Val Chiavenna, because of his war with the Emperor and the Germans. Further that you will make a league with the Florentines to strengthen your confederacy. That at the end of May he will find himself towards France with his army to make war on the King of France. He has arranged this with King Edward, who will cross at that time with 40,000 combatants on the one side, and the Duke of Brittany on the other.

Louis might always have preferred to rely on his skill as a diplomat to get him out of tight corners, but he did not neglect common-sense military and naval precautions. On 13 April, he wrote this one of a group of letters to the people of Harfleur:

Dear and well beloved,

In order to resist and prevent the invasion and damnable plan that the English and our long-standing enemies, rebels, and disobedient subjects have plotted and intend to carry out against us, our kingdoms, lands, and manors and against our good and loyal vassals and subjects, and in order to injure and attack them with all our might, with the help of God our Creator, we have decided, as soon as the truces expire, to send a large army to sea. In order to do this, we have arranged for all the big ships in our country of Normandy to be armed and fitted with guns, and afterwards victualled for four months, and this includes the ship called *Magdalene* of Harfleur. And because we cannot supply sufficient victuals without the help of our good and loyal subjects, because of the other great expenses we must meet, we require that you will contribute up to 600 livres tournois for the victualling of the aforesaid ship called *Magdalene* of Harfleur . . .

The Franco-Burgundian truce expired on 1 May 1475. Immediately Louis invaded the Netherlands. Commines commented, 'the King regretted it greatly for he would much rather have had an extension of the truce', and there is plenty of evidence to show that Louis was a very worried man throughout May and June. Commines recorded that the Emperor was threatening to make peace with Duke Charles if Louis did not fulfil a promise to invade the duchy of Burgundy, and also that Louis was keeping an anxious eye on negotiations between Edward and Francis, duke of Brittany. There is a note of relief in a letter Louis wrote at the end of June: 'the English are now treating the Bretons as enemies at sea, and say that they have betrayed them'. But Edward's military preparations were Louis's chief worry. Towards the end of June he decided that the invasion would not be in Normandy but in Picardy north of the Somme. He wrote to the grand-maître:

My lord grand-maître,

I came into Normandy in great haste, as you know, believing to find the English ready to invade. But I find that, the day before I arrived, the ships had withdrawn and sailed up the coast.

When I saw that we could do nothing, it seemed to me that, in order to defeat the English plan to invade Normandy, that I ought to send my troops into Picardy in order to destroy the countryside in which the invaders must find their food. And I sent them by the bridge at Remy [on the Somme] because the bridge at Gué is not safe for a big company. And they have gone as far as the sea, and have devastated from the Somme as far as Hesdin and the outskirts of Hesdin, and from there they have come, all the time carrying out their work, to Arras. . . .

. . . Our troops have retreated. I will send 400 lances to Eu, and will have all the grain, both of the town and the whole countryside, sent to Dieppe in order that the English shall find nothing . . .

By 15 July Louis knew that the duke of Burgundy was marching into Picardy to join Edward, but, he admitted, 'we do not know for certain whether the king of England has landed; and if he has landed it was with so small a company that he made so little noise that the prisoners who were taken yesterday at Abbeville know nothing of it and do not believe it has happened'. But about ten days later he learned the truth, that Edward had been in Calais for the last three weeks. On 28 July he ordered Doullens, north of Amiens, to be destroyed so that

Edward would find it in ruins, and three days later instructed the bailiff of Amboise to strengthen the fortifications of Reims.

I am advised that the king of England and the duke of Burgundy intend to march into Champagne to Reims, to the intent, God forbid, that the king of England shall be crowned at Nôtre Dame. And because of this, for the love you bear me, make all haste to fortify Reims. And tell the townsfolk that if they do not quickly make the town safe, it will be burned down. . . .

The townsfolk responded well. On 4 and 12 August Louis wrote them encouraging letters, bidding them hurry with their task of digging a wide moat round the city.

Edward had crossed to Calais on 4 July. According to Commines, Burgundy sent 500 ships to Dover to help transport the English army across the Channel, and the whole operation took three weeks. Looking back on these events years later, Commines was of the opinion that if only Louis had understood naval warfare as well as he did land fighting, Edward would never have been able to make so leisurely a crossing. As it was Edward's fleet met no opposition: 'a single ship from Eu captured two or three of the little transports'. Commines wrote enthusiastically about Edward's army:

. . . never had a king of England gathered together so powerful an army . . . nor one so well equipped to fight. Without exception all the English noblemen were there. There could well have been 1,500 men-at-arms, which is a big number for an English army, all well equipped and well supported, and 14,000 mounted archers carrying bows and arrows, and sufficient other men on foot serving the fighting troops. And in the whole army there was not a single page.

Yet this workmanlike army was destined to do little fighting. Charles maintained the siege of Neuss to the last minute. He met Edward at Calais on 14 July, but was not at all ready to campaign with him. He rushed back to Bruges to remonstrate with the Estates of Flanders for not voting him sufficient money, and soon after he had rejoined Edward in Picardy, he decided he must go off again to take command of his forces in Lorraine.

The count of St Pol, nominally a Burgundian, greeted Edward's arrival at St Quentin with shooting instead of the expected bell-ringing, and on top of these cumulative disappointments, relentless rain destroyed what remained of Edward's zeal for the campaign.

During the second week of August, through the good offices of a released prisoner, Edward established contact with Louis at Compiègne. Heralds carried safe-conducts for commissioners, and negotiations began in earnest on 15 August. Four days later, when a very angry Charles turned up at the English camp, he found himself too late to save the situation. The agreements had been signed. According to Pietro Panicharolla who sent a report to Milan from Namur, Burgundy put the blame partly on Edward's cowardice and partly on Brittany's indecision.

'It would cut him [Burgundy] to the quick if he had reason to enter such a vile agreement, made without ever seeing the face of the enemy. If he had not trusted to the backing of the English, he would have made other provision against the enemy . . . The duke of Brittany had aroused these suspicions in the English because, when at his request they sent him 2,000 English archers, he would not accept them, but temporized when he should have disclosed himself . . .

The Anglo-French agreement included arrangements for a personal meeting between the two kings and a formal sealing of the documents. Louis wrote to his chancellor:

My lord chancellor,

I am sending you copies of the letters that my lord of Saint Pierre has written me, from which you will be able to learn of the good news I have, for which I praise God and Our Lady and St Martin. And make sure that you have all our money at Amiens by Friday evening, as well as anything else which will be of use to my lord of Havart and the others who have the arrangements in hand. And in this matter, as you value my safety, my honour and that of the king-dom make haste and do not fail me, for if you did, you would do me irreparable harm.

It is necessary to have the great seal for the confirmation of these matters, for they will have no faith in any other. And for this, if you yourself cannot come so soon, send it immediately you have read these letters by some reliable man. And let there be no mistake, so that they will have no excuse to repudiate what has been agreed.

Written at La Victoire les Senlis, 23rd day of August.

Loys.

The meeting between Edward and Louis took place on a bridge across the Somme at Picquigny, nine miles from Amiens. Commines, Lord Howard, and others carefully chose the site, for neither side trusted the other, and the historically-minded recalled how John the Fearless, duke of Burgundy, had been treacherously murdered on just such another occasion in 1419. Commines described the occasion in his memoirs:

In the middle of the bridge was built a strong wooden lattice, similar to that with which lions' cages are made. The hole between the bars was just wide enough to take a man's arm, the top was only sufficiently covered with boards to keep off the rain, and the structures on each side were big enough to hold ten or twelve men. To prevent any person from by-passing it on one side or the other, the bars of the trellis ran across to both sides of the bridge. In the river there was only one little boat manned by two men to row such as required to cross.

As an extra precaution Commines, who walked at Louis's side, wore similar clothes to the king, and when they reached the trellis, they discovered that three or four of Edward's party were dressed in cloth of gold like Edward. The kings greeted each other with elaborate courtesy, and then, no doubt with considerable difficulty, embraced through the trellis. Commines recalled Louis's welcoming words:

My lord, my cousin, you are heartily welcome. There is no other person in the world I wanted to see so much, and God be praised that we have met on so good an occasion.

Edward, said Commines, returned the compliment in good French.

The anonymous writer of the misnamed *Chronique scandaleuse* also described the meeting:

Upon the bridge at Picquigny the king had ordered two large penthouses to be erected opposite each other, one for himself, and the other for the king of England. In the middle between these penthouses a large wooden grating, something like a lion's cage, was built breast high, so that the two kings could lean over it and speak together. . . . While Louis waited for Edward at the bridge, it began to rain heavily. This did considerable damage to the housings and furnishings that the French nobles and officers had specially provided for this meeting, and they were rich and magnificent . . .

On 12 September, a fortnight after the interview, the Florentine ambassador wrote from Lyons:

Ultimately they [Edward and Louis] both ratified what had been arranged in public and in secret by their ambassadors, and when they had finished, the barriers were broken down and the two kings took leave of each other amid great festivities and friendliness.

There is no confirmation of this detail, which seems unlikely to be true.

A fortnight later still, Panicharolla sent news of the interview to Milan from Luxemburg. He described how the two kings had embraced through the trellis, and added,

That done, the king of France drew his naked sword and offered it to the said king, who did not appear to take much notice of it, but told him to sheathe it. They interpret this act here in various ways, but incline to consider it one of submission . . .

From the secretary's report, the English seemed the more friendly and finer troops than those of the king of France, who, however, had his massed together, especially all the guns, for the safety of his person at this conference.

Thus this king will return to England. He remarked to the secretary that he had heard that when the duke [of Burgundy] heard of this agreement, he tore up the Garter with his teeth into more than six pieces. This is not true, but his Majesty has already committed such an affront, because he wore the Golden Fleece [a Burgundian honour] before the king of France, who assured him that he desired nothing but peace with the duke of Burgundy. . . .

The details of the agreement made at Picquigny are to be found once again in the invaluable *Foedera*. There are three documents. The first arranged for Edward to withdraw his army to England once Louis had paid him 75,000 golden crowns; the second concluded a seven-year truce, during which neither Englishmen in France nor Frenchmen in England would require safe conducts; and by the third the two kings promised not to enter into any alliance without the other's knowledge and consent. But as everyone knows, official words on official occasions do not always represent true feelings. Louis was certainly relieved that he had been able to make peace. In his enthusiasm he said that Edward must come and stay with him in Paris. Edward's ready acceptance took him aback, and he studiously avoided all mention of this invitation again. Later in Amiens he spoke his true mind to Commines:

He is a very handsome prince, a great admirer of the ladies. Who knows some of them may appear to him so charming that they will give him a desire to make us a second visit. His predecessors have already been too often in Paris and Normandy, and I do not care for his company so near. But on the other side of the water, I shall esteem him my friend and good brother. . . .

Commines's considered judgement on the treaty was:

Hardly anything was carried out that was promised there. The whole show was pretence. It is true that they never warred against one other because the sea divided them, but there was never any real friendship between them.

Edward returned to Calais on 4 September, and to London at the end of the month. Not everybody in England was pleased that he had signed the treaty. Many noblemen felt they had been cheated of booty and ransoms, but probably Sir John Paston spoke for the majority when he wrote from Calais, 'Blessed be God, this voyage of the king's is finished for this time.'

3. LAY CHRONICLERS

We have seen from the letters they wrote that many middle-class English men and women of the fifteenth century were literate enough to write frequently and fairly freely in English. The founding of chantry schools and grammar schools – a charitable work which remained fashionable throughout the century – steadily made education more easily available to children from those fairly well-to-do households which did not maintain a chaplain-tutor. Most of these children eventually earned their living farming or trading. A few studied law or medicine: as the century progressed there is little doubt that the proportion of lay students increased at Oxford and Cambridge. The church still provided the teaching, however, and the study of theology still remained the goal of all learning, but literacy and academic knowledge were more widespread among the laity than they had ever been. Before the turn of the century, such noblemen as Humphrey, duke of Gloucester, William de la Pole, duke of Suffolk, and James Butler, earl of Ormonde, were showing an active interest in learning and the arts, yet the most noticeable progress and enthusiasm was not in the aristocracy but among the merchants and the smaller estate holders.

The chronicles of the century reflect this social change as clearly as do the letters. In almost every monastery – Croyland and St Albans are the outstanding exceptions – the monks of the fifteenth century neglected their traditional task of maintaining annals and chronicles. Fortunately, in the same century, a substantial number of laymen took an interest in keeping records. The most important group of them came from London. As C. L. Kingsford has demonstrated in detail, it is difficult to determine how many original manuscripts there were, for what have come down to us are the manuscripts of editor–copyists, who have not hesitated to add to, subtract from, and summarize parts of the original. Some thirty versions and fragments are extant. No two are exactly alike, but most of them divide into groups, the members of each of which undoubtedly had a common source which no longer exists. If one chronicle could claim to be more fundamental than any of the others, it

would be the *Brut*. Manuscript copies seem to have been widely
dispersed, and as early as 1480 Caxton printed a version of it
under the title *Chronicles of England*. Apparently it began as a
fourteenth-century Norman-French chronicle telling the story
of Britain from the usual mythical founding by Brutus until the
beginning of Edward III's reign. During the minority of
Henry VI another hand added a continuation to carry events as
far as 1419, and thence, at intervals until the end of the century,
several other writers contributed new continuations. Most of
the later additions seem to have been based on the same sources
as some of the London chronicles, but, in turn, they provided
raw material for other writers to use and shape for themselves.
Much of the revised *Brut* appeared across the Channel in the
pages of *Recueil des Croniques d'Engleterre* written by Jean
Wavrin, the Burgundian chronicler, and once Caxton had
published his printed version, the *Brut* became still more popular
and influential.

Fabyan's Chronicle is another well-known work which
illustrates this widespread editorial-copying. Robert Fabyan,
alderman and sheriff of London, set out to follow the traditional
route from the Creation to his own day, but, as usual, it is only
the last part of his work that has historical value. Fabyan based
his story of fifteenth-century England on a London chronicle
which has not survived. But careful comparisons with other
works dependent on the same source show that he did not just
copy what was in front of him. He condensed some passages,
and here and there introduced information from other written
sources, and probably, as William of Worcester and others did,
from personal information and memories. His own description
of his work was 'a concordance of chronicles'. He brought his
narrative as far as 1485, and the work, entitled *The New
Chronicles of England and of France*, was printed in 1516, three
years after his death. Later in the sixteenth century, writers such
as Hall and Holinshed published chronicles derived in part from
secular chronicles of the fifteenth century, and in Elizabeth's
reign Stow, in such works as *Summarie of English Chronicles*

and *Annales of England*, not only copied the work of his fifteenth-century predecessors but still continued to use their prosaic method of presenting facts. For none of these lay chroniclers can be considered embryonic historians. They did not try to present a theme or assess the importance of events. They remained annalists, recording major and minor facts with impartiality, repeating gossip without considering its truth or falsity, and making no attempt to reconcile contradictory versions of the same event.

During the last quarter of the nineteenth and the first years of the twentieth centuries, James Gairdner and C. L. Kingsford edited a number of these London chronicles and had them printed. Until then the manuscripts had been preserved in college libraries or private collections. None of them were signed, and it was clear that some of them had been written by more than one hand. Gairdner attributed one to William Gregory, mayor of London from 1451 to 1452, and Flenley, a slightly later editor, named another *Bale's Chronicle*. But the remainder continue to be known by their library catalogue numbers, some of which, like Cleopatra C IV and Julius B I, sound unexpectedly romantic.

It had been the custom, at least from the second half of the thirteenth century, for the city of London to keep a brief, semi-official chronicle of events. In the fifteenth century the writers of these annals gradually became more expansive. They began to give information other than the names of the mayor and aldermen and the usual terse statements about disasters or the deaths of kings. They wrote comparatively full accounts of events which they had witnessed, and of news that had reached the capital, and they occasionally recorded contemporary opinion. Not unexpectedly their main interests remained predominantly parochial: for example, in the following account of events for the year October 1456 to October 1457 when Thomas Cannings was mayor of London, the writer of the version known as Vitellius A XVI seems to have been more concerned with the Newgate riot and the fish caught in the

Thames than he was with the French attack on Sandwich or even with the invention of printing.

In this year was the earl of Salisbury discharged of his Chancellorship [a mistake: archbishop Bourchier surrendered the chancellorship to William Waynflete in October 1456]. And after, the Duke of York, and the said earl, with the earl of Warwick, were sent for by the privy seal to Coventry where they were all near entrapped. And in this year were taken between Erith and London four great fishes, whereof one was called 'mors maryne', and the second a swordfish, and the other two were whales. And this year were certain affrays between the lord Egremont and the earl of Salisbury's son: the said lord Egremont, being committed to Newgate, this year broke prison. And this year died the earl of Richmond [Edmund Tudor], brother unto king Henry by the mother's side. And this year was likely to have been an affray between the Duke of Somerset and Sir John Neville, knight, son of the earl of Salisbury; which by sad [serious] provision of the Mayor of the City of London with keeping of sufficient watches it was letted [prevented]. Also this year Frenchmen entered Sandwich and took there great goods, and went away unpunished. Item this year the earl of Warwick with his wife went to Calais to take possession of the Captainship of Calais. Also this year began the Craft of Emprinting of Books, which was founded in a town called 'magounce' [Mayence or Mainz] in Almayne [Germany]. In this year was the battle of Saint John Capistrane, a friar, which destroyed an innumerable number of Turks. Also this year the prisoners of Newgate broke their prison and went upon the leads, and fought against the Citizens and kept the gate a great while: but at the last they were overcome, and after sore punished with Irons and Fetters.

Weather and prices are recurrent themes in all these London chronicles. The author of Julius B 11, which was probably written about 1435, not only repeated from an earlier manuscript that the years 1202 and 1270 witnessed most violent tempests – 'fire Dragons and Wicked Spirits were many seen, marvellously flying in the air' – but also recorded, probably from living memory, that in 1363–4 there 'was the great wind, that overthrew many houses and steeples in England', and, probably from his own experience, that in 1408 there 'was a great frost, and long [en]during, for men might go over Thames upon the ice'. The only thing the author of Cleopatra C IV recorded about the year 1428 was the continual heavy rain which destroyed hay and corn crops, and the author of Vitellius A XVI, has left us a curious description of St Paul's struck by lightning in February 1443

upon the Candlemas Eve before by a great tempest of thunder and lightning at afternoon the Steeple of St Paul's church was set on fire about the middle of the Shaft in the timber; which was quenched by great labour, and specially by the great diligent labour of the morrow-mass priest of the Bow in Cheap, which was thought impossible except [by] the grace of God.

Natural though it was to comment on extraordinary weather, it was just as natural for a London citizen to comment on prices, especially when they were high. According to Cleopatra C IV, 1439 'was a right dear year of corn of all manner [of] corn throughout all England'. Wheat rose to 3s. 4d. and oats to 8d. a bushel; malt was bringing between 13s. and 14s. a quarter. The chronicler wryly commented, 'men ate more beans, and pease, and barley that year than ever was eaten in England a hundred winter before'. The author of Vitellius A XVI gives us quite a range of what appear to be normal prices for 1494 – wheat 6d. a bushel, malt 3s. 4d. a quarter, white herrings 2s. 8d., and sprats 6d. 'a corde', Gascony wine £6 a tun, salt from the Bay of Biscay 3½d., but Nantwich salt 6d., a bushel – and between notices of the death of the bishop of London and the punishment of a heretic, he sandwiched the information that in Lent 1496 almonds were selling for 14d. a pound and 'good Flanders herring' for 3s. 4d. a barrel. Under the mayoral year, October 1464 to October 1465, William Gregory, if he were indeed the author of *Gregory's Chronicle*, explained how Edward IV devalued the coinage. The manoeuvre was designed to help the king to meet his immediate financial difficulties, but Gregory makes plain the trouble it caused in London.

And this year was it ordained that the noble of 6s. 8d. should go for 8s. 4d. And a new coin was made. First they made an angel and it went for 6s. 8d., and half an angel for 40d.; but they made no farthings [quarters] of that gold. And then they made a greater coin and named it a royal, and that went for 10s., and half a royal for 5s., and the farthing for 2s. 6d. And they made new groats not so good as the old, but they were worth 4d. And then silver rose to a greater price, for an ounce of silver was set at 3s., and better of some silver. But at the beginning of this money men grudged passing sore, for they could not reckon that gold not so quickly as they did the old gold. And men might go throughout a street or through a whole parish ere that he might change it. And some men said that the new gold was not so good as the old gold was, for it was alloyed.

The outlook of the London chroniclers might have been parochial, but of course, then as now, many of the events which happened in London 'parish' had national and even international significance. It is not surprising, therefore, that the London chronicles can be successfully searched for information upon such widely varied topics as the growth of nationalism, the strength of Lollardism and other heresies, the political events of the Wars of the Roses, and the visits of foreign embassies to England. In no place in fifteenth-century England could feeling be more readily roused against foreigners than in London. In 1456 there were some ugly riots against the Lombards. The author of Vitellius A XVI explained how one of them began, and how narrowly the authorities avoided provoking a major revolt.

The cause began of a young man that took a dagger from a stranger and broke it. Wherefore the young man was sent for unto the Mayor and Aldermen being at Guildhall, and there by them he was committed for his offence to one of the contours [prisons]; and then the Mayor departing from the hall toward his mansion to dinner, in Cheap [there] met with him a great company of young men of the mercery [trade of the mercers], as apprentices and other loose men; and tarried the Mayor and Sheriffs still in Cheap, not suffering him to depart till they had their fellow, being in prison, as is aforesaid, delivered; and so by force delivered their fellow out of prison. Whereupon the same evening the hand crafty-men ran unto the Lombards' houses, and robbed and despoiled divers of them. Wherefore the Mayor and Sheriffs, with the assistance of good and well-disposed people of the City, with great jeopardy and labour drove them thence, and committed some of them that had robbed to Newgate.... upon this came down an oyer et terminer, for to do justice upon all them that so had rebelled in the City; upon which sat that time with the mayor the Duke of Buckingham with divers other great lords for to see execution done. But the Commons of the City did arm them secretly in their houses, and were in purpose to have rung the Common Bell, called Bow Bell; but they were let [prevented] by sad [discreet] and well-advised men, which when it came to the knowledge of the Duke of Buckingham and other lords there being with him, they incontinently arose, fearing longer to abide; for it was shown to them that all the City would arise upon them. But yet notwithstanding in conclusion 2 or 3 misdoers of the City were adjudged for the robbery, and were hanged at Tyburn; and this done the king and the queen and other lords rode to Coventry, and withdrew them from London for these causes.

This outburst of violence in 1456 had several precedents, and it was by no means the last time the Londoners expressed their mistrust and hatred of foreign traders. Indeed throughout the fifteenth century, increasing numbers of men and women were becoming dissatisfied with a wide range of conventions and traditions. Questioning accepted ideas and trying to formulate new ones always proves disturbing, and on occasions in the fifteenth century restlessness expressed itself in active opposition. At the beginning of the century Lollardy was a popular form of protest, which church and state wished to suppress. Wycliffe himself died in his bed, but *Gregory's Chronicle* records how, nearly fifty years later, the authorities, because they were incensed by the activities of his followers, exhumed and burned his remains. Several chroniclers related how Sir John Oldcastle, a leading Lollard, was arrested in 1413. He escaped from the Tower, but five years later was captured in the Welsh marches, brought to London and hanged. Most of the chroniclers told the story in their usual impersonal way, but the author of Julius B 11 allowed his detestation of Lollards to peep through his report. Of the events in 1413 he wrote:

. . . Sir John Oldcastle was damned for a Lollard and a heretic by all holy church, and committed to the Tower of London; and there he broke out within a few days.

And soon after he and his affinities [fellows], that were of his sect conjected [plotted] and conspired not only the death of the king and of his brethren, but also the destruction of all holy church; for they purposed them to have assembled together by night in St Giles Field, a mile out of the city, and there to have gathered the strength to have fulfilled their cursed purposes.

But, blessed be God, the king and his lords were warned of their purposes; and took the field rather than they, and awaiting after their coming; and so they took many of their priests and clerks and other low [humble] men, that were of their sect, coming thither, expecting to have found there Sir John Oldcastle, but they failed of their purpose.

And soon after there were drawn and hanged 36 upon one day, upon new gallows made for them upon the highway fast beside the same field . . .

This destruction of Lollards was the only thing the writer thought fit to record for that mayoral year. In the year 1417–18 he proclaimed a double triumph – the end of the Great Schism in the church and the execution of Oldcastle. His account gives the impression that the second item of news pleased him as much as, if not more than, the first:

In this same year, thanked be Almighty God, the general council was ended and union made in holy church: and a pope chosen at Constance upon St Martin's Day by the assent of all the general council, and he is called Martin V. Also in the same year was Sir John Oldcastle, called the Lord Cobham, taken in the Marches of Wales and brought to the City of London, the which was chief lord and maintainer of all the Lollards in this realm, and ever about to destroy to his power holy church. And therefore he was first drawn, and afterwards hanged, and burnt hanging on the new gallows besides St Giles with an iron chain about his neck, because that he was a lord of [by] name. And so there he made an end of his cursed life.

Heresy trials were common enough throughout the century. Every few pages the London chroniclers slipped in a line to convey such news as 'two heretics were abjured at Paul's Cross', or as 'there was burnt at Smithfield an old man for heresy'.

Londoners involved in commerce only approved of war if it brought rapid conquests and new trading opportunities overseas. All other types of war damaged trade, and occasioned unwelcome demands for loans and taxes. Therefore, they showed no partisan enthusiasm for either side in the Yorkist–Lancastrian struggle. They did not wish to be involved: above all they wanted to keep the fighting well away from the capital. They found it expedient to accept the party in the ascendant. In 1461 the Londoners eagerly welcomed Edward, Earl of March, fresh from his victory at Mortimer's Cross, because they hoped that he and Warwick commanded strong enough forces to save their homes from being pillaged by the undisciplined northerners who had recently won the battle of St Albans. *Gregory's Chronicle* conveys some of the excitement in the city:

Then came tidings of the coming of the Earl of March unto London; then all the city were fain, and thanked God, and said that

> He that had London forsake
> Would no more to them take,

and said, 'Let us walk in a new wine yard, and let us make us a gay garden in the month of March with this fair white rose and herb, the Earl of March.'

Vitellius A XVI relates how, on the first Sunday in March, the Londoners loudly proclaimed their newly-found loyalty to the house of York:

And upon the Sunday after, all the host mustered in St John's Field, where was read among the people certain articles and points that king Henry had offended in. And then it was demanded of the people whether the said Henry was worthy to reign still; and the people cried, Nay! Nay! And then they asked, if they would have the Earl of March to be their king, and they said, Yea! Yea! And then certain captains were sent to the Earl of March's place at Baynard's Castle, and told to the earl that the people had chosen him king; whereof he thanked God and them, and, by the advice of the Bishops of Canterbury and of Exeter, and the Earl of Warwick with other[s], he took it upon him.

Ten years later, after Edward had fled to Flanders, the same London crowd lined the streets to watch Warwick and Clarence bring Henry VI from the Tower into the City. They particularly approved of the arrest and condemnation of the unpopular earl of Worcester:

And as he was coming from Westminster toward his execution the people pressed so fast about him that the officers were fain to turn into the Fleet [prison] with him; and there he rested that night and till upon the Tuesday at afternoon, which was St Luke's Day and the 18th day of October, he was brought through the City, and so to the Tower Hill upon his feet; and there beheaded; upon whose soul and all Christian [souls] Jesu have mercy. Amen!

John Warkworth, the master of Peterhouse, Cambridge, attempted an explanation of this apparent fickleness. He described how the bishop of Winchester, acting as emissary for Warwick and Clarence, released Henry from the Tower and 'restored him to the crowd'. He then went on:

Whereof all his good lovers were full glad, and the most part of the people. Nevertheless, before that, as he was put out of his realm by King Edward, all England for the more part hated him, and were full glad to have a change; and the cause was the good Duke of Gloucester was put to death, and John Holland, Duke of Exeter, poisoned, and that the Duke of Suffolk, the Lord Saye, Daniel Trevylian, and other mischievous people that were about the King, were so covetous toward themselves, and did no force of the King's honour, nor of his weal, nor of the common weal of the land, where King Henry trusted to them that they should do, and labour in time of innocence ever for the common weal, which they did contrary to his will; and also France, Normandy, Gascony, and Guienne was lost in his time.

And these were the causes, with others, that made the people grudge against him, and all because of his false lords, and never of him; and the common people said, if they might have another king, he should get all again and amend all manner of things that was amiss, and bring the realm of England in great prosperity and rest. Nevertheless, when King Edward IV reigned, the people looked after all the foresaid prosperities and peace, but it came not; but one battle after another, and much trouble and great loss of goods among the common people; as first, the fifteenth of all their goods, and then a whole fifteenth, but yet at every battle to come far out [of] their countries [districts] at their own cost; and these and such others brought England right low, and many men said that King Edward had much blame for hurting merchandise. . . .

Party politicians will readily appreciate Warkworth's argument, for none know better than they that the existence of an alternative government in opposition, or exile, encourages criticism of the government in power, and, despite previous bitter disappointments, without fail raises hopes that a change of control will bring about a miraculous improvement in social conditions.

As we have seen, all medieval chroniclers were credulous, indiscriminate, and only partially informed. Moreover, because they were human, they could not prevent their own attitudes and preferences from colouring their work. Yet, in the second half of the fifteenth century, a number of writers, in their enthusiasm for either the Yorkist or the Lancastrian faction, produced more partisan writing than their predecessors had ever done. Much of their bias appears to have been unconscious. They usually related the sequence of events accurately according to their information, but they displayed their prejudices by hints and innuendoes, by their distribution of emphasis, and by reporting rumours and opinions which favoured their cause. No chronicler was better able stealthily to plant ideas in his readers' mind than the author of *Davies's Chronicle*, who, soon after the accession of Edward IV, wrote a continuation of the *Brut* from 1440 to 1461. He was a Yorkist. He particularly disliked Margaret of Anjou and everyone who had ever befriended her. Therefore, without question he accepted the view that the parliament which met at Bury St Edmunds in February 1447 'was made only for to slay the noble duke of Gloucester, whose death the false duke of Suffolk, William de la Pole, and Sir James Fiennes, Lord Saye, and others of their assent, had longtime conspired and imagined'. Humphrey, duke of Gloucester, certainly died a few days after arriving at Bury. He was elderly, and journeying in that 'fervent cold weather' probably proved too much for him. The chronicler did not directly accuse Suffolk of murdering Gloucester, as later the Tudor historians did, but he made some gratuitous guesses at what might have been the cause of his death.

And the third day after, he died for sorrow, as some men said, because he might not come to his answer and excuse him of such things as were falsely put on him; for the said duke of Suffolk and Lord Saye, and others of their assent, so stirred and excited the king against the said duke of Gloucester that he might never come to his excuse; for they had cast among them a privy conclusion, the which as yet is not come to the knowledge of the common people, and they wist well that they should never bring it about till he were dead, but the certainty of his death is not yet openly known, but there is nothing so privy, as the gospel saith, but at last it shall be open.

The same chronicler reported the death of the earl of Devonshire at Abingdon in January 1458. He put in parenthesis 'poisoned as men said', and then added, apparently inconsequentially, 'being there at that time with Queen Margaret'. He was ready to believe any slanderous rumours against the queen, and wrote down hostile opinions and speculations as if they were proved facts. The blame for the crown's shortage of money in 1459 he placed on Henry's innocent simplicity – 'all the possessions and lordships that pertained to the crown the king had given away' – and on Margaret's criminal cupidity:

The queen with such as were of her affinity ruled the realm as she liked; gathering riches innumerable. The officers of the realm, and especially the earl of Wiltshire, treasurer of England, for to enrich himself, peeled the poor people, and disinherited rightful heirs and did many wrongs. The queen was defamed and beslandered, that he that was called Prince, was not her son, but a bastard gotten in adultery; wherefore she dreading that he should not succeed his father in the crown of England, allied unto her all the knights and squires of Cheshire for to have their benevolence, and held open house among them; and made her son called the Prince give a livery of Swans to all the gentlemen of the country, and to many others throughout the land; trusting through their strength to make her son king; making privy approaches to some of the lords of England for to stir the king that he should resign the crown to her son: but she could not bring her purpose about.

It is not clear whether the chronicler was alleging that Prince Edward was the illegitimate son of Henry or of Margaret, but there is no doubt that he wished to convince his readers that the queen was an evil influence. Virtue for this writer was with one political faction only. After the Coventry Parliament had attainted the chief Yorkists of treason, he described how Ludlow was robbed to its bare walls, and how 'the noble duchess of York unmanly and cruelly was entreated and spoiled'. He claimed that, after the second battle of St Albans, the Lancastrians executed Lord Bonville in spite of Henry's promise that he should suffer no harm:

... nevertheless notwithstanding that surety, at instance of the queen, the duke of Exeter, and the earl of Devonshire, by judgement of him that was called the Prince, a child, he was beheaded at St Albans.

Later, he described the reckless retreat of the Lancastrians:

The which Northernmen as they went homeward did harms innumerable, taking many carts, wains, horses and beasts, and robbed the people and led their pillage into the North country, so that the men of the shires that they passed by had almost left no beasts to till their land.

Probably he did not exaggerate. During these civil wars, many ladies suffered cruelly for their husband's political mistakes, solemn pledges were often ignored, and pillaging troops spared nothing and nobody. But, contrary to what this chronicler would seem to infer, such evils did not lie only at the Lancastrian door.

T – H

A few fifteenth-century writers openly argued a case. Despite the obvious dangers of indiscretion in the turbulent days of civil war, merchants and professional men must have frequently debated political issues, and, as ever, it was possible honestly to hold very contrary views on the same events. The action taken by Richard of York against Henry VI and his ministers during the later fifties, example, could be seen either as a public-spirited campaign to oust corrupt self-seekers from positions of authority, or as an attempt by mischief-making, selfish, and ambitious men to seize power. One unknown Lancastrian, probably a lawyer, had no doubt of the truth. He argued:

I have a rotten tooth in my mouth that vexeth me night and day. Is it better to pull him out and so make a gap in my mouth, the which I wot well is not good, or else to plaster him to the confusion and undoing of all the others, and at last he will fall according to his nature and do to me a shrewd turn? For sooth if the king had no more lords in this land than they [York and his supporters] yet were it better without comparison to give them to the hands of Satan in perpetual subversion than to reconcile them, for the restoring of them were none other but a wilful submission and exposing of the king to their will, the which was never good nor never shall be.

The author of the chronicle of the *Rebellion in Lincolnshire* used a slightly less straightforward way of putting his case. He told a chronological story of events, but he made it clear enough that his purpose was to win sympathy for Edward and expose Warwick and Clarence as double-crossing traitors. He began by stating this theme:

First, how be it that our said sovereign lord, as a prince inclined to show his mercy and pity to his subjects rather than rigour and straitness of his laws, pardoned of late to his said rebels all treasons and felonies, trespasses and offences committed and done by them against his highness afore the feast of Christmas last past . . . yet they unnaturally and unkindly, without cause or occasion given to them by our said sovereign lord, falsely compassed, conspired, and imagined the final destruction of his most royal person and of his true subjects taking part with him in assisting his highness. . . .

The author then related how Sir Robert Welles, encouraged by Warwick and Clarence, roused the people of Lincolnshire to revolt, but now and again he momentarily button-holed his reader, or at least wagged a finger at him, to press home his point that Edward trusted the word of Warwick and Clarence and that they basely deceived him.

. . . which message so sent by the duke was false dissimulation, as by the works [events] after it appeared. Nevertheless, the king, not understanding no such doubleness, but trusting that they meant truly as they showed, sent unto the said duke and earl incontinent his several commissions . . . Where it appeareth clearly that by all this time the said duke and earl dissembled falsely with the king . . . Also the said duke dissembled right untruly with the king . . . That the duke thus dissembled . . . The king, not understanding these false dissimulations, but, of his most noble and rightwise courage, with all speed purposing to go upon his said rebels, early on the Monday afore day drew him to the field. . . .

History of the Arrival of Edward IV is another such Yorkist *apologia*, this time concerning the restoration of Edward in 1471. Yet, although the main intention of these two short chronicles was avowedly to justify political and military action, both documents give us detailed narratives. Without them we should know far less of what happened in Lincolnshire in March 1470, and of the details of the campaigns which led to Edward's victories at Barnet and Tewkesbury.

The ballads and political verses of the period often display a cruder and more violent partisanship. The fifteenth century cannot boast poets of the calibre of Chaucer and Langland, but the victories of Henry V in France inspired many popular verses. Agincourt won special praise:

> Our King went forth to Normandy,
>   With grace and might of chivalry:
> There God for him wrought marvellously,
>   Wherefore England may call and cry –
> *Deo gratias Anglia redde pro victoria!*

> Then forsooth that knight comely
>   In Agincourt field he wrought manly:
> Through grace of God most mighty
>   He had both the field and the victory.

John Page wrote a long poem about the siege of Rouen, which came to a grim end in January 1419. Page took part in the siege, and he spared his readers few of the horrors experienced by the besieged.

> They ate dogs, they ate cats,
>   They ate mice, horse, and rats.
> For a horse's quarter, lean or fat,
>   A hundred shillings it was at.
> A horse's head for half a pound;
>   A dog for the same money round;
> For thirty pence went a rat.
>   For two nobles went a cat.
> For sixpence went a mouse;
>   They left few in any house.

Some twenty years later, when the war had turned sour and there was nothing to relieve the monotony of constant demands for money and the occasional news of defeat, an unknown Londoner wrote another poem, *The Libel of English Policy*. He urged the king's government to be more ruthless with foreign competitors. He declared it to be economic folly to continue the war –

> Hath done us harm, and doth us every day . . .
> . . . Our money spent all to little avail . . .

and then argued strongly that England would be well advised to hold Calais and build a strong navy to give her control of the Channel.

> Keep then the sea about in special
>   Which of England is the round wall:
> As though England were likened to a city,
>   And the wall environ were the sea.
> Keep then the sea, that is the wall of England,
>   And then is England kept by God's sending.

In the middle decades of the century John Harding wrote a verse chronicle. He spoke openly against the lack of order and justice in England, and on the eve of the Wars of the Roses offered this advice to Henry VI:

> Withstand, good lord, beginning of debate,
>   And chastise well also the rioters,
> That in each shire be now consociate
>   Against your peace, and all their maintainers;
> For truly else will fall the fairest flowers
>   Of your crown and your noble monarchy,
>   Which God defend and keep through his mercy.

Such poems allow us to assess the current opinions of the middle class. We know that most of the leaders of the aristocracy in the fifteenth century were still thinking in feudal terms, but the thought behind these poems is much more modern. It recognized commercial profits, and not ransoms, as the wealth for which Englishmen should strive overseas, and at home upheld the rule of law, and not an independent baronage, as the basis for sound government. It was forward-looking, anticipatory of convictions that were going to develop very strongly during the next century.

The civil war itself provoked some bitter political satire. According to the verses that have survived, the unpopular duke of Suffolk suffered particularly badly. He was attacked straightforwardly –

> God keep our King – aye, and guide him by grace,
>   Save him from Suffolk and from his foes all –

and under thin disguises, which any contemporary with the slightest political knowledge could easily penetrate. The author of the following, for example, used the transparent cloak of heraldry.

> The Rote [Bedford] is dead, the Swan [Gloucester] is gone,
>   The fiery Cressest [Exeter] hath lost his sight;
> Therefore England may make great moan,

> Were not the help of God almight. . . .
>   The White Lion [Norfolk] is laid to sleep
>   Through the envy of the Ape-clog [Suffolk]. . . .

Suffolk's arrest and banishment were greeted with approval, and his murder at sea brought laughter instead of tears.

> In the month of May, when grass groweth green,
>   Fragrant in her flowers with sweet savour,
> Jack Napes [Suffolk] would on the sea a mariner to have been,
>   With his clog and his chain, to seek more treasure.
> Such a pain pricked him, he asked [for] a confessor.
>   Nicholas [he sailed in *The Nicholas of the Tower*] said:
> 'I am ready thy confessor to be'.
>   He was holden so that he passed not that hour.

Edward IV's early successes inspired some joyful Yorkist verses, and, although Henry VI was spared the satirist's darts, Queen Margaret continued to be a favourite target even after she had been forced into exile. In 1462–3 a political poet attacked her once again:

> . . . She and her wicked affinity certain
>   Intend utterly to destroy this region
> For with them is but death and destruction,
>   Robbery and vengeance, with all rigour,
> Therefore all that hold of that opinion,
>   God send them a short end with much languor.

From Towton until Bosworth there was little to encourage verses in favour of the Lancastrians, though in 1483 some brave propagandist managed to fasten this scurrilous couplet on the door of St Paul's:

> The Cat [Catesby], the Rat [Ratcliffe], and Lovel our Dog,
>   Rule all England under a Hog [Richard III].

After Bosworth the political satirist had to be most circumspect. He could defile the memory of Richard III with safety, and no one was likely to protest if he added yet another to the numerous slanders against Queen Margaret. But to stray far from such well-trodden paths was to run the risk of being silenced for ever.

Bibliography of Fifteenth-Century Documents

Collections of letters referred to in this chapter are:

Original Letters Illustrative of English History, 1418–1726, H. Ellis, 11 vols. (1824–46).

Lettres de rois, reines et autres personnages des cours de France et d'Angleterre, J. J. Champollion-Figeac, 2 vols. (1839–47).

The Cely Papers, ed. H. E. Malden, Vol. 1, Camden Third Series.

The Stonor Letters and Papers, ed. C. L. Kingsford, Vols. 29, 30, and 34, Camden Third Series.

Plumpton Correspondence, ed. T. Stapleton, Vol. 4, Camden Old Series.

Paston Letters, ed. J. Gairdner, 6 vols. (1904).

Lettres de Louis XI, roi de France, ed. J. Vaesen, 11 vols. (1883–1909).

Foreign chronicles referred to are:

The Chronicle of Froissart, translated Lord Berners, ed. W. P. Ker, 6 vols. (1901–3) and 8 vols. (1927–8).

Histoire des règnes de Charles VII et de Louis XI, ed. J. Quicherat (1859).

Oeuvres, G. Chastellain, ed. K. de Lettenhove, 8 vols. (1883–4).

Mémoires, P. de Commines, ed. J. Calmette and G. Durville, 3 vols. (1924).

Chronique, M. d'Escouchy, ed. G. du Fresne de Beaucourt, 3 vols. (1863–4).

Mémoires, O. de la Marche, ed. H. Beaune and J. d'Arbaumont, 4 vols. (1883–8).

Chronique, J. de Molinet, ed. J. A. Buchon (1827).

Receueil des croniques, J. de Wavrin, ed. W. Hardy and E. L. C. P. Hardy, 5 Vols., Rolls Series (1864–91).

Chronique scandaleuse, ed. B. de Mandrot, 2 vols. (1894–6).

The collections of Italian state papers are:

Calendar of State Papers and Manuscripts existing in the archives and collections of Milan, ed. A. B. Hinds, Vol. 1, 1385–1618 (1912).

Calendar of State Papers and Manuscripts relating to English Affairs Preserved in the archives of Venice, ed. R. Brown, Vol. 1, 1202–1509 (1864).

English Historical Literature in the Fifteenth Century, C. L. Kingsford (1913) is an invaluable guide to the English chronicles.

The following are the chief sources:

The Arrival of King Edward IV, ed. J. Bruce, Vol. 1, Camden First Series.

The Brut, ed. F. W. D. Brie, Vol. 131, Early English Text Society.

Collections of a London Citizen, ed. J. Gairdner, Vol. 17, Camden Second Series (For *Gregory's Chronicle*).

English Chronicle, 1377–1461, ed. J. S. Davies, Vol. 64, Camden First Series.

The New Chronicles of England and of France, R. Fabyan, ed. H. Ellis (1811).

Six Town Chronicles, R. Flenley (1911).

Chronicle, J. Harding, ed. H. Ellis (1812).

Chronicles of London, ed. C. L. Kingsford (1905).

Three Fifteenth-Century Chronicles, ed. J. Gairdner, Vol. 28, Camden Second Series.

Chronicle, J. Warkworth, ed. J. O. Halliwell, Vol. 10, Camden First Series.

Political Poems and Songs, T. Wright, 2 vols., Rolls Series (1859–61).

THE SIXTEENTH CENTURY

I. HISTORIES AND OTHER WRITINGS

The reign and character of Richard III are subjects which bristle with difficulties. Scholars as well as fanatics can argue for hours about the degree of truth in Shakespeare's portrait of the king. Did Richard, because he could not 'prove a lover', determine to 'prove a villain'? Did he clothe his 'naked villainy with odd old ends stolen forth of holy writ', and so seem a saint when most he played the devil? Was he 'deformed, unfinished, sent before my time into this breathing world, scarce half made up'? Today, nearly five hundred years after Richard reigned, conscientious research and endless discussion have not yet produced widely-accepted answers to such questions.

The Tudor historians are the real villains in the story. It is possible to plead that they were villains by necessity, but there is no denying that they obscured the truth so effectively that we can still only see Richard's reign through a glass darkly. If they had not painted Richard a black-hearted scoundrel, then it would have been impossible for them to hail Henry Tudor as a national saviour and deliverer. After the battle of Bosworth it became imperative to avoid the slightest suggestion that Henry was anything less. By descent he had a comparatively poor claim to the throne. To justify his acceptance of the crown he exalted both the 'divine right' manifested by his victory at Bosworth and the authority of the act of parliament which confirmed his accession. But every would-be St George has need of a dragon. William the Conquerer had used Harold's broken oath: Adolf Hitler was later to choose the Treaty of Versailles. Henry VII's dragon could only be Richard III. His political supporters quickly established Richard's image as that of an evil usurper, and the historians consolidated the tradition. Thomas More wrote his condemnatory *History of King Richard*

III about 1513, and Polydore Vergil, in his *Anglica Historia* which first appeared in print in 1534, ended his account of Richard's reign with this judgement:

Suddenly the wretched man met a fate such as regularly befalls those who confound right, law, and decency with wilfulness, disloyalty, and wickedness.

They and their followers, particularly Edward Hall and Raphael Holinshed, did their work so well that Shakespeare had no need to invent a single detail. He could portray Richard as evil incarnate, and justify each detail by reference to one historian or another. 'Every tale condemns me for a villain', protested Shakespeare's Richard III. During the Tudor period this was literally true. Yet, although we know that all the Tudor historians displayed this strong political bias, we cannot reveal the truth by merely reversing their judgement. Just as it is probable that Harold did break a solemn promise, and just as we have to admit the harshness of some of the clauses of the treaty of Versailles, so it is likely that there was a measure of villainy in Richard's heart. But how much villainy and how much virtue we are not likely to determine by studying the work of sixteenth-century historians.

Their well-known fault of condemning all the political opponents of the Tudors does not render the writings of More, Vergil, Hall, and the others useless. On the contrary, their histories have a double value, for in their pages, which were printed and widely disseminated, they have preserved for us details gathered from sources now lost, and also given us direct evidence of Tudor political thinking. Their work is at once history and partisan politics, and any scholar using it has to keep this double attribute well in mind. But it is no easy task to sift truth from exaggeration, or justified criticism from vituperation. How much reliance, for example, can historians put in the following passages, the first More's account of the murder of the princes in the Tower, and the second Polydore Vergil's twin portraits of Henry VI (whose heir Henry Tudor claimed to be) and his queen, Margaret of Anjou?

Now fell the mischiefs thick. And as the thing evil gotten is never well kept, through all the time of his [Richard III's] reign, never ceased there cruel death and slaughter, till his own destruction ended it. But as he finished his time with the best death, and the most righteous, that is to wit his own; so began he with the most piteous and wicked, I mean the lamentable murder of his innocent nephews, the young king and his tender brother. . . . I shall rehearse you the dolorous end of those babes, not after every way that I have heard, but after that way that I have so heard by such men and by such means, as me thinketh it were hard but it should be true. King Richard after his coronation, taking his way to Gloucester to visit, in his new honour, the town of which he bare the name of his old [honour] devised as he rode to fulfil that thing which he before had intended. And forasmuch as his mind gave him that, his nephews living, men would not reckon that he could have right to the realm, he thought therefore without delay to rid them, as though the killing of his kinsmen could amend his cause, and make him a kindly king. Whereupon he sent one John Green, whom he specially trusted, unto Sir Robert Brackenbury constable of the Tower, with a letter and credence also, that the same Sir Robert should in any wise put the two children to death . . .

[Brackenbury refused to obey. Therefore, Richard ordered Brackenbury to surrender the keys of the Tower to Sir James Tyrell.]

. . . After which letter delivered and the keys received, Sir James appointed the night next ensuing to destroy them [the princes], devising before and preparing the means. The prince, as soon as the protector left that name and took himself as king, had it shown unto him that he should not reign, but his uncle should have the crown. At which word the prince, sore abashed, began to sigh and said: 'Alas I would my uncle would let me have my life yet, though I lose my kingdom.' Then he that told him the tale used him with good words, and put him in the best comfort he could. But forthwith was the prince and his brother both shut up, and all other removed from them, only one called Black Will or William Slaughter except, set to serve them and see them sure . . . Sir James Tyrell devised that they should be murdered in their beds. To the execution whereof, he appointed Miles Forest, one of the four that kept them, a fellow fleshed [initiated] in murder before time. To him he joined one John Dighton, his own horse-keeper, a big, broad, square, strong knave. Then all the others being removed from them, this Miles Forest and John Dighton, about midnight (the sely [innocent] children lying in their beds) came into the chamber, and suddenly lapped [wrapped] them up among the clothes, so bewrapped them and entangled them, keeping down by force the feather bed and pillows hard unto their mouths, that within a while smothered and stifled, their breath failing, they gave up to God their innocent souls into the joys of heaven, leaving to the tormentors their bodies dead in the bed.

King Henry was a man of mild and plain-dealing disposition, who preferred peace before wars, quietness before troubles, honesty before utility, and leisure before business; and to be short, there was not in this world a more pure, more honest, and more holy creature. There was in him honest 'shamfastnes', modesty, innocence and perfect patience, taking all human chances, miseries, and all afflictions of this life in so good a part as though he had justly by some his offence deserved the same. He ruled his own affections, that he might more easily rule his own subjects; he gaped not after riches, nor thirsted for honour and worldly estimation, but was careful only for his soul's health. . . .

On the other side, Margaret his wife, a woman of sufficient forecast, very desirous of renown, full of policy, counsel, comely behaviour, and all manly qualities, in whom appeared great wit, great diligence, great heed and carefulness: but she was of the kind of other women, who commonly are much given and very ready to mutability and change. This woman when she perceived the king her husband to do nothing of his own head, but to rule wholly by the duke of Gloucester's advice, and that himself took no great heed or thought as concerning the government, determined to take upon her that charge, and by little and little to deprive the duke of that great authority which he had; lest she also might be reported to have little wit, who would suffer her husband being now of perfect years to be under another man's government.

If Tudor historians display so much bias and feeling in writing of people and events in the fifteenth century, can historians rely upon what they have to say about their own times? Polydore Vergil's *Anglica Historia*, which he began to write at Henry VII's command, is avowedly a justification of the accession and the policy of the Tudors, and Edward Hall's *The Union of the Two Noble and Illustre Famelies of Lancastre and Yorke* is a panegyric of Henry VIII and the establishment of a national church in England. Stow and Holinshed were no less partisan. Yet three of these four authors lived through many of the years about which they wrote. They were eye-witnesses of some of the events they described, and their ears were wide open to current opinion and debate. Moreover, they were deliberately trying to write history, and not merely keeping annals or a diary of events. For them, unlike for most of the chroniclers, all facts 'were not born free and equal'. Some had significance, others had not: events required examining and analysing as well as narrating. In much the same way as the first telephones resembled speaking tubes, the form of the work of these historians is reminiscent of the chronicle, but its avowed purpose was more profound. It was carefully considered history such as had never before been written in English.

Clearly, historians today must welcome Vergil's and Hall's evidence on the reigns of Henry VII and Henry VIII just as historians in the future will be thankful for the equally partial *Second World War* by W. S. Churchill or for the many partisan studies of the inter-war and post-war years which have been written by politicians and commentators of all political parties. Polydore Vergil knew Henry VII well. His description tells us more of the man than either Michel Sittow's portrait in the National Portrait Gallery or Torrigiano's sculptured image on the king's tomb in Westminster Abbey.

His body was slender but well built and strong; his height above average. His appearance was remarkably attractive and his face was cheerful, especially when speaking; his eyes were small and blue, his teeth few, poor and blackish; his hair was thin and white; his complexion sallow. His spirit was distinguished, wise, and prudent: his mind was brave and resolute and never, even at moments of the greatest danger, deserted him. He had a most pertinacious memory. Withal he was not devoid of scholarship. In government he was shrewd and prudent, so that no one dared to get the better of him through deceit or guile. He was gracious and kind and was as attentive to his visitors as he was easy of access. His hospitality was splendidly generous; he was fond of having foreigners at his court and he freely conferred favours on them. But those of his subjects who were indebted to him and who did not pay him due honour or who were generous only with promises, he treated with harsh severity. . . .

Hall in his *History* described many occasions in the reign of Henry VIII in eyewitness detail. Obviously he loved spectacle, and he was ever anxious to impress his reader with the magnificence of the court and the state occasions. His word-pictures are arrestingly vivid. The following is part of his description of the coronation ceremonies in June 1509:

And the morrow following being Saturday, the xxiii day of the said month, his Grace, with the Queen, departed from the Tower, through the city of London, against whose coming, the streets where his Grace should pass, were hanged with Tapestry and cloth of Arras. And the great part of the south side of Cheap, with cloth of gold, and some part of Cornhill also . . . His Grace wore in his upperest apparel, a robe of Crimson Velvet, furred with Ermine, his jacket or coat of raised gold, the placard embroidered with Diamonds, Rubies, Emeralds, great Pearls, and other rich Stones, a great Baldric about his neck, of great Balases. The Trapper of his Horse, Damask gold, with a deep purfle of Ermine. . . .

The morrow following being Sunday, and also Midsummer Day, this noble Prince with his Queen, at time convenient, under their Canopies borne by the Barons of the five Ports, went from the said Palace [Westminster] to Westminster Abbey upon cloth, called vulgarly cloth of Ray, the which cloth was cut and spoiled by the rude and common people immediately after their repair into the Abbey, where, according to the sacred observance and ancient custom, his Grace with the Queen were anointed and crowned, by the Archbishop of Canterbury. . . .

For the more honour, and ennobling of this triumphant coronation, there were prepared, both Jousts and Tourneys, to be done in the Palace of Westminster, where, for the King's Grace, and the Queen, was framed a fair house, covered with tapestry, and hanged with rich cloths of Arras. . . . And out at several places of the same Castle, as well the day of the coronation as the said days of the Jousts and Tourney, out of the mouths of certain beasts, or gargoyles did run red, white, and claret wine. . . .

Topical comment and topographical descriptions by these Tudor historians and other contemporary writers are equally valuable. Polydore Vergil was born in Italy. He came to England in 1502 as a young man, and so he saw the country through foreign eyes. Here are his comments upon the origin of the agricultural crisis of his day:

For half a century or more previously, the sheep-farming nobles had tried to find devices whereby they might increase the annual income of their lands. As a result the yeomen had incurred very considerable losses. The sheep farmers, cultivating pasturage (after the manner of Arabs) rather than arable, began everywhere to employ far fewer agricultural labourers, to destroy rural dwelling-houses, to create vast deserts, to allow the land to waste while filling it up with herds, flocks and a multitude of beasts; in like fashion they fenced off all these pastures to keep them private, thus establishing in their own right a monopoly of wool, sheep and cattle. From this three evil consequences ensued for the state. First, the number of peasants, upon whom the prince chiefly relies for waging war, was reduced. Second, a larger number of villages and towns, many stripped of inhabitants, were ruined. Third, the wool and cloth which was then produced, as well as the flesh of all kinds of animals which is fit for human consumption, began to sell much more dearly than it used to do, so that the price has not really dropped even to this day. . . .

Another Italian, this time unknown but suspected to be a Venetian, has left us in *A Relation of the Island of England* a lively description of his impressions of the people of Tudor England. These tart comments are typical of the whole manuscript:

The English are, for the most part, both men and women of all ages, handsome and well proportioned; though not quite so much so, in my opinion, as it had been asserted to me, before your Magnificence went to that kingdom; and I have understood from persons acquainted with these countries, that the Scots are much handsomer; and that the English are great lovers of themselves, and of everything belonging to them; they think that there are no other men than

themselves, and no other world but England; and whenever they see
a handsome foreigner, they say that 'he looks like an Englishman,'
and that 'it is a great pity that he should not be an Englishman;' and
when they partake of any delicacy with a foreigner, they ask him,
'whether such a thing is made in *their* country?' They take great
pleasure in having a quantity of excellent victuals, and also in remaining a long time at table, being very sparing of wine when they
drink it at their own expense. And this, it is said, they do in order to
induce their other English guests to drink wine in moderation also;
not considering it any inconvenience for three or four persons to
drink out of the same cup. Few people keep wine in their own houses,
but buy it, for the most part, at a tavern; and when they mean to
drink a great deal, they go to the tavern, and this is done not only by
the men, but by ladies of distinction. The deficiency of wine, however, is amply supplied by the abundance of ale and beer, to the use
of which these people are become so habituated, that, at an entertainment where there is plenty of wine, they will drink them in prefer-
ence to it, and in great quantities.

Erasmus was another distinguished visitor to the England of
Henry VII and Henry VIII. In several early letters he wrote
kindly about the country, but as he was given to extravagant
and flattering comment, it is wise to take such passages as this
with a pinch of salt. In 1499 he wrote to Robert Fisher, an
English friend living in Italy:

But how do you like our England, you will say. Believe me, my
Robert, when I answer that I never liked anything so much before. I
find the climate both pleasant and wholesome; and I have met with
so much kindness, and so much learning, not hackneyed and trivial,
but deep, accurate, ancient, Latin and Greek, that but for the curiosity
of seeing it, I do not now so much care for Italy. When I hear my
Colet, I seem to be listening to Plato himself. In Grocin who does
not marvel at such a perfect round of learning? What can be more
acute, profound, and delicate than the judgement of Linacre? What
has Nature ever created more gentle, more sweet, more happy than
the genius of Thomas More?

In a more sober letter to a friend in Paris in 1505, he still admitted
that there were five or six men in London, 'who are accurate

scholars in both tongues [Latin and Greek], such as I think even Italy does not at present possess', but in the privacy of letters to Italian friends he exploded about the meanness and dirtiness of the cold English houses, the monotony of the food, and the lack of safety on the roads. He and Andrea Ammonio, an Italian who became one of Henry VIII's secretaries, exchanged such confidential comments as these: 'About St Paul's there is, as you know', wrote Ammonio, 'a college of some learned men, who are said to fare well; I reckon it living in a sewer.' 'For while these people', wrote Erasmus from Cambridge, 'are nothing but Cyprian bulls and dung-eaters, they think they are the only people who feed on ambrosia and Jupiter's brain.' Even so, Erasmus had a real affection for this country. In his fifties he told Archbishop Warham that 'he proposed to remove to England as a sheltered and distant retreat', and to his friend John Fisher, bishop of Rochester, he described England as 'a locality out of the world, and perhaps the least tainted part of Christendom'.

John Skelton, the scholar and poet who helped to tutor the future Henry VIII, thought this 'least tainted' England tainted enough. He joined in the general paean of praise for the young king –

> But now will I expound
>   What nobleness doth abound
> And what honour is found
>   And what virtues be resident
> In our royal regent,
>   Our peerless president,
> Our king most excellent . . .

but he was most critical of the court and the leaders of the church.

> Laymen say indeed
>   How they [the clergy] take no heed
> Their silly sheep to feed,
>   But pluck away and pull

> The fleeces of their wool . . .
>   All to have promotion
> There is their whole devotion,
>   With money, if it will hap
> To catch the forked cap [mitre]. . . .

He was particularly bitter when attacking Wolsey. He detested
the cardinal's power and pride, and could not overlook either
his humble birth or his lack of the highest academic honours.
There is an odd mixture of old-fashioned medieval and
up-to-date Renaissance thinking in *Why come ye not to court?*,
which he wrote in 1522.

> But however he [Wolsey] was born,
>   Men would have the less scorn
> If he could consider
>   His birth and room together,
> And call to his mind
>   How noble and how kind
> To him he hath found
>   Our sovereign lord . . .
> For he was, pardee,
>   No doctor of divinity,
> Nor doctor of the law,
>   Nor of none other saw;
> But a poor master of arts
>   God wot, had little part
> Of the quatrivials [*quadrivium*]
>   Nor yet of trivials [*trivium*]
> His Latin tongue doth hobble,
>   He doth but clout and cobble
> In Tully's [Cicero's] faculty
>   Called humanity.
> Yet proudly he dare pretend
>   How no man can him amend. . . .

The publication of this poem, a more direct attack on the cardinal than *Speak, Parrot* which had appeared the year before, so
angered Wolsey that Skelton thought it prudent to seek sanctuary in Westminster Abbey. Few critics would attribute a

high degree of poetical skill to Skelton, but for the historian his verses have the same kind of value as have Dryden's *Absalom and Achitophel* or Pope's *Dunciad*.

Enthusiasm for the new learning characterized several aristocratic and many middle-class families during the long reign of Henry VIII. The printed book helped both to satisfy and stimulate this enthusiasm, so that a widening stream of books flowed steadily from the presses. A number of them can now be regarded as primary historical documents. The first third of the sixteenth century was a period of thinking and rethinking. Venerable established beliefs and practices in politics, theology, education, science, and economics were all being questioned or denied, and scores of people were raising their voices and using their goose quills either to defend the old, thrust forward the new, or try to find a compromise between the two. We cannot overhear what these disputers said, but in the pages of their books, we can still appreciate their arguments and seek reasons for their actions. Sir John Fortescue's *Governance of England*, written in Yorkist times but still influential a couple of generations later, More's well-known *Utopia*, Edmund Dudley's *The Tree of Commonwealth*, and William Tyndale's *Obedience of a Christian Man* must remain obligatory reading for all who would master the political thinking of the age. Eliot, More, and the Spaniard, Vives, have left us treatises on education, one of the subjects most discussed by their contemporaries, and Fitzherbert's *Boke of Husbandry* is one of the most useful of the many books and pamphlets written at that time on farming. The growth of patriotism in Tudor times led naturally to a curiosity about England's countryside and its inhabitants. Geography and topography began to interest an increasing number of people, and, though the first county maps were not produced until Elizabeth's reign, John Leland, one of Henry VIII's household officials, undertook a series of exploratory journeys in England and Wales between 1534 and 1539. He never wrote the travel book which he intended, but his notes have been preserved in his *Itinerary*. He whets our appetite for more detail, but we must be thankful that his jottings and field notes were preserved. These two extracts, typical examples of his writing, concern Manchester and Tenby.

Here about I passed over Medlock river, and so within less than a mile to Manchester. Manchester on the south side of the Irwell river standeth in Salfordshire [Salford hundred], and is the fairest, best builded, quickest, and most populous town of all Lancashire, yet is in it but one parish church, but is a college and almost throughout double aisled out of square, hard-wearing stone, whereof a goodly quarry is hard by the town. There be divers stone bridges in the town, but the best of three arches is over Irwell. This bridge divideth Manchester from Salford, the which is a large suburb to Manchester. On this bridge is a pretty little chapel. The next is the bridge that is over the Irk river, on the which the fair builded college standeth as in the very point of the mouth of it. For hard thereby it runneth into Irwell. On Irk river are divers fair mills that serve the town. In the town be two fair market places. And almost two flight-shots without the town beneath on the same side of Irwell yet be seen the dikes and foundations of Old Man Castle in a ground now enclosed. The stones of the ruins of this castle were translated toward making of bridges for the town. It is not long season since the church of Manchester was collegiated. The town of Manchester standeth on a hard rock of stone, else Irwell, as well appeareth on the west bank, had been harmful to the town. Irwell is not navigable but in some places, for weirs and rocks.

From Swansea to Kidweli a 12 miles. From Kidweli to Tenby a 16 miles. Tenby is a walled town hard on the Severn Sea in Pembrokeshire. There is a bay and a pier made for ships. The town is very wealthy by merchandise, but it is not very big having but one parish church. One thing is to be marvelled at. There is no well in the town, as it is said, whereby they be forced to fetch their water at St John's without the town.

John Stow wrote a detailed account of Tudor London in his *Survey of London*. English men and women of the sixteenth century were particularly proud of their capital, which even the contemporary Scottish poet, William Dunbar, described as 'sovereign of cities'. It is true that Stow only wrote his book in the last decade of Elizabeth's reign, but he was so conscious of London's history and development that the *Survey* is an excellent guide to the city that existed nearly a century earlier.

2. ACTS OF PARLIAMENT AND OTHER OFFICIAL RECORDS

One of the perennial difficulties which face the historian is the dispersal of his raw material. The Public Record Office, the British Museum, the Houses of Parliament, university and major public libraries, county record offices, cathedrals, parish churches, lawyer's offices, business houses, and the muniment rooms of landed families can all be storing the documents which he seeks to consult. The lists, guides, and calendars issued by the more professional of these different repositories are helpful and time-saving, but no historian can ever be sure that he has inspected every significant document relevant to the period or subject he is studying. Many have had the mortifying experience of discovering 'new' basic or illuminating material for the very topic on which, a few weeks earlier, they have published a book or an article. Hence, in the long run, no work is more helpful to historical scholarship than printing texts and calendars of collections of documents. It is a gigantic and expensive task. Nineteenth-century scholars were the first to tackle the job systematically, and each successive generation has continued the work. Such official bodies as the Record Commissioners and the Royal Commission on Historical Manuscripts, such national societies as the Harleian and the Camden, as well as some fifty or sixty county or regional societies have each published scores of volumes. The enthusiasm for the work is as good as ever, but what has already been achieved, most valuable though it is, is no more than a beginning. For decades yet to come researchers will still have to travel from one collection of documents to another not only to check transcripts made by their predecessors – always a wise precaution – but also to read through boxes of uncalendared documents to see if they contain any material they require.

Historians interested in England in the early sixteenth century, therefore, are particularly fortunate in that good collections of official and semi-official documents have already been printed for the reigns of Henry VII and Henry VIII. In addition to the calendars of patent rolls, close rolls, and inquisitions *post mortem*, to the collections of Scottish, Irish, Spanish, Milanese, and Venetian papers relating to English affairs, and to Rymer's *Foedera* and other collections of official documents which cover considerably longer periods than these two reigns, successive generations of Tudor scholars have brought together and printed documents from a scatter of sources. In 1858 James Gairdner edited for the Rolls Series a Henry VII miscellany, which included a life of the king written by Bernard André, a contemporary scholar and courtier. Three years later, in the same series, he published the first of two volumes entitled *Letters and papers illustrative of the reigns of Richard III and Henry VII*. In the 1870s William Campbell edited two more volumes of *Materials for a history of the reign of Henry VII*, and just before the First World War, A. F. Pollard produced, in three volumes, *The Reign of Henry VII from Contemporary Sources*. Together, these collections cover the chief official records, the London chronicles, and contemporary literature, and the editors searched for material abroad as well as in the main archives in London. Even so, the printed sources for the years 1485 to 1509 look thin when compared with the thirty-eight large books which contain *Letters and papers, foreign and domestic, of the reign of Henry VIII*. The first volume was published by the Public Record Office in 1862, the last in 1932. J. S. Brewer, J. Gairdner, and R. H. Brodie were the three scholars most responsible for this remarkable compilation. In its thousands of pages they included, either in full or in summary, all the chancery and exchequer papers they could find in the Public Record Office, official and private letters, relevant papers from collections in the British Museum and in foreign archives, details of court revels and jollifications, and descriptions of contemporary maps and drawings. The general historian could hardly imagine a more useful collection for his purpose: even the specialists, however obscure their speciality, cannot ignore it.

Between 1810 and 1834, in six folio volumes, the Record Commissioners published *Valor Ecclesiasticus*, a kind of ecclesiastical Domesday Survey compiled by Sir Thomas Audley's officers in 1535. Parliament had decreed that, annually from 1535 onwards, the crown should take as tax a tenth of the net incomes of all spiritual benefices. This necessitated an immediate survey of church wealth, and, in January 1535, Henry VIII's chancellor, Audley, sent out commissioners, armed with questionnaires and specific injunctions, to list in each county the lands, buildings, tithes, benefactions, and other sources of income possessed by cathedrals, parish churches, monasteries, and friaries. No previous visitation had been anything like so comprehensive, nor had it been carried out chiefly by laymen as this one was. Audley's commissioners worked rapidly. They handed in most of their information by midsummer, and early in 1536 the summarized and edited report was ready for the king. Not all of the original has survived. The details of Berkshire, Cambridgeshire, Essex, Hertfordshire, Northumberland, Rutland, and some parts of Middlesex and Yorkshire are missing but the summary of all benefice incomes is complete. The manuscript shows signs of haste, but though the commissioners made shrewd guesses at many of the details of the valuation, the result, as far as it can be checked by other documents, seems to be reasonably accurate. It tended to underestimate incomes, but it served Thomas Cromwell admirably when, almost simultaneously, he began to plan the phased dissolution of the monasteries.

Valor Ecclesiasticus and Domesday Survey are alike both in intention – to provide an up-to-date basis for taxation – and in form, except that the administrative units of the *Valor* were not counties and hundreds but dioceses and archdeaconries. Both manuscripts were written in abbreviated Latin, both recorded the essential facts in the minimum number of words. The length of each entry varied with the economic importance of the institution. Parish churches, such as Millom in Cumberland, were dispensed with in a few lines:

The monastery of Furness is rector; Edmund Staneforth incumbent.
  The aforesaid vicarage is worth in

	£	s.	d.		£	s.	d.
House with garden and orchard per annum		6.	8				
Tithes of corn and hay	4.	6.	8	⎫			
wool and lambs		13.	4	⎬	8.	15.	0
piglets and chickens ..		5.	0	⎪			
Lenten payments	3.	3.	4	⎭			

Repayments, namely to			
Synod 3s. 0d.	⎫		
Proctor [of Furness Abbey] 6s. 8d.	⎭	9.	8

	£	s.	d.
Net value	8.	5.	4

Richer churches from more prosperous parts of England took a little more space. These are the figures for the receipts in the parish of North Cerney in the diocese of Gloucester:

		£	s.	d.
In the parish 96 acres of arable land	—	1.	4.	0
70 acres of pasture	—		14.	0
tithes of corn	—	10.	6.	0
the benefice and offerings	—	1.	6.	11½
hay	—	1.	0.	0
wool	—	6.	0.	0
lambs	—		17.	0
cows and calves	—		8.	1
flax, eggs, fruit, piglets and geese	—		5.	10

	£	s.	d.
In all	22.	1.	10½

Against this the commissioners acknowledge necessary payments of 11s. 5d., so that the net annual value of the parish for tax purposes was £21 10s. 5½d.

Cathedrals and the larger monasteries were far more complicated to assess. They held scattered temporalities, in the form of arable land, meadow, buildings, woods, rents, and services, and equally scattered spiritualities, in the form of tithes, offerings, pensions, and other traditional payments. The following extracts from the assessment of the Benedictine monastery of Peterborough illustrate how complicated monastic income had become by the end of the Middle Ages, and how thoroughly the commissioners probed the accounts in the short time available. Peterborough, in 1535, was still part of the diocese of Lincoln: it was not until after the dissolution that the monastic buildings were transformed into Peterborough Cathedral.

Temporalities within the county of Northampton.
The site of the aforesaid monastery of Peterborough
with the approaches, gardens, orchards, and
various houses within the precincts, and also the demesne,
meadow and pastures in the hands of the abbot and
community, with the tithes of the same demesne, assessed by
the king's commissioners as is fully contained in the
declaration made therein

				£	s.	d.
				55.	3.	10

Rents of assize with the rents and farms of tenants in
various lordships, vills, hamlets, and parishes in the same:
The abbot's demesne

				£	s.	d.
The lordship of Peterborough	..	..	..	70.	6.	8
Boroughbury [in Peterborough]	..	..	..	63.	15.	1½
Eye	..	..	..	63.	3.	10
Thorpe	..	..	..	41.	3.	10
Castor	..	..	..	34.	9.	2½
Werrington	..	..	..	35.	19.	2
Walton	..	..	..	16.	1.	8
Glinton	..	..	..	57.	13.	8½
Stamford [Baron]	..	..	..	18.	14.	4

	£	s.	d.
Kettering	97.	8.	$9\frac{3}{4}$
Irthlingborough	33.	8.	$1\frac{1}{2}$
Stanwick	21.	15.	$6\frac{1}{2}$
Oundle	88.	18.	$0\frac{1}{2}$
Ashton	21.	16.	10
Warmington	49.	6.	$5\frac{1}{4}$
Cottingham	45.	17.	4
The hundred of Nassaburgh	15.	0.	$5\frac{3}{4}$
The hundred of Polebrook and Navisford	10.	18.	$1\frac{1}{2}$
The hundred of Huxloe	11.	18.	$0\frac{1}{2}$

The portion of the community

The cellarer

In the vill of Burgh [Peterborough]	7.	2.	8
Belsize	5.	0.	0
Glinton	6.	0.	0

The sacrist

In the vill	11.	11.	11
Paston	5.	0.	0
Polebrook	8.	6.	$2\frac{3}{4}$

The almoner

In the vill	14.	8.	$7\frac{1}{2}$
Sutton	14.	12.	$0\frac{1}{2}$
Maxey	5.	6.	1
Clapton	3.	8.	$5\frac{1}{2}$
Warmington	2.	4.	$0\frac{1}{2}$

The bursar

In the vill	28.	3.	$4\frac{1}{4}$
Gunthorpe	11.	1.	$9\frac{1}{2}$
Southorpe, with its members	8.	4.	11
Luddington	8.	6.	$0\frac{1}{2}$

The warden of the Lady Chapel

In the vill	7.	11.	$1\frac{1}{2}$

The chamberlain

In the vill	7.	3.	6
Northborough	5.	19.	1

The subsacrist, in the vill	2.	1.	2
The warden of Oxney	4.	4.	5

The monk of the works

	£	s.	d.
Pilsgate	21.	13.	$0\frac{1}{4}$
The infirmarian, in the vill	6.	2.	$8\frac{1}{2}$
The pittancer, in the vill	5.	6.	2
The guest-master, in the vill	1.	5.	6
The refectorian, in the vill	2.	15.	0
Warden of the altar of the Holy Cross, in the vill..	4.	6.	2
Precentor, in the vill		18.	4
As is clear from the declaration made therein and examined			
Total	1,005.	17.	$6\frac{1}{4}$

[SIC]

The commissioners then listed incomes from mills, tolls, markets, woods, fines, and perquisites of courts. The total of all the monastery's temporalities in Northamptonshire was £1,088 10s. $7\frac{3}{8}$d. The list of its spiritualities, parcelled out to the various obedientiaries or office holders in the monastery, began thus:

	£	s.	d.
Profits from:			
Oundle rectory, leased by indenture to Robert Baker	54.	6.	8
Warmington rectory, assessed with the cellarer's office, leased to Miles Forest	34.	0.	0
Maxey rectory	13.	16.	8
Gunthorpe, the tithe of sheaves of corn therefrom, assessed with the almoner's office	11.	0.	0
The vill of Burgh, the tithe of sheaves of corn therefrom, assessed with the sacrist's office, leased to William Alger, and	18.	0.	0
Eye, the tithe of sheaves of corn in this hamlet, assessed with [the office of] the warden of Oxney	5.	0.	0
As is clear from our examination of the said declaration thereon	136.	3.	4

The commissioners found another £45 12s. 8d. in pensions and tithes in Northamptonshire alone. From Lincolnshire, Leicestershire, Huntingdonshire, Rutland, Nottinghamshire, and

Middlesex came further payments, mostly temporalities, so that the gross annual revenue of the monastery eventually reached £1,979 7s. 5⅝d. Against this the commissioners allowed a long list of rents, fees, pensions, and alms amounting in all to £299 11s. 9d., and, as the report concluded, leaving the monastery a net assessment of £1,679 15s. 8⅝d. It was the net figure which primarily interested Henry VIII and Cromwell, but all the items in the accounts are of interest to historians. They give the ecclesiastical historian a comprehensive view of the estates of the church, the economic historian useful details of the distribution of wealth throughout England and Wales, and the local historian the pattern of landholding and the relative importance of different crops and stock – all on the eve of events which were destined to transform the whole picture. One might almost say that *Valor Ecclesiasticus* gives historians their farewell view of medieval England.

Had the first two Tudors decided to legislate through orders in council and to tax by royal writ, they would have been acting in line with current European ideas about the function of monarchy and the art of good government. It is most unlikely that there would have been any immediate substantial protest from their people, so long as they continued to ensure order at home and protection from enemies overseas. Yet both kings chose to follow English constitutional practice and make laws by sealing acts of parliament, and levy taxes on the authority of parliamentary grants. This does not mean that the Tudors were constitutional sovereigns in the usual modern interpretation of that term. For them parliament was still a court with the king sitting in the seat of the chief judge. The Star Chamber, the Duchy Chamber Court of Lancaster, and, a little later, the Court of High Commission were among the important courts which issued orders and decrees as well as made judicial decisions. Each of them had its own restricted field of administration, but Henry VIII especially recognized no limits to the authority of the High Court of Parliament. Usually through members of the council, he called on the two houses favourably to consider a wide variety of proposals concerning every aspect of temporal and ecclesiastical government. Lords and commons discussed the king's suggested legislation, and then framed their reply in the form of a petition to the crown. If it was favourable to his wishes – and it usually was – the king turned the petition into a statute by the simple process of accepting it. By force of tradition, which had grown strong since the fourteenth century, all England recognized that nothing had greater authority than an act of parliament. Nothing could countermand it except another act passed on a later occasion.

The form of some of these early Tudor acts, such as the acts of attainder against Catherine Howard and the duke of Buckingham, is identical with that of a judicial court's verdict. In 1531, for example, Richard Roose was found guilty of attempting to poison Bishop Fisher. He was condemned to a horrible death as part of an act passed against poisoners.

The King's Royal Majesty calling to his most blessed remembrance that the making of good and wholesome laws and due execution of the same against the offenders thereof is the only cause that good obedience and order hath been preserved in this realm, and his Highness having most tender zeal to the same, among other things considering that man's life above all things is chiefly to be favoured, and voluntary murders most highly to be detested and abhorred, and specially of all kinds of murders poisoning, which in this realm hitherto, our Lord be thanked, hath been most rare and seldom committed or practised; and now in the time of this present Parliament ... one Richard Roose ... of his most wicked and damnable disposition did cast a certain venom or poison into a vessel replenished with yeast or barm standing in the kitchen of the Reverend Father in God John, Bishop of Rochester, ... with which yeast or barm and other things convenient porridge or gruel was forthwith made for his family ... whereby not only the number of 17 persons of his said family which did eat of that porridge were mortally infected and poisoned. ... Our said Sovereign Lord the King ... hath ordained and enacted by authority of this present Parliament that the said poisoning be adjudged and deemed as high treason, And ... that the said Richard Roose shall be therefor boiled to death without having any advantage of his clergy. And that from henceforth every wilful murder of any person or persons by any whatsoever person or persons hereafter to be committed and done by mean or way of poisoning shall be reputed, deemed, and judged in the law to be high treason. . . .

Henry VIII's matrimonial ups and downs caused him to manipulate and remanipulate the order of succession. In 1536 he decided to secure the throne for the unborn child of Jane Seymour. The act which put his will into force reads as if he were graciously submitting to the pleadings of his people:

And forasmuch as it standeth at this present time in the only pleasure and will of Almighty God whether your Majesty shall have heirs begotten and procreated between your Highness and your said most dear and entirely beloved wife Queen Jane, or else any lawful heirs and issues hereafter of your own body begotten by any other lawful wife, and if such heirs should fail (as God defend) and no provision made in your life who should rule and govern this realm for lack of such heirs, that then this realm after your transitory life shall be destitute of a Governor, or else percase encumbered with such a person that would covet to aspire to the same whom the subjects of this realm shall not find in their hearts to love, dread, and obediently serve as their Sovereign Lord . . . For reformation and remedy whereof, we your most bounden and loving subjects . . . Do therefore most humbly beseech your Highness that it may be enacted, for avoiding of all ambiguities, doubts, divisions, and occasions in that behalf, by your most royal Majesty, by the assent of us the Lords spiritual and temporal and the Commons in this your present Parliament assembled and by authority of the same, That your Highness shall have full and plenar power and authority to give, dispose, appoint, assign, declare, and limit, by your letters patents under your great seal or else by your last Will made in writing and signed with your most gracious hand, at your only pleasure from time to time hereafter, the imperial Crown of this realm and all other the premises thereunto belonging. . . .

Whatever form these acts might assume, however, their text is really the voice of the king speaking to his subjects. With the advice and assent of the lords, spiritual and temporal, and of his

faithful commons, he, king and sovereign lord, announces his will. And what the king wills has the force of law. For this reason the preface of an act, which sets out the need, or at least the official need, for its enactment, is worth as careful study as the clauses which follow. Henry VII usually contented himself with comparatively pithy statements, but, especially in his more controversial acts, his son thought it wise to begin with a detailed explanation and justification. The following two short prefaces are to the Beggars Act of 1495, Henry VII's first attempt to solve the chronic problem of vagabondage, and to the well known Statute of Liveries of 1504.

Forasmuch as the King's Grace most entirely desireth amongst all earthly things the prosperity and restfulness of this his land and his subjects of the same to live quietly and surefully to the pleasure of God and according to his laws, willing and always of his pity intending to reduce them thereunto by softer means than by such extreme rigour therefor purveyed in [the Beggars Act of 1383], considering also the great charges that should grow to his subjects for bringing of vagabonds to the gaols according to the same Statute and the long abiding of them therein, whereby by likelihood many of them should lose their lives, In moderating of the said Statute his Highness wills by the authority of this present Parliament it be ordained and enacted, That . . .

The King our Sovereign Lord calleth to his remembrance that where before this time divers statutes for punishment of such persons that give or receive liveries, or that retain any person or persons . . . have been made and established, and that notwithstanding divers persons have taken upon them some to give and some to receive liveries and to retain and be retained . . . and little or nothing is or hath been done for the punishment of the offenders in that behalf, Wherefore our Sovereign Lord the King . . . hath ordained, stablished, and enacted that all his statutes and ordinances afore this time made against such as make unlawful retainers and such as so be retained, or that give or receive livery, be plainly observed and kept and put in due execution.

Compared with these straightforward statements, the prefaces to such acts as the Restraint of Annates in 1532 or the Dissolution of the Lesser Monasteries in 1536 read like opening speeches in favour of the motion. They plead, and sometimes overplead, the cause. They served the king's government in much the same way that a party political broadcast serves the government today: they were a mixture of truth, half-truth, and bland, inconsequential statement.

Forasmuch as it is well perceived by long approved experience that great and inestimable sums of money be daily conveyed out of this realm to the impoverishment of the same, and specially such sums of money as the Pope's Holiness, his predecessors, and the Court of Rome by long time have heretofore taken of all and singular those spiritual persons which have been named, elected, presented, or postulated to be archbishops or bishops within this realm of England, under the title of Annates, otherwise called firstfruits . . . By occasion whereof not only the treasure of this realm hath been greatly conveyed out of the same, but also it hath happened many times by occasion of death unto such archbishops and bishops so newly promoted within two or three years after his or their consecration, that his or their friends by whom he or they have been holpen to advance and make payment of the said Annates or firstfruits have been thereby utterly undone and impoverished; And for because the said Annates have risen, grown, and increased by an uncharitable custom grounded upon no just or good title . . . The noblemen therefore of this realm and the wise, sage, politic commons of the same assembled in this present Parliament, considering that the Court of Rome ceaseth not to tax, take, and exact the said great sums of money under the title of Annates or firstfruits as is aforesaid to the great damage of the said prelates and this realm, which Annates or firstfruits were first suffered to be taken within the same realm for the only defence of Christian people against the infidels, and now they be claimed and demanded as mere duty, only for lucre, against all right and conscience, insomuch that it is evidently known that there hath passed out of this realm unto the Court of Rome since the second year of the reign of the most noble Prince of famous memory King Henry VII unto this present time . . . the sum of eight hundred thousand ducats, amounting in sterling money at the least to eight score thousand pounds, besides other great and intolerable sums which have yearly been conveyed to the said Court of Rome by many other ways and means, to the great impoverishment of this realm; And albeit that our said Sovereign Lord the King and all his natural subjects as well spiritual as temporal be as obedient, devout, Catholic, and humble children of God and Holy Church as any people be within any realm christened, yet the said exactions of Annates or firstfruits be so intolerable and importable to this realm that it is considered and declared by the whole body of this realm now represented by all the estates of the same assembled in this present Parliament that the King's Highness before Almighty God is bound as by the duty of a good Christian prince, for the conservation and preservation of the good estate and commonwealth of this his realm, to do all that in him is to obviate, repress, and redress the said abusions and exactions of Annates or firstfruits; And because that divers prelates of this realm be now in extreme age and in other debilities of their bodies, so that of likelihood bodily death in short time shall or may succeed unto them; by reason whereof great sums of money shall shortly after their deaths be conveyed unto the Court of Rome for the unreasonable and uncharitable causes abovesaid, to the universal damage, prejudice, and impoverishment of this realm, if speedy remedy be not in due time provided; It is therefore ordained, established, and enacted by authority of this present Parliament that the unlawful payments of Annates or firstfruits . . . shall from henceforth utterly cease . . .

Forasmuch as manifest sin, vicious, carnal, and abominable living, is daily used and committed amongst the little and small abbeys, priories, and other religious houses of monks, canons, and nuns, where the congregation of such religious persons is under the number of 12 persons, whereby the governors of such religious houses and their convent spoil, destroy, consume, and utterly waste, as well their churches, monasteries, priories, principal houses, farms, granges, lands, tenements, and hereditaments, as the ornaments of their churches and their goods and chattels, to the high displeasure of Almighty God, slander of good religion, and to the great infamy of the King's Highness and the realm if redress should not be had thereof; And albeit that many continual visitations hath been heretofore had . . . yet nevertheless little or none amendment is hitherto had, but their vicious living shamelessly increaseth and augmenteth, and by a cursed custom so rooted and infested that a great multitude of the religious persons in such small houses do rather choose to rove abroad in apostasy than to conform them to the observation of good religion; so that without such small houses be utterly suppressed and the religious persons therein committed to great and honourable monasteries of religion in this realm, where they may be compelled to live religiously for reformation of their lives, there can else be no reformation in this behalf: In consideration whereof the King's most Royal Majesty, being Supreme Head in earth under God of the Church of England, daily finding and devising the increase, advancement, and exaltation of true doctrine and virtue in the said Church . . . considering also that divers and great solemn monasteries of this realm wherein, thanks be to God, religions is right well kept and observed, be destitute of such full numbers of religious persons as they ought and may keep, hath thought good that a plain declaration should be made of the premises as well to the Lords spiritual and temporal as to other his loving subjects the Commons in this present Parliament assembled; whereupon the said Lords and Commons . . . most humbly desire the King's Highness that it may be enacted by authority of this present Parliament, that His Majesty shall have and enjoy to him and to his heirs for ever all and singular such monasteries, priories, and other religious houses of monks, canons, and nuns, of what kinds or diversities of habits, rules, or orders so ever they be called or named, which have not in lands or tenements, rents, tithes, portions, and other hereditaments, above the clear yearly value of two hundred pounds. . . .

We have no journals for the House of Commons for the years before the reign of Edward VI, and such records of the House of Lords that have survived for the years before 1547 are scrappy and uninformative, but preambles such as these help us to estimate the content of the speeches by which members of the council conveyed to parliament the king's will and intention.

3. THE END OF THE MIDDLE AGES

The Middle Ages never existed: they were invented. No era could be *middle* until the following age had established itself, and consequently no generation ever considered itself to be medieval. Nineteenth-century historians adopted the terms *Middle Ages* and *medieval* because they found them convenient labels for those centuries which, in the western half of Europe, separated the Ancient World from the capitalist, technological, rationalist Europe of nation states, which they, if not the general public, called *modern*. No one doubts the usefulness of these divisions in time. Each age has its recognizable characteristics and atmosphere. It is just as possible to define the outlook, the philosophy, or the economy of the people of the Middle Ages, as it is to recognize a painting, a building, a poem, or a style of dress as medieval. Nevertheless, it remains true that there are no 'natural breaks' in time: all the beginnings and endings which we use and take for granted – 1 January, the twenty-first birthday, the end of a century – are man-made and to that extent artificial.

To indicate a dream or a lapse of time, film producers often use the device of simultaneously fading out one picture and introducing another. For a few seconds both pictures are on the screen, and it is usually not possible to determine the exact moment when the second picture becomes dominant or the first disappears altogether. One image merges into another. In the same way the Ancient World merged into the Middle Ages, and the Middle Ages into the Modern Age. For some years the old and the new existed together. But though examiners, textbook writers, cataloguers, and others recognize this fact, they find it more practical to make an arbitrary decision and choose precise dates for the birth and death of the Middle Ages.

The politically-minded historians of the nineteenth century thought 1485 the most convenient date of death. It marked the last decisive battle of the Yorkist–Lancastrian struggle, and the beginning of Tudor rule. Today, when more research has revealed that Edward IV anticipated much of the 'modern' outlook hitherto associated with Henry VII, the year 1485, even in political history, does not seem so clear a dividing mark as it once did. In ecclesiastical history the battle of Bosworth indicates no change whatever. The church *in* England was as strong and wealthy under Henry VII as it had been under Richard III or Edward IV: the church of England, a separate unit in Christendom, only came into existence with the Act of Supremacy in 1534. In *England in the Late Middle Ages*, the fourth volume of *The Pelican History of England*, A. R. Myers argued that 'this triumph of the Crown over the Church in the fifteen-thirties marks the close of the Middle Ages in more spheres of life than the ecclesiastical'. The distribution of monastic lands among the upper- and middle-class laity after the dissolution of the monasteries can well be viewed as the economic beginning of modern England, although it could not have had the same commercial, industrial, and social effects had not a middle class, drawing its chief income from trade, been steadily growing stronger and more numerous during the previous two centuries. And the distinctive pattern of modern social life can be held to date from the middle decades of the sixteenth century when it became much more usual to build houses in stone, when other towns as well as London began to grow, and when far more smallholders were earning part of their living either digging coal, spinning and weaving, or making small metal goods at their cottage forge. Probably one cannot get nearer the truth than to say that Henry VIII, a colossus indeed, bestrode the medieval and the modern worlds. During the half century through which he lived much of medieval England perished and much of modern England came to life.

Historical records were not unaffected by these changes. During the 1530s Thomas Cromwell laid the foundations of the modern bureaucratic method of government. Out of an amorphous collection of king's councillors he distilled the Tudor Privy Council, a firmly constituted body which met regularly, kept minutes, and employed a permanent clerk. He transformed the secretary of the royal household into a more authoritative official, the secretary of state, and in his reorganiz-ation of national finance he created new administrative bodies such as the court of augmentations to look after the surrendered monastic lands, and the court of wards and liveries to manage the king's feudal income. These basic changes in national administration entailed changes in the pattern of national records. Some existing series, such as the patent rolls, were unaffected; others such as the charter rolls, ceased; and each new department began to keep records and accounts of its own. But more important still, there was greater administrative efficiency and a marked change of emphasis. The proceedings of the Privy Council, systematically recorded, are extant from 1540 onwards. Inquisitions *post mortem*, a feudal record, and the papers of the Star Chamber, a comparatively recent judicial body, remained important documents until both the holding of land by knight's fee and the Star Chamber disappeared during the legal and administrative reforms of the mid seventeenth century. The more personal crown records declined in national significance, but parliamentary records gained in importance as one reign followed another.

In local records the change is even more clearly marked. From 1538, thanks to Cromwell again, the king required parish churches to keep registers of baptisms, marriages, and burials. Not all the incumbents obeyed, and many of the earliest records, which were often haphazardly kept on separate sheets of paper, have not survived. But parish registers of Elizabeth's reign are far more plentiful, and historians concerned with the Stuarts and Hanoverians take them for granted. Wills and inventories have a similar history. Just as it is possible to find fragmentary records of births and burials before 1538, so there have survived a number of wills and inventories made before the Statute of Wills in 1540. But from that year wills were systematically filed in the consistory court of each diocese, and no executor could obtain probate until he had given the court a detailed inventory of the deceased's possessions. Economic and social historians, as well as genealogists, find these voluminous records most helpful. They also have available the lieutenancy papers, for Protector Somerset in 1551 placed the control of the armed forces of the shire in the hands of the lord lieutenant, a new official, and the genealogist has an additional useful source of information in the records of heraldic visitations which cover the years from the middle of Henry VIII's reign to that of James II.

The Tudors did not invent either justices of peace or quarter sessions. Both date from the fourteenth century. But the Tudors used the justices and their court far more extensively than any previous kings. They increased their judicial powers to cover all felonies but treason, and they piled on their shoulders all kinds of administrative duties – responsibility for the care of bridges and roads, arresting vagrants, fixing local wage rates, indenturing apprentices, enforcing the recusancy laws, administering houses of correction, licensing gamekeepers and public houses, and supervising the work of all parish officers. In most counties the extant quarter sessions records go back to the sixteenth century. They are easily the most comprehensive and valuable body of local records before the nineteenth century. What is more, because the justices required all parish officers who handled public money to submit to them a careful record of expenditure, the files of accounts of churchwardens, constables, overseers of the poor, and surveyors of the highways provide the modern historian with a treasure house of detailed local information.

Nothing of this is available to the medieval historian. But he has no need to covet his colleague's possessions, for he has not yet exhausted all his own resources.

Bibliography of Sixteenth-Century Documents

The work of the contemporary historians and commentators has been published in the following editions:

History of Richard III, T. More, ed. J. R. Lumby (1883).

Anglica historia (1485–1537), Polydore Vergil, ed. D. Hay, Vol. 74, Camden Third Series.

The Union of the Two Noble and Illustre Famelies of Lancastre and Yorke, E. Hall, ed. C. Whibley, 2 vols. (1904).

Chronicles, R. Holinshed, ed. H. Ellis (1807–8).

Survey of London, J. Stow, ed. C. L. Kingsford (1908).

A relation, or rather a true account, of the island of England . . . about the year 1500, ed. C. Augusta, Vol. 37, Camden Old Series.

The Epistles of Erasmus, ed. F. M. Nichols, 3 vols. (1901–17).

The Complete Poems of John Skelton, ed. P. Henderson (1949).

Itinerary, John Leland, ed. L. T. Smith, 5 vols. (1906–10).

Collections of early Tudor documents are:

Memorials of King Henry VII, ed J. Gairdner, Vol. 10, Rolls Series.

Letters and Papers illustrative of the reigns of Richard III and Henry VII, ed. J. Gairdner, 2 vols., Rolls Series (1861–3).

Materials for a history of the reign of Henry VII, ed. W. Campbell, 2 vols., Rolls Series (1873–7).

Letters and papers, foreign and domestic, of the reign of Henry VIII, ed. J. S. Brewer, J. Gairdner, and R. H. Brodie, 38 vols. (1862–1932).

The Record Commission published the Latin text of *Valor Ecclesiasticus*, edited by J. Caley, in 6 volumes, between 1810 and 1834. A few county societies have since published translated extracts. The full report on Peterborough Monastery, part of which is quoted above, will be found in Vol. 12 of the publications of the Northamptonshire Record Society (1947).

The full text of the early Tudor statutes will be found in Vols. 2–4 of the *Statutes of the Realm*, 11 vols. (1810–28), but substantial extracts are printed in J. R. Tanner, *Tudor Constitutional Documents, 1485–1603* (1922).

GLOSSARY OF ARCHAIC AND TECHNICAL WORDS USED IN THE TEXT

ADVOWSON
: The right of patronage or of presenting a clergyman to a living

AID
: A periodic payment made by a feudal vassal to his lord

ALB
: A full-length white linen vestment worn by the priest celebrating communion

ALIENATION
: The transference of land from one holder to another

ALMONER
: Monastic official responsible for the collection and distribution of alms

AMERCEMENT
: A fine levied by a court

ASSART
: An area of arable land won from the forest or waste

ASSIZE
: A statutory regulation or law

AUGER
: A tool for boring holes in wood

AVENTAIL
: Mail armour hanging from the helmet to protect the throat and shoulders

BALDRIC
: Sword belt hung from the shoulder across the body

BANNERET
: A knight commanding a group of men-at-arms in battle

BARBETTE
: Strip of linen worn under the chin by women in the later Middle Ages

BASCINET
: Cloche-shaped helmet made of PLATE (q.v.). Popular in the later fourteenth century

BEAVER
: Piece of PLATE ARMOUR (q.v.) designed to protect the throat

BEREWICK
: Subsidiary or outlying estate

BORDAR
: A cottager and smallholder who owed services to his lord

BOVATE
: The eighth part of a CARUCATE (q.v.). Sometimes called an oxgang

CALENDAR
: A list of documents with summaries of their contents. Usually arranged in chronological order

CANON
: Originally a secular priest, but after the Norman Conquest an increasing number of canons (canons regular) lived monastic lives, e.g. Augustinian and Premonstratensian canons

CARTULARY	A list or record of lands and privileges granted by charters
CARUCATE	Another name for ploughland. Originally an area of arable land which a plough team could keep in cultivation, but by 1086 a unit of tax assessment rather than of land measurement
CELLARER	Monastic official or OBEDIENTIARY (q.v.) responsible for food supplies and outside trading
CHAIN MAIL	Armour made from numerous small links of metal, each forged separately and then riveted together
CHAMBER	A household organization created by Edward II, after his barons had compelled him to abandon the independent WARDROBE administration (q.v.)
CHANCELLOR	The head of the CHANCERY (q.v.). Eventually the king's chief minister
CHANCERY	The royal secretariat
CHAPTER	The chapter of a religious house consisted of all the full members. The part of the Rule read daily in the chapter house was also called the chapter
CHASUBLE	Short, outer vestment worn by a priest celebrating communion
CLERK	A word of several meanings in the Middle Ages: any clergyman; a man in minor orders; one in charge of accounts or records; a scholar
COIF	Close-fitting helmet made of CHAIN MAIL (q.v.)
COMMISSION OF ARRAY	Instruction addressed by the king to a group of local gentlemen to call out the SHIRE LEVY (q.v.)
COURT LEET	A local court authorized by royal grant to hear cases of petty jurisdiction. Courts leet were often responsible for the view of FRANKPLEDGE (q.v.)
COURT ROLL	The record of a court's activities, so called because the parchment on which the record was written was filed as a roll
DARREIN PRESENTMENT	Judicial cases concerned with ADVOWSON (q.v.)
DEMESNE	Part of the manor land which the lord farmed directly. The 'home-farm'
ESCHEATOR	The royal officer responsible for holding INQUISITIONS *post mortem* (q.v.)

ESQUIRE or SQUIRE	A knight's 'apprentice'
ESSOIN	An excuse for non-attendance at a court
EXCHEQUER	The royal counting-house
EXTENT	A detailed valuation of land and property
FARM	The rent or service paid for landholding
FEE SIMPLE	Land held in fee simple was held without restriction on inheritance
FEODARY	One who holds lands on condition of homage and service to an overlord. Also an officer concerned with inheritance of land
FEUDAL HOST	The army which assembled when the king required his tenants in chief to support him in war
FEUDALISM	Social organization based on holding land in feud or fief, i.e. from a superior on specified terms of service
FINAL CONCORD	A legal agreement or settlement
FINE	Two meanings – a fee or an end (*finis*). Often applied to a final agreement or decision concerning landholding. Such fines were written in triplicate. Copies went to the disputants, and the third copies, feet of fines, were filed in the records of the court of common pleas
FINE ROLLS	Records of payments made for writs issued by the crown
FOREST	Area reserved for game and hunting. Special laws, forest laws, governed these areas, which were far from being all woodlands
FORESTER	Officer in charge of the king's (or his lord's) forest lands and game
FRANKPLEDGE	The system by which the householders of a manor or village were grouped into TITHINGS (q.v.), in order that each tithing could be held corporately responsible for the good behaviour of its members. Cases of lawbreaking were heard twice a year at a view of frankpledge
GELD	A tax. Particularly associated with English and Norman taxes of the tenth and eleventh centuries
GILD	A corporation of merchants or craftsmen inside a borough
GOTHIC	The art and architectural style of the later Middle Ages

GRAND ASSIZE	A group of neighbours sworn to give evidence and judgement concerning disputed land-holding. In Henry II's reign this was an alternative method of settlement to ORDEAL by combat (q.v.)
GREAT SCHISM	Division in the papacy, which began in 1378 and ended with the election of Martin V as pope in 1417
GREAVES	PLATE ARMOUR (q.v.) designed to protect the legs below the knee
HAYWARD	Manor or parish officer responsible for fences and enclosures
HIDE	An area of land, which differed considerably in size in different counties. By 1086 it had become a tax assessment unit rather than a measurement
HOBELAR	A lightly-armed horseman usually used for foraging and scouting
HOLDING LAND	Since all land belongs to the crown, no subject can *own* it. Tenants-in-chief *held* it directly from the crown; subtenants *held* from a superior lord. *Teneo:* I hold
HOMAGE	Acknowledgement of allegiance to a superior
HUMANIST	Student of the new learning (i.e. the classical literatures of Greece and Rome) during the Renaissance
HUNDRED	An administrative subdivision of a county
INDENTURE	An agreement written two, three, or more times on a single parchment. To insure against forgery, the copies – one for each party to the agreement – were separated by irregular, wavy cuts
INFANGENTHIEF	The right sought by borough and manor courts to apprehend and punish anyone caught thieving within the boundaries of their jurisdiction
INFIRMARIAN	Monastic official responsible for the infirmary or sick quarters
INQUISITION	An inquiry. Inquisition *post mortem* was an inquiry into the holdings, services, and succession of a deceased person, who held land of the king
INVESTITURE	Putting a priest or deacon in possession of a benefice. The Investiture Dispute in the eleventh and twelfth centuries concerned the right of lay rulers to receive homage from ecclesiastics
ITINERANT JUSTICE	A royal judge who moved from centre to centre hearing pleas of the crown

JOUST	A duelling match between two armed horsemen
JUPON	Tight-fitting garment worn over armour, chiefly in the later fourteenth century
JUSTICE IN EYRE	A judge commissioned by the crown to undertake a journey, or eyre, in order to hear all pleas at certain county centres
JUSTICIAR	The king's chief minister during the late twelfth and early thirteenth centuries
KNIGHT'S FEE	Originally a grant of land in exchange for undertaking to supply a lord with the services of a fully armed knight and his necessary servants for forty days each year. Eventually, payment was made by rent, and knight's fees were often divided among several tenants
LASTAGE	Charges for lading, i.e. putting goods on board ship
LETTERS CLOSE	Private letter or letters
LETTERS PATENT	Open letter or letters
LIBERATE ROLLS	Records of writs which authorized the spending of the king's money
LIMITER	A begging friar
MANOR	A feudal freehold estate. Manors varied considerably in size, but usually the lord of the manor, or his deputy, presided over a manor court, which administered the manor lands and controlled the manor tenants. Since manors were held in FEE SIMPLE (q.v.), they passed automatically from the lord to his heir
MERCY	To be in mercy was to be liable to punishment for an offence
METES	Boundaries
MOIETY	One of two parts into which an estate was divided: not necessarily a half
MORT D'ANCESTOR	Judicial cases concerned with claims of inheritance
MOTA	Moot hall
MOTTE AND BAILEY CASTLE	A Norman castle, built of wood on an artificial mound of earth (the motte) and adjoining a stockaded living area (the bailey)
NOVEL DISSEISIN	Judicial cases concerned with dispossession of land
NOVICE	A probationary member of a monastic community

OBEDIENTIARY	A monk in charge of an administrative department inside a monastery
ORDEAL	A means of submitting a case to 'divine judgement'. The English and the Normans both used the ordeals of fire and water. The Normans added ordeal by combat for knights
OYER ET TERMINER	To hear and give judgement. A court of oyer et terminer was one of final judgement usually held by one of the king's judges
PALLIUM	A strip of white woollen cloth worn by an archbishop across the shoulders as a symbol of rank
PANNAGE	The right to feed pigs in the woods. Also the payment made to hold that right
PASSAGE	Tolls on passengers or goods
PINDER	The villager responsible for putting stray animals in the pinfold or pound
PIPE OF WINE	Large cask of wine
PIPE ROLL	Record of payments made to the EXCHEQUER (q.v.)
PITTANCER	Monastic official responsible for supplying pittances, the extra food given to the community on feast days
PLATE ARMOUR	Armour made from sheet metal. In the later thirteenth century pieces of plate were used to protect shoulders, elbows, and knees. By the fifteenth century complete suits of articulated plate armour had become common
PLEA	Action at law. Pleas of the crown were cases reserved for the king's justices. The court of common pleas heard civil actions only
PLOUGHLAND	See CARUCATE
POKE	A half-filled sack of wool
PONTAGE	Bridge tolls
POTTLE	Half a gallon
PRECENTOR	The priest responsible for conducting choir services in a cathedral or monastery
PROTONOTARY	Chief clerk in certain courts of law
PURPRESTURE	An encroachment, especially on to deer pastures in the forest
QUADRIVIUM	The four more advanced subjects taught in medieval schools – arithmetic, music, geometry, and astronomy

QUIT RENT   Money payment made by a small landholder in place of traditional services

RECUSANCY   The legal offence of refusing to attend the established church. *Recuso:* I refuse

REEVE   A deputy. The shire reeve (sheriff) was the king's deputy in the county: the manor reeve the lord's deputy in the manor court

REFECTORIAN   Monastic official in charge of the refectory or *frater*

REGULAR CLERGY   Clergy living according to a religious rule. Monks and friars were regulars

ROMANESQUE   The art and architectural style of the Norman and Angevin period

SAC AND SOC or SAKE AND SOKE   The right to hold a court and require tenants to attend it

SACRIST   The official responsible for the utensils used in divine service

SARCENET   Fine silk material

SARPLER   Sack of wool

SCRIPTORIUM   The part of a monastery, often the north walk of the cloisters, set aside for study and writing

SCUTAGE   A money payment made to the king instead of personal military service. Scutage became increasingly usual from the reign of Henry II onwards

SECULAR CLERGY   Priests who live among laymen and not in a religious order. Bishops, parish priests, and curates are all seculars

SEIGNIORIAL BOROUGH   A borough which received its charter from an earl, baron, or local landholder, i.e. not from the crown

SEIZE   Possess. A freeholder was said to be *seized* of his land. To be *disseized* was to be dispossessed

SENESCHAL   Steward

SERF   An unfree servant; a slave

SERJEANTY   To hold land by serjeanty was to hold it in exchange for an agreed service other than military duties

SHIRE LEVY   The defence force provided for by the assize of arms, 1181. In Anglo-Saxon times, the fyrd

SOCAGE   Tenure without servile obligation; the tenant usually paid a rent

SOKEMAN or SOCMAN	A free tenant, who came under the lord's jurisdiction
SPIRITUALITIES	Tithes, gifts, and other ecclesiastical sources of income belonging to a bishop or religious house
SYNOD	An ecclesiastical council or assembly
TALE	Count or total
TALLAGE	A tax, usually levied arbitrarily by a lord on his vassals
TEMPORALITIES	Lands, buildings, and other secular sources of income belonging to a bishop or religious house
T.R.E.	*Tempore regis Edwardi:* in the days of King Edward. Used in Domesday Survey to mean the day of Edward the Confessor's death
T.R.W.	In the days of King William. Used in Domesday Survey to mean the year 1086
TENANT-IN-CHIEF	One who held land directly from the crown
THEGN	An Anglo-Saxon retainer of noble birth. By 1086, however, many thegns owned little land and enjoyed few privileges
TITHE	Payment to the church of a tenth of the produce of the land. In a parish the great tithes, i.e. tenths of the main products, went to the rector, and the small tithes to the vicar
TITHING	A group of householders in the FRANKPLEDGE system (q.v.). Originally a tithing had ten members, but eventually numbers varied considerably
TOLL AND THEAM	Two rights granted in most borough charters – to exact toll from strangers bringing goods to the market, and to compel a receiver of stolen property to disclose how he got it
TOURNEY	A jousting tournament
TRIVIUM	The three basic subjects taught in medieval schools – grammar, rhetoric, and logic
VIEW OF ARMS	A six-monthly inspection of the arms held by the SHIRE LEVIES (q.v.)
VILL	A settlement; a hamlet
VILLEIN	An unfree peasant or villager, who usually farmed strips in the common fields, and, therefore, was better off than a serf

VIRGATE   Quarter of a HIDE (q.v.). Yardland is an alternative name

WARD   The seasonal closing of pasture land

WARDROBE   The more personal household administration developed by Henry III and Edward I to by-pass the heavy administrative machine of the CHANCERY and EXCHEQUER (q.v.). Edward III used the wardrobe, by then a subsidiary of the exchequer, as his war treasury overseas

WIMPLE   A woman's head-dress which also covered her cheeks, chin, and neck. Fashionable in the fourteenth century

WITAN or   The king's council in Anglo-Saxon England.
WITENAGEMOT   The Norman kings transformed it into the Great Council, the assembly of feudal magnates

INDEX

Dates following names of kings are dates of their reign. Dates following other names are of birth and death, or death alone, or period when most active.

*More about Penguins
and Pelicans*

If you have enjoyed reading this book you may wish to know
that *Penguin Book News* appears every month. It is an
attractively illustrated magazine containing a complete list
of books published by Penguins and still in print, together
with details of the month's new books. A specimen copy
will be sent free on request.

Penguin Book News is obtainable from most bookshops;
but you may prefer to become a regular subscriber at 3s
for twelve issues. Just write to Dept EP, Penguin Books
Ltd, Harmondsworth, Middlesex, enclosing a cheque or
postal order, and you will be put on the mailing list.

The latest volume in the Pelican History of England is
described overleaf.

Note: *Penguin Book News* is not
available in the U.S.A.

DAVID THOMSON

To many of us figures like Asquith and Lloyd George already seem almost as remote as Walpole and Pitt.

Fifty years have provided two world wars, countless revolutions, a world slump, the rise and fall of the dictators, and scientific and technical advances on an unprecedented scale. During this time England has become more fully a democracy, has pioneered the concept of the Welfare State, and laid the foundations of a multi-racial Commonwealth.

It is easy to see that the story of Britain in our century can hardly fail to be as fascinating and dramatic as it is important. In telling this story in a new volume of the Pelican History of England the Master of Sidney Sussex College, Cambridge, has not only managed to stand back from the times: he has also accomplished an extraordinary feat of compression and, in describing an age of revolution, underlines the significance of continuity.

Also available in this series: